D1789181

George Hunte

JAMAICA

B. T. Batsford Ltd, *London*

First published 1976

Copyright © George Hunte 1976
Printed and bound in Great Britain
at The Pitman Press, Bath
for the Publishers, B. T. Batsford Ltd,
4 Fitzhardinge Street, London W1H 0AH
ISBN 0 7134 3147 4

Contents

Acknowledgements

During forty years I have met so many Jamaicans from so many walks of life that I find it impossible to say to whom I am most indebted for the impressions I have sought to convey in this book. Statesmen, civil servants, journalists, teachers, artists, writers have all contributed in some degree to my perception of a few of the many strands of experience imprinted through centuries upon an island which American Indians accurately described as a place of woods and running water.

Perhaps the most fitting acknowledgement for me to make here would be a general statement to the effect that I have always found Jamaicans generally courteous, friendly, patient and accessible. These qualities I certainly discovered in men as eminent as Sir William Bustamante, Norman Manley, Sir Philip Sherlock, Theodore Sealy, H. N. Nethersole, Rex Nettleford, His Excellency Dr Arthur Wint, who, among others, have let me share in some degree a portion of their own rich stores of knowledge about their island.

More particularly in connection with the foreground of this book I would like to give special thanks for assistance to Doug Littlejohn, Alec Sanguinetti and G. G. Machado of Air Jamaica; to Hope Sealy, Norman Brunskill and other officials of the Jamaica Tourist Board; to the managers of Half Moon Bay, Jamaica Inn, Club Caribbean, Goblin Hill and Skyline Hotel; to Carlton Proute of the Daily News and to Jamaica's last English governor general Sir Kenneth Blackburne. I am deeply grateful to my wife Emma who has patiently transcribed my difficult handwriting into legible typescript.

For the illustrations in this book the author and publishers would like to thank Anne Bolt (nos. 11, 12, 14, 17, 18, 20, 21, 22, 24); the British Museum (no. 1); Robin Farquaharson (no. 15); the Jamaican Tourist Board (nos. 8, 9, 10, 16, 19, 23); the National Portrait Gallery (no. 3); Henry Sotheran Limited (no. 7); the Victoria and Albert Museum (nos. 4, 6, 13).

Illustrations

JAMAICA

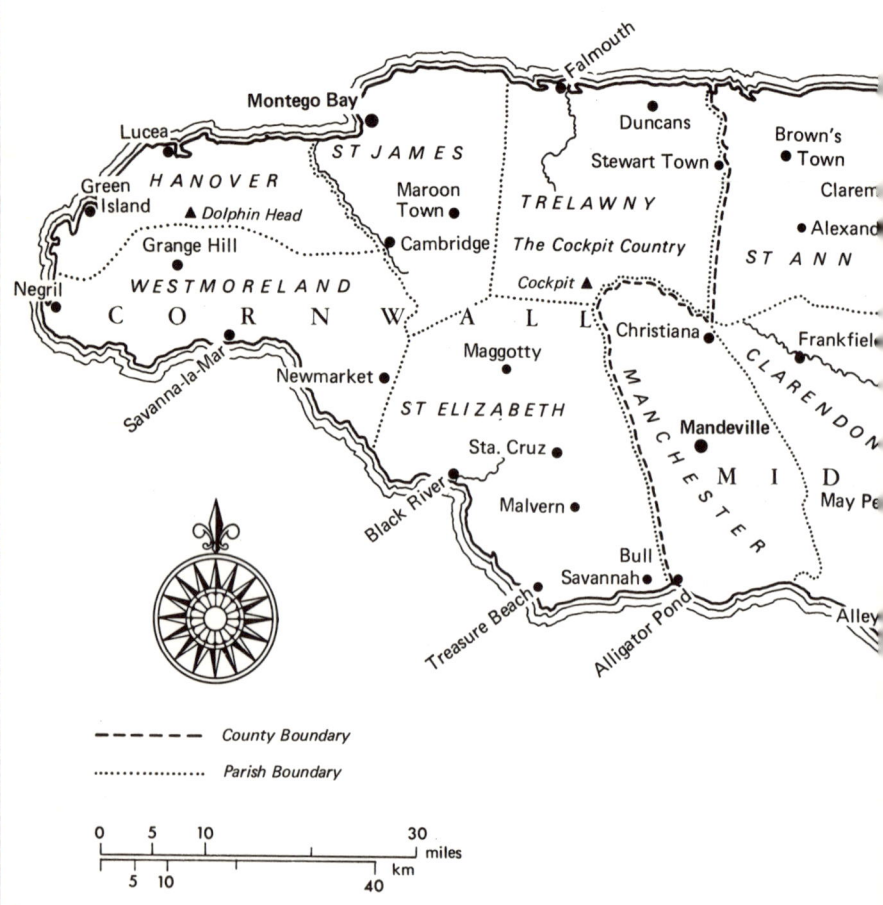

CARIBBEAN SEA

Falmouth

Montego Bay ●

Lucea ●

Duncans ●

Brown's
● Town

Green
● Island

ST JAMES

Stewart Town ●

Clarem

HANOVER

▲ *Dolphin Head*

Maroon
Town ●

TRELAWNY

● Alexand

Grange Hill ●

● Cambridge

The Cockpit Country

ST ANN

Negril ●

WESTMORELAND

Cockpit ▲

Christiana ●

Frankfiel ●

C O R N W A L L

Savanna-la-Mar

Newmarket ●

Maggotty ●

M A N C H E S T E R

C L A R E N D O N

ST ELIZABETH

Mandeville ●

M I D

Sta. Cruz ●

Black River

Malvern ●

May Pe

Bull
Savannah ●

Treasure Beach

Alligator Pond

Alley

- - - - - -   *County Boundary*

· · · · · · · · · ·   *Parish Boundary*

0	5	10		30	

miles

	5	10			km

40

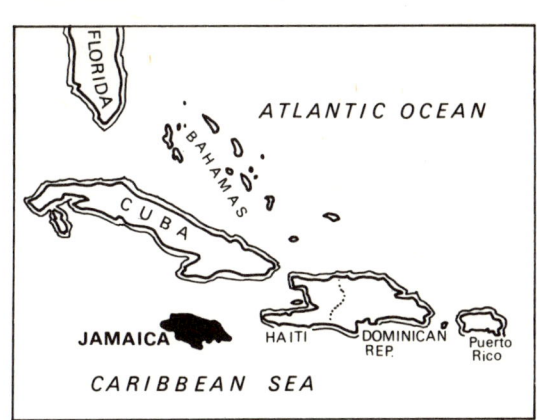

ATLANTIC OCEAN

FLORIDA

BAHAMAS

CUBA

JAMAICA HAITI DOMINICAN REP. Puerto Rico

CARIBBEAN SEA

n's Bay

Ocho Rios

Oracabessa

Port Maria

ST MARY

Annotto Bay

Buff Bay

Hope Bay

Port Antonio

Long Bay

Manchioneal

Hector's River

endship

Richmond

oneague

Castleton

PORTLAND

Linstead

Newcastle

SURREY

iidas Vale ST

CATHERINE ST ANDREW

ST

THOMAS

KINGSTON

Spanish Town

Seaforth

Port Morant

Golden Grove

ESEX

Old Harbour

Port Royal

Yallahs

Morant Bay

Bowden

Portland Cave

CARIBBEAN SEA

For Silvio and Antonella

Introduction

I first visited Jamaica in the uniform of a British soldier. I was on leave in the West Indies from Naples when the American Lend Lease programme ended, and could only return to the Mediterranean on a British plane. The plane which took me from Piarco airport left me for two days in Kingston while it made a call at Belize. This unscheduled stop gave me the opportunity to stay in an old style West Indian guest house near Up Park Camp where the British army was in residence. Kingston was at the time a leisurely place where walking was comparatively pleasant. It had no industrial districts then and most of the road leading to the Palisadoes airport ran alongside open water. When nearly five years later I saw Jamaica again I landed at Montego Bay where a few modern hotels had been provided for discriminating tourists. I remember being very much impressed on that occasion by the facts that there was a large cemetery close to these hotels and that the famous Doctor's Cave Beach was remarkably small. I travelled by car from Montego Bay to Kingston and, like many other visitors since, I delighted in the natural beauty of the north coast. It was easy to understand why Ian Fleming and Noel Coward had chosen to work in such surroundings. Other impressions of that drive were the deserted appearance of Falmouth, the rolling pasturelands where cattle grazed among fruit trees, the twisting ascent and descent of roads through the hills and the frequent presence of water and woodland. Jamaica had not yet experienced the big bauxite revolution. Kingston too was still a very staid, almost English provincial town where

I lunched in the privacy of the men's club, slept in an old world nineteenth-century hotel (The Myrtle Bank) and walked through wide shopping streets and avenues spaced with enormous villas and well tended gardens.

The taxi which took me from my hotel to King's House and the car in which I was driven up to Mona revealed, as I watched through the windows, how solid were the middle class foundations of a city which had been moulded by imperial traditions. I heard, it is true, much talk about a new emerging nation but the new nation was to be a West Indian dominion which would take its rightful place in a British-led Commonwealth.

Underneath the apparent quiescence of a sleeping outpost of empire, Jamaica was however seething with ferment of social strivings which were to explode in continuous bursts of political, social and economic change over the next three decades. The influences shaping this emerging Jamaica were coming from many directions; from neighbouring islands, from North America, from England and from within the complex society itself.

Anyone who seeks to measure modern Jamaica's achievement must begin with humility and patience to study the many strands of human experience which differentiate Jamaica's people from other islanders of the former British West Indies. So much larger than other British islands, Jamaica had enough room for several communities to develop separately.

Those who travel exclusively for pleasure in Jamaica today ought to be particularly wary of snap judgments about the island drawn from personal experiences of any particular place. The Jamaican holiday is not easily broken down into a single component which is common. Apart from the large Kingston hotels where there is a variety within a definite pattern, the accommodations available on Jamaica are so variegated that the choice of hotel, inn, guest house or apartment can be the decisive factor affecting a holiday.

Unlike small West Indian islands where the amenities for tourists are relatively easily accessible to all visitors, the tourist in Jamaica is much more dependent on those amenities which are close to the place selected. On the other hand activities for visitors in Jamaica are organised to appeal to the greatest number of visitors, and Jamaica is very well served by more than one sightseeing tour operator.

There are two main ingredients to a Jamaican holiday; the common Caribbean mixture of warm sea and sandy coastline; and the superb natural scenery and vegetation of the interior. The mountains above the Rio Grande valley have been likened to 'North Wales, clothed with the trees of Worcestershire', but everywhere, as the same writer William Lloyd M.D. said in 1837 'beauty is before' the traveller, 'and spicy odours at his right hand; in short to sum up there are balmy mornings, scorching noons, placid evenings, starlit nights.' These observations remain true today of an island whose transition to the twentieth-century world is perhaps most obviously expressed by the gaily painted colourful flying birds of Air Jamaica which take increasing numbers of visitors from Europe each year to the country whose sincerest form of approval is the invitation to 'walk good'. Whether taken literally by the pedestrian or figuratively by others who seek greater speed of propulsion, Jamaica is undoubtedly a place where the reward for movement is the unfolding of larger canvases of natural beauty.

From Columbus to Cromwell

Friendly Indians told Christopher Columbus about Jamaica during his first voyage to the Indies. They called it Yamaye and said it was ten days journey from Terra Firma by canoe. Columbus was also told, and noted in his diary, that gold pieces as large as 'broad beans' had been picked up in Jamaica by Indians who lived there. It was therefore in certain hope of finding gold that he dropped anchor in Santa Gloria Bay (St Ann's) on 5 May 1494. His reception was far from friendly. No less than 70 large canoes filled with hundreds of Arawak men came against the Spaniards and tried to drive them away. Columbus then frightened them off by firing an unloaded cannon. No gold was found and on the next morning Columbus left the 'glorious' bay of the most beautiful and graceful of the islands in search of better fortune in some other part of Jamaica. Six miles westwards at Puerto Bueno larger numbers of Indians were waiting for the Spaniards. They attacked them by hurling volleys of pointed sticks, and were only discouraged by the discharge of Spanish crossbows. Impressed by these weapons which caused the death of some of their fellows and wounded others the Indians of Puerto Bueno sent a delegation of six men to Columbus on the next day bearing gifts of food but not gold. Disappointed for the second time Columbus continued his westward journey as far as the gulf of Buen Tiempo (Montego Bay) where he obtained the services of a native Indian before setting sail for Cuba. Some months afterwards he returned to the bay of Buen Tiempo from where he continued a leisurely inspection of the Jamaican coastline, not-

1

ing its dense vegetation close to the sea, its natural harbours and the heavy downpours of rain each evening. About 20 miles west of today's Port Royal he anchored at Portland Bight and called it Bahia de la Vaca. There an Indian caicque tried unsuccessfully to persuade Columbus to take him to Spain so that he might see the land from which the explorers came. The Admiral refused the request but his interest was aroused by gold trinkets he noticed on the bodies of some Indians.

Nine years later, on his last voyage to the Indies, Columbus and the crew of two waterlogged ships were forced to take refuge in Puerto Seco (Dry Harbour). Finding neither water nor provisions there, the Spaniards with difficulty coaxed their almost sinking vessels eastwards to St Ann's Bay where they ran them aground. They stayed upon their 'floating pontoons' for nearly a year, using dried palm leaves to protect them from rain and sun. From the neighbouring Indian village of Maima the Spaniards got water and food in exchange for trinkets and other articles brought from Spain.

Columbus did not go to Jamaica by choice on this second visit. He was a reluctant exile and had to cope as best as he could with rebellious Spaniards and resentful Indians. He was also for a long period uncertain as to the fate of the chief notary Diego Mendez and the Genoese Bartolome Fieschi who had rowed across 170 kilometres of sea in two open piraguas with six Spaniards and 12 Indians to seek help and a rescue ship from Hispaniola. Believing them drowned, two brothers, Francisco and Diego Porras, revolted against Columbus' authority and persuaded 48 other Spaniards to attempt an escape in ten ill-constructed canoes. Their attempt failed but the rebels later brought discredit on Columbus by raiding Indian settlements in the interior. The Indians took their revenge by cutting off supplies to Columbus and his men. Columbus escaped this new danger by playing God. He found in his cabin a book, *Ephemerides Astronomiche,* that foretold the date of an imminent eclipse of the moon. The man who had tricked his own sailors by falsifying the records of his ship's daily mileage across the Atlantic had lost none of his cunning over the years. He called the Indian chiefs together and warned them that God was very angry with them for witholding rations from the Christian Spaniards. As a sign of God's anger the sky would be darkened. When the eclipse occurred the terrified Indians begged Columbus to petition the heavenly power on their behalf. Knowing that the eclipse would soon pass Columbus promptly promised to obtain a pardon for them and almost immediately 'the sign of God's displeasure' disappeared from the sky. Columbus had ensured food for his men by his cunning but because of the absence of news from Hispaniola another conspiracy was hatched by a man named Bernal. In the nick of time a caravel arrived with supplies from Hispaniola thereby giving proof that Mendez's mission had been successful. However, salted pork and casks of wine were considered very poor substitutes for a rescue ship and another serious rebellion had to be put down by Diego Colon who captured the chief trouble maker Francisco Porras. Wisely Columbus pardoned the rebels and on 29 June 1504, in a ship finally brought over by Diego Mendez from Hispaniola, Columbus and the Spanish exiles sailed 'with no regrets' from the land of wood and waters. He left no one behind to go on calling the island by the name which he had given it, Santiago.

It is generally believed that the Indians whom Columbus met in Jamaica were Arawaks. They were of a brown colour, short with broad faces. They grew maize, cassava and potatoes for their main diet, and ate fish and the flesh of birds, agoutis, iguanas, snakes and manatees. They used nets and pointed spears as well as bone and turtle shell hooks for fishing, built wooden stools and made arms and other instruments of stone. They were skilful sailors who traded along the coasts of large islands and crossed the seas to other islands. They travelled in canoes which were carved and painted in bow and stern. Their canoes varied in size and were sometimes as long as 96 feet. They were dug out of branches of cedar or silk cotton trees. Arawak women knitted from locally-grown cotton, hammocks which served as beds and the brief garments they wore. Men smoked locally-grown tobacco in 'pipes' and drank lavishly at festivals of singing and dancing known as Areitos. Liquor was made from cassava or other food crops. A favourite sport of the Arawaks was a ball game known as 'bato'. The purpose of the game seems to have been a struggle for points between two sides of up to 20 each. Both sides in turn tried to keep aloft a ball or object which was light enough to stay in the air for some seconds before falling to the ground.

Arawaks believed in supernatural beings, but built no temples. Their priests fulfilled the role of medicine men and they paid special honour to Zemis, which were images of departed spirits that were kept in caves or special straw-covered houses. They lived in tentlike structures supported by a central pole and surrounded by small posts. The walls were made of dried wild cane tied tightly together by withes or vines, and dried grass or palm leaves provided roofs.

At the time of Columbus' arrival about 60,000 Arawaks of Jamaica were probably living on the island in one hundred or more settlements governed by chiefs and sub-chiefs. Their early resentment against the Spaniards was undoubtedly due to tales traders had brought back of Spanish behaviour towards the Arawaks on Hispaniola. The Indians were no doubt delighted to see Columbus leave their shores on 29 June 1504 and hoped that life would resume its normal pattern. They were doomed to disappointment for although they were never to see Columbus again, some of his fellow exiles returned in 1509 under command of Juan de Esquivel, the first governor appointed by Columbus' son Diego Colon, heir to Jamaica.

Esquivel had been with Columbus on his second expedition to the New World and had fought against Indians in Hispaniola. In commemoration of his birthplace, Seville, he called the settlement which he established close to St Ann's Bay, Sevilla La Nueva (New Seville). The Jamaican Indians who had welcomed neither Columbus nor his men during their accidental exile on Jamaica now began to experience the rigours of Spanish rule. They were made to realise that they were no longer free to follow their previous way of life but had to help the Spaniards search for gold or till virgin soil for planting around New Seville. They did not suffer the Spaniards gladly. Some took to the mountains, others escaped by boats, some committed suicide by drinking the poisonous juice of cassava, others contracted European diseases and died, others died of overwork and Spanish brutality. But Esquivel succeeded just the same in establishing a secure settlement on Jamaica. Reports of the amazing fertility of the island and its capacity to support swarms of swine, mountain goats and beef cattle attracted the attention of the Spanish king. Jamaica, he decided, needed a direct royal representative who could act as his *Teniente* and protect his economic and political interests. He appointed Francisco de Garay as royal governor and put under him four officials, a treasurer, a contador, a factor and a veedor to look after his *Hacienda Real.* Always hopeful that gold would be found in Jamaica, the King was also impressed by the role he thought Jamaica could play as a supply base for Spanish expeditions to the mainland where large numbers of Indians had to be subdued before permanent Spanish settlements could be established.

Soon after Garay's appointment in 1514 the question of the spiritual welfare of the people of Jamaica was also considered and in 1515 the first abbot Don Sancho de Matienzo, President of La Casa de La Contratacion in Seville was appointed. He never actually visited the island, but his appointment made it possible for progress to be made. His third successor in office, Pedro Martire de Angleria, who wrote of Jamaica as his 'spouse', began the erection of a Christian temple built of stone. During these relatively progressive years, funds provided by the Spanish Crown had made possible the building of some stone houses at New Seville and strengthening of the fortress which had been erected by Esquivel. Garay also founded a second settlement at Oristan near Bluefield's Bay on the south-western shores of the island. Under Esquivel the Spanish settlers had concentrated largely upon husbandry and cotton growing. Garay continued to foster planting of food crops but also encouraged the keeping of cows, sheep and other livestock. He probably founded Oristan because the savannahs on that side of the island were suited to cattle raising or because he may have decided that New Seville had proved unhealthy because of its nearness to swamps. As early as 1519 Pedro de Mazuelo, the King's treasurer, asked permission from the King to 'found a people to the south' because of 'pestilential bogs' between New Seville and the sea. A heavy mortality rate of children at New Seville eventually led to its complete abandonment and the foundation of La Vega by Mazuelo in 1534. Garay's administration ended in 1523 when he left Jamaica to go on an expedition to Mexico. With this departure there ended what might be described as the only period in which Jamaica received anything like adequate support from the authorities in Spain. Once Mexico and Peru had been reduced to subjection, huge lands lay open for Spanish colonisation and Jamaica's role as a prime supplier to expeditions finished. It also lost several of its early settlers who sought greater opportunities on the mainland.

A slight resurgence of interest occurred in 1546 when the Duke of Veragua employed Jamaica's resources to assist the development of his property on the mainland but from that year until the conquest by the English in 1655 Jamaica remained a neglected Spanish colony.

Although no abbot took up residence in Jamaica until 1581 some strenuous attempts had been made to build churches. In 1525 the first stone temple was begun on orders from the absentee abbot Peter Martyr. His church was never finished, but it was designed as a splendid Gothic temple with three naves and buttresses. In 1533 the King, who had supplied 100,000 maravedis for its construction requested that the chapel at least should be completed. It was, but a year later the people of New Seville left for La Vega. The settlement grew until, according to a report issued in 1554, there was a church, a monastery and a number of stone and tiled-roof houses. The first abbot, Sammano, to live in La

Vega in 1539 left in the same year after a clash with the governor. No more abbots were appointed until 1556. In Spain at the beginning of the sixteenth-century about 125,000 persons controlled the country from above. By establishing peace in the peninsula Ferdinand and Isabella had stabilised property in a country where almost all the land was then owned by 1.5 per cent of the population. Revenues were divided on the basis of one third to the king, one third to the nobility and one third to the Church (whose hierarchy was largely drawn from the nobility). From the ranks of the lower nobility, too, Ferdinand and Isabella recruited the royal governors of the cities with whose help a rigid authoritarian mould was given to the Castilian state. Castile made history in the New World because Ferdinand and Isabella wanted to rule the Indies without any interference from Catalan, Aragonese, or Valencian nobles or merchants who did not conform to the Castilian mould. The Spanish monarchs recognised a Castilian sense of mission, a vitality and an acceptance of nomadic life which would be useful in the Indies. At the same time the Castilians who first went to the Antilles, then to the Isthmus and later to Mexico and Peru were quite willing to escape from the tensions of centralised authoritarian government at home and were avidly hopeful of finding quick riches overseas. Especially did the myth of gold appeal to the hidalgos who had been ruined by the great landowners whose sheep destroyed their prosperous agricultural holdings.

The disillusionment which followed in the early years of discovery did not extinguish the spark of Castilian vitality nor quench the insatiable desire for gold. Seeds and flocks, tools and utensils were sent to the Antilles where the search for gold and pearls continued for at least two decades. Then after Cortez had subdued the Aztecs in 1524 more gold was shipped from Mexico to Spain in one year than had been sent in all the years since 1492. Castilians began to emigrate in greater numbers from Spain to the Antilles in search of new wealth and the stream turned to a flood when in 1534 they heard news of temples covered with gold and of treasures amassed by the Incas whom Pizarro had brought under the dominion of Castile. For some years after the Peruvian gold rush the Antilles were practically depopulated.

During the first seven decades which followed Columbus' discovery the umbilical cord between Europe and America had been nurtured by about 80 Spanish ships a year. These ships were very small, seldom more than 100 tons in size and on each voyage had to brave perils from turbulent seas and tempests and pirates. From 1521 coastguard ships had to be commissioned to protect transatlantic ships and later two guardships accompanied all convoys when the system of fleets was established after 1563.

Castile's determination to keep the Indies and Americas as an exclusive patrimony seriously restricted the numbers of Spaniards available for overseas settlement and created in America a social hierarchy whose power was based on control of property, concession of titles of nobility, connection with the higher bureaucracy and the right to bear arms. How relatively small was the number of the ruling minority may be gauged from the fact that no more than 69,000 Spaniards are known to have emigrated to America by 1570, while only 120,000 are believed to have gone there during the whole course of the sixteenth century. These figures are all the more staggering when set against the 25 million Indians who are thought to have inhabited Central Mexico in the period before Cortez. They demonstrate also how feeble a grip the Spaniards must have had upon the island of Jamaica, which until 1640 was considered primarily as a *latifundia* or huge property of the heirs of Columbus. Jamaica had suffered from plagues of locusts during the first half of the sixteenth century and agriculture was seriously affected by the increase in cattle population. Some 40,000 cattle roamed the plains of the south in the early years of the seventeenth century. Wild cattle, which the Spaniards called *ganado cimarron* are thought to have given the name to the 'maroons' who took to the mountains at the time of the English attack upon Jamaica in 1655. Most of the Indian population had 'disappeared' by 1515 and small numbers of

Africans were introduced into Jamaica to replace them. The Spanish Crown had authorised the slave trade in 1510, and then banned it in 1516, but it was accepted during the early years of the reign of Charles V and a contract system was inaugurated in 1527 to replace the earlier system of licences. There was never any large number of African slaves in Jamaica during the nearly 150 years of Spanish occupation, the maximum number probably never exceeding 1,000. All negroes were not slaves. At the beginning of the seventeenth-century when La Vega was still the only urban centre on Jamaica and had a total population of 1,510 souls, Abbot Don Bernardo de Balbuena reported the presence in the town of 558 slaves and 107 negroes. The remainder of the city dwellers were described as 523 Spaniards, 107 children, 75 foreigners and 74 Indians. Most of the island's population then lived at La Vega, the rest of the island being a rural conglomeration of cattle farms. There were two main trails in use by the Spaniards, one on the southern coast and another beside river beds extending from St Ann's Great River over the Golden Spring Gap to Alderston and then down to the St Catherine's Plain.

The Africans who remained loyal to the Spaniards over the five years in which guerilla operations were conducted against the English invaders proved by their actions that they had been reasonably treated by their masters. Evidence of good treatment seems to have been given by Abbot Mateo de Santiago in a letter to King Philip II. The Abbot, writing in 1574, reported that slaves were living outside matrimony 'creating little sons and daughters as if man and wife'. Abbot Bernardo de Balbuena writing in 1612 put forward another reason for lenient treatment of slaves. The people of La Vega were, he says 'lazy and idle' and only the negro could work in the hot and humid climate. Sugar had been grown in the Antilles soon after 1506 but the first *ingenio* erected on Jamaica does not appear to have worked until 1534, the year of the founding of La Vega. It is probable that African labour had been especially introduced a little earlier to prepare the canefields. But sugar production in Jamaica never developed much under the Spaniards, who used horses to drive the mills which made all the sugar they wanted for local consumption. Sugar cane, like bananas, citrus and grapes were cultivated to 'sweeten' the diet of the resident Spaniards rather than as economic export crops. The chief exports were cattle, hides and lard produced from the annual slaughter of swine.

During the first half of the sixteenth century privateers lay in wait for Spanish ships returning from America over a triangle of sea lying between the Canaries, the African coast and Cape St Vincent. Gradually those who sought Spanish treasure at sea grew more venturesome and by the middle of the century French sailors were bold enough to anchor in uninhabited coves or harbours of the Spanish Caribbean. In 1556 a French ship spent nearly three weeks in Puerto Caguaya, the nearest port to La Vega. Six years later Hawkins began a series of 'trading' visits to Spanish possession in the Americas which excited the anger of Philip II and encouraged other 'illicit' visits by a trail of Tudor seamen like Drake, Raleigh, Gilbert, Oxenham, Grenville, Barker and Cavendish. Jamaica lay wide open to attack in these years, but neither Britain nor France then had navies capable of protecting Caribbean or American territories from Spanish counter-attacks. It was the age of the hit-and-run seafarer. English aggression in the Spanish Indies was intensified, however, after 1572 when Elizabeth felt she could actively encourage piracy and seek Spanish plunder because she had secured a defensive alliance with Charles IX of France at a time when the Spaniards were faced by a major rebellion in the Netherlands. English rage against Spain's dominance and Spanish control of world trade boiled over danger point when in 1580 Philip II acquired Portugal and its immense Eastern network of commerce. Sooner or later a trade war had to break out between Spain and England unless English entrepreneurs were going to be for ever content with the profits of contraband and piracy, or with whatever concessions they might receive from Spanish colonists illegally. The struggle for supremacy at sea became active in the year 1585 when Drake sacked Vigo, attacked the Canaries and the Cape Verde islands, plundered San Domingo, assaulted Carthagena and moved against St Augustine in Florida. He took back to England that year an enormous booty from his wide ranging exploits valued in the currency of the time at £671,000! Philip II could not overlook such outrageous assaults upon his overseas possessions and prepared to send a huge fleet against England in 1587 when Elizabeth's judicial murder of Queen Mary allowed him to claim the English throne for himself. By sending Drake to Cadiz, where he destroyed 13,000 tons of Spanish shipping, Elizabeth probably saved England from Spanish rule because a new Armada was not ready to attack the English fleet until 1588 and by that time Philip's best admiral had died.

The English defeat of the Spanish Armada advertised to all of Spain's enemies in Europe that her ships could no longer give adequate protection to Spanish settlements overseas. Jamaica especially was vulnerable to attack. Anthony Shirley landed 250 men at Port Caguaya in 1597 and then marched inland to find La Vega deserted, its inhabitants having fled to the hills. A Spanish historian of this century noted with surprise that Shirley's title of 'Sir' did not prevent him 'from being a pirate'. Some years later when La Vega was under attack by Christopher Newport and 1,500 English sailors, the Spaniards there, encouraged by a friar who rode alongside on a horse chanting hymns, successfully resisted the invaders. From this time, it seems, the town began to be called St Iago de la Vega because its inhabitants attributed their deliverance from Newport's men to the intercession of St James (Iago).

Foreign seamen who never had any intention of attacking Spanish settlements increasingly made use of the natural harbours of the island to repair their ships and to obtain supplies of fresh food and water. Some overstayed their welcome, as happened in 1626 when three Dutch ships remained for so long at Negril Point on the west coast that the abbot of St Iago de la Vega organised groups of citizens to dislodge the 'Dutch pirates' from Jamaican shores. The Spanish government must have decided later that there was a grave risk of Jamaica being lost under the proprietorship of the Duke of Veragua (who was also Marquis de la Vega) because in 1640 Jamaica was placed under full control of the Crown. Change of over-lordship did not, however, save La Vega from the fury of Captain Jackson's onslaught in 1643. This experienced privateer, who held a commission from the Earl of Warwick, had been wreaking vengeance on Spanish possessions for nearly three years. From La Vega, which was then a town of about 400 houses, he stole 7,000 pieces of eight and carried off large quantities of food.

Continuous alarms and recurrent invasions by English or Dutch 'pirates' had increased the problems of the Spanish settlers on Jamaica. Their men had to abandon work on farms for long periods and patrol the beaches like frontier soldiers. A report sent to Spain in 1644 observed that 'if two ships are seen off the port, without waiting to know where they are from, they (the inhabitants of La Vega) remove the women and their effects to the mountains'. The report criticised such behaviour because it wasted time and gave 'the enemy opportunity to return and occupy the town without resistance'.

Invasion from the sea was not the only threat to the Spaniards on Jamaica in the decade preceding the British invasion of 1655. They had also to put up with high-handed governors like Don Pedro Caballero. He was only 28 when he became governor in 1646 and quickly fell out with the Abbot of La Vega. Don Pedro insisted on putting a large bed with draperies into the church where his son was being baptised although he was forbidden to do so by the abbot. Later he called the abbot a 'garlic eating clown', thereby inviting the excommunication which he duly received. The arrogance of the young governor was ended by his death at the hands of an assassin. The man who succeeded him in office died in prison. Civil and religious affairs on Jamaica had reached so low an ebb that old-established families left the island for Cuba and the Holy Office appointed an *alguacil* whose powers took precedence over lay rulers. After more than 140 years the island from which Columbus had expected much gain for himself and his family when he first saw it, was still largely underdeveloped and lacked a population adequate for its defence. It is estimated that no more than 2,500 persons were living in Jamaica when the British army of 7,000 arrived in the fleet of 38 ships which dropped anchor in Hunt's Bay near Passage Fort on the morning of 10 May 1655. Most of the population then lived at La Vega or its environs, but others lived on ranches or *hatos* beyond today's Clarendon Plain in Guatibacoa and Pereda. There had also been some settlements at the eastern and western ends of the island.

The accession of the peace-loving James I to the throne of England after Elizabeth's death in 1603 had given the Spaniards a respite from British armed aggression by sea. The Dutch however seized every opportunity to take advantage of the Spaniards during the official truce with Spain from 1609-21. The early decades of the seventeenth century saw Holland surpassing all countries in the world in the accumulation of capital. From 1590 onwards ships of the Hollanders flooded into Mediterranean countries, laden with European and colonial merchandise. Dutch traders also predominated in Baltic ports and some had set up centres on French soil, as at Nantes, for the purpose of supplying French settlements in Canada, West Africa and the Caribbean. Amsterdam soon became the centre of Dutch East Indian and West Indian trade. After the end of the truce with Spain in 1621, Holland's great resources were employed to finance the West India Company, which was formed with the deliberate intention of striking at the sources of Spanish wealth in the Americas. By 1636 the Dutch West India Company had destroyed 547 Spanish ships, while Piet Hein had in 1628 captured an entire Plate fleet off Mantanzas Bay, near Cuba, with a treasure valued at 15 million guilders! This huge flow of money to Amsterdam financed the Dutch invasion of Brazil in 1630. The period of Dutch ascendancy in the Caribbean came to an end in 1648 when the terms of the Treaty of Munster, which concluded the Thirty Years' War in Europe, stopped Dutch privateering at Spanish expense in the Americas.

Although Dutch finances were largely drained away in efforts to sustain a settlement in Brazil, Piet Hein's victory did mark the end of Spanish naval supremacy in the Caribbean sea and prepared the way for the later reign of the Buccaneers. Spain never really recovered from the disgrace of losing its armada during the attempted invasion of Britain in 1588 and a decline in its naval supremacy was accompanied by a fall in maritime trade which progressively fell into the hands of foreigners. Between 1610 and 1640 Spanish ships to the Indies grew smaller and smaller in number and as early as 1590 the fleet of Portugal had to be called in to assist the Atlantic service. In 1648 when Spain bought peace from the States of the Netherlands by acknowledging their independence, doors were also opened for Dutch traders to do business in Spanish overseas possessions.

By the time that Cromwell became Protector in 1653 England was already engaged in a trade war with the Dutch. Having got the better of the Dutch at sea, Cromwell had to choose between France and Spain as the greatest threat to England's trade. Mazarin, the chief minister in France, wanted peace at any price in order to protect his country from renewed disturbances by the Frondeurs, and because France was still at war with Spain, Cromwell thought he saw a golden opportunity to give a death blow to Spain's supremacy in the Americas. His Western Design, launched in late 1654, was more than a continuation of Elizabethan-style privateering and much more than a revenge for the Spanish recapture of the Puritan colony of Providence off Nicaragua in 1641. It was the despatch of a large army against Spanish America with a purpose stated by Cromwell as 'securing and increasing the interests of this Commonwealth in those parts and for opposing and weakening and destroying that of the Spaniards'. Surprisingly in view of the difficulties of the enterprise the army was not selected from seasoned troops in Britain but was drawn partly from civilians recruited in

England and largely from dissatisfied settlers or servants impressed in Barbados and the Leeward islands. Of a total of more than 8,000 men only 2,500 were from England. In addition to Robert Venables who was chosen as general and commander in chief of the army and General William Penn commander in chief of the fleet, Cromwell appointed three other men, Edward Winslow, Daniel Searle and Gregory Butler, to be their fellow commissioners 'for the better ordering and managing of "the operation" for the best advantage of the State and for the improvement of the whole design.'

It is hard to imagine how a battle could have been won anywhere in Europe with such an army, so Cromwell probably had swallowed hook, line and sinker, the exaggerated reports of his chaplain Thomas Gage, a renegade Dominican priest, that any large body of men would be enough to conquer Spaniards living in the West Indies or the Spanish Main. Not content with formulating a divisive command Cromwell made matters worse by giving Venables no clear instructions. He was left to talk about possible landfalls with Penn and his other fellow commissioners and then to attack the Spaniards wherever the five commissioners decided was best. In case the commissioners had no ideas of their own, Cromwell volunteered two or three possible lines of action. One was to attack Hispaniola and Puerto Rico, and then to take Havana, 'the backdoor of the West Indies'. Another was to aim at Carthagena on the mainland after taking places on the way. A third course was to take Santo Domingo or Puerto Rico, or both, and then to capture Carthagena. With such detailed guidance from the Lord Protector is it surprising that the commissioners followed his 'two or three ways' to the best of their ability, only choosing Jamaica instead of Puerto Rico when their attempt on San Domingo failed disastrously?

Venables remained in Barbados from 29 January until 31 March. That island was put under martial law and compelled to provide men, arms and large quantities of food. Cromwell's misuse of Barbados as a garrison for his army was a complete violation of the charter of liberties promised to the islanders when the Royalists there surrendered in 1652. At the same time news of the presence of so huge an army and fleet quickly spread throughout the Caribbean and gave the Spaniards plenty of time to prepare for the British invasion of their territories. No attempt seems to have been made to keep the probable destination of the army secret. Writing to his mother in London ten days before the army set sail from Barbados, Charles Sparke told her that because of debts incurred on the island he was joining the army as an ensign to Captain Stephen Noell in the regiment of Colonel Lewis Morris, all islanders, and was likely bound 'for Highespaniola in the first place, then to Cuba, thence to Carthagena'. If Ensign Sparke could identify his probable destination with Cromwell's third suggestion to Venables there is little doubt that the Caribbean grapevine had also passed the message to the Spaniards who were living in the places mentioned. Venables later blamed Penn for landing the troops more than 30 miles from the city of San Domingo, but the attack on Hispaniola never stood much chance of success because of the lack of elementary precautions against rains and diseases. Death by sickness and enemy attacks reduced Venables' army by approximately 1,000 men whereas the Spaniards on Hispaniola lost less than 50 men. If Venables, who had taken his wife on the expedition with him, displayed any military ability on this unsuccessful assault upon the Spanish Indies it was in getting the majority of his troops afloat before the Spaniards captured or killed them all.

Having failed to reduce Hispaniola the commissioners showed prudence in selecting Jamaica as their face-saving target. Jamaica had been invaded by the English several times before and its defences were known to be poor. They justified their decision when on 11 May their soldiers entered St Iago de la Vega and found it deserted. Little resistance had been made by the defenders of Passage Fort on the day before and none was met on the six-mile march to the capital of the island. On 16 May the Spanish Governor Ramirez

1. Arawak wood carving from Jamaica.

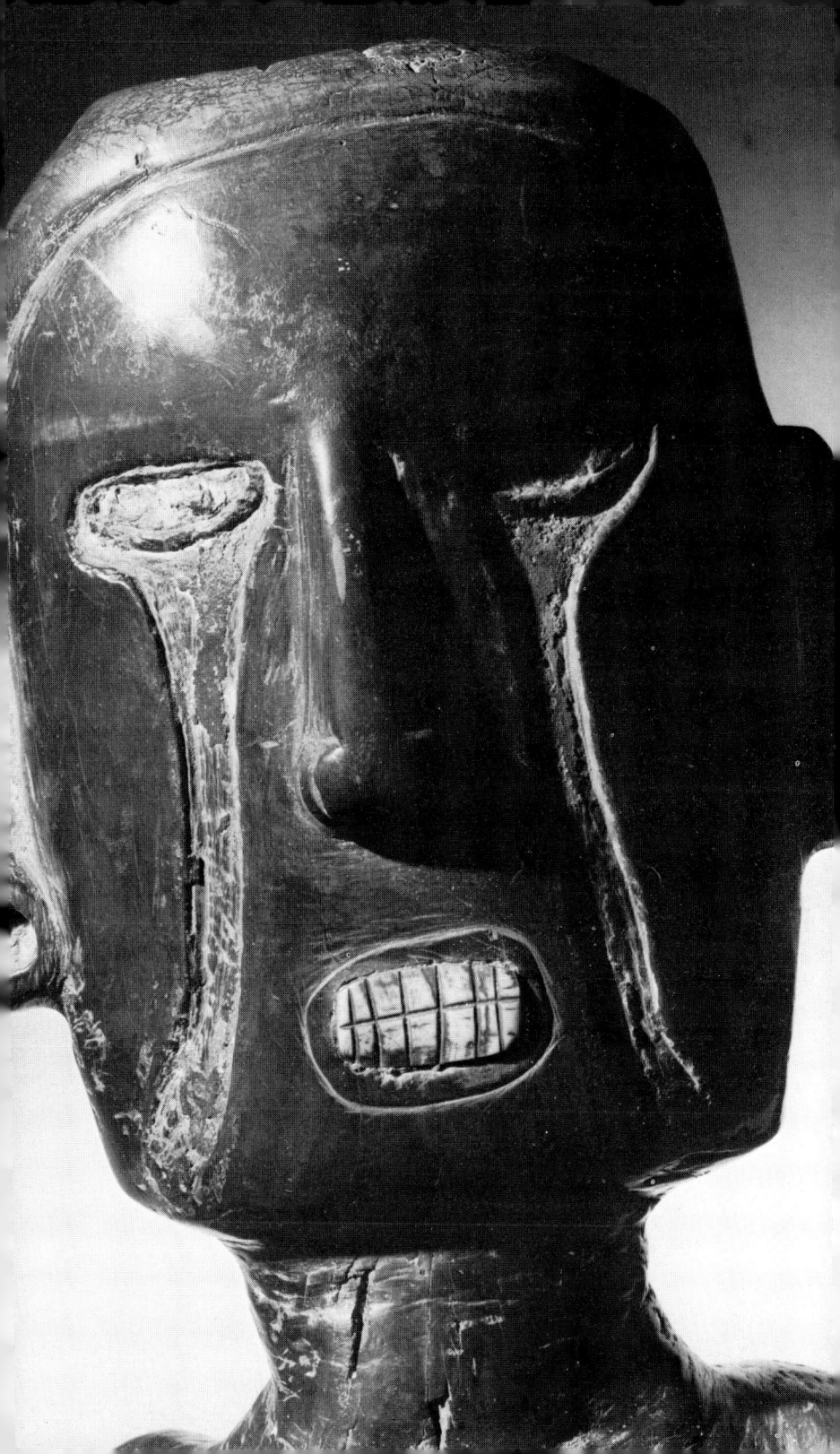

returned to La Vega to sign articles of surrender. According to an eye-witness he was a sorry sight, although carried in a hammock, between negroes upon a pole, with two men on horseback to wait on him. He was 'so rotten and so much eaten out with the pox that he could neither go, stand, nor seat, nor well lie; he was a very sad creature and the enemy were ashamed that we should see him'. The sad creature agreed upon abject conditions of surrender which gave the Jamaican Spaniards a choice of being transported to some other Spanish territory or submitting to directives from the conquerors. They opted for neither, but fled with their possessions into the mountains, driving their horses and much of their cattle ahead of them. Venables had occupied an empty city but his army, already short of adequate rations, was forced to eat the flesh of whatever horses, stray cats, dogs or donkeys they could surprise in the vicinity of the town. Bad diet and insanitary conditions caused sickness, and deaths became so frequent that many men remained unburied for days. In desperation Venables later distributed lands to regiments for cultivation, ordering that whatever food was produced by an individual soldier would be for his own use. Not all the soldiers were turned into farmers, however. Some had to be mounted as guards to protect their fellows in the fields from sudden attacks by bands of Spaniards who raided from their strongholds in the mountains, or from negro cow-killers who hunted in the plains. For years after the so-called capture of Jamaica the British forces effectively occupied only a small portion of the island; the major land area remained available for use by Spanish guerillas and their allies, the negro huntsmen.

Without receiving orders from London, Penn decided in June that his role as commander of the fleet had been accomplished and left Jamaica on the 25th of that month. Venables followed on 4 July. Both commanders were sent to the Tower by Cromwell soon after their arrival in England, but were soon released after acknowledging that they had been guilty of deserting their posts without instructions. Cromwell's sense of righteousness never failed him. He had

2. The pacification with the maroon negroes, 1739, from Bryan Edwards' *History of the British West Indies.*

received the disastrous news of San Domingo with the comment 'the Lord hath greatly humbled us', but he wrote to Goodson, who succeeded Penn in command of the Jamaican fleet telling him to 'set up [his] banners in the name of Christ' and to fight 'the Lord's battles' against the 'Roman Babylon of which the Spaniards is the great underpropper'. What the soldiers of the Lord wanted in Jamaica was radically different from Cromwell's visions. They wanted to be paid, they wanted clothes and especially tools and instruments of a far higher quality than had been issued to them. The officers begged for bread, flour, brandy, arms, shot and medical supplies. They wanted Scotch servants and ratification by Cromwell of the land grants made by Venables. Many wanted to go home. At a meeting called soon after Venables had deserted his post a Council of War passed a resolution calling upon Cromwell to establish a constitution and laws to govern and administer the settlement. Other requests approved for transmission to the Lord Protector at the time concerned a supply of settlers from England and British colonies and the grant of the necessary authority to draw bills of exchange on the public treasury up to £10,000 in order to purchase necessities from ships calling at Jamaica with greater frequency than the occasional army transports from England.

The men on the spot wanted to get on with the urgent task of settlement, but Cromwell continued to think of Jamaica only as the door he had finally opened to fight the Lord's battles against the Spaniards in the lands from which their treasure came. While Cromwell dreamed his visions, his soldiers in Jamaica continued to die of dysentery and malaria, sometimes as many as 140 a week. When Sedgwick, who had succeeded to Venables' command, reported to Secretary of State Thurloe on the condition of the troops in October 1655 he described the commanders as 'some having left them, some dead, some sick, some in indifferent health; the soldiery many dead, their carcasses lying unburied in the highways, and among the bushes . . . many of them that were alive walked like ghosts or dead men . . . they lay groaning and crying out bread for the Lord's sake . . . the truth is God is angry and the plague is begun'. At the time of Sedgwick's report only 3,710 of the 7,000 men who had captured Jamaica remained alive. Sedgwick's scathing remark about the quality of those who had survived seems strangely irrelevant to modern ears. Unpaid, badly led, poorly fed and exposed to attacks by guerillas and haunted by the fear of epidemics, could soldiers have been expected to be other than 'lazy and idle . . . slothful' or desirous to die rather 'than to live'? Cromwell's method of dealing with the pitiful condition of his army of the Lord was to send out more regiments to endure the same hardships with a supply of food for 6,000 men to last four months. The rations were all gone by April 1656 and his commander Sedgwick also died of fever on 23 May. Before he died Sedgwick had written to Thurloe that the Spaniard was not a considerable enemy but the blacks 'must either be destroyed or brought in upon some terms or other, or else they will be a great discouragement to the settling of a people here'. Sedgwick's assessment of the Spanish guerillas seems unrealistic in view of the fact that the king of Spain had recognised the leader of the Spanish resistance in Jamaica, Ysassi with the title of Governor in 1656. Fear of a Spanish attack from Carthagena had also led Sedgwick to build a fort on the Cay de Carina which the English after the Restoration renamed Port Royal. A ground fort was completed on the cay by 1657 and British military headquarters were set up there. Prize ships taken by the fleet were also unloaded at the cay which was visited from time to time by trading ships from New England and Bermuda. D'Oyley, who succeeded Sedgwick as military commander, also began to encourage the off-loading there of prizes taken by English buccaneers living on Tortuga. The seamen who used the cay which was to become famous as Port Royal were eventually to do more damage to Spain's American sources of wealth than Cromwell's soldiers ever achieved. As early as 1659 Myngs, who succeeded Goodson as commander of the fleet in Jamaica, brought back a treasure from the Spanish Main valued at 1,500,000 pieces of eight.

Towards the end of June 1657 a Spanish invasion force of more than 200 men arrived in the port of La Maguana (Ocho Rios) from Cuba. They were met by Ysassi and some Spanish soldiers who brought the strength of the force up to 400 men. The invasion army achieved very little mainly because of divisions among senior officers and from lack of clear objectives. That they remained on Jamaica for months before D'Oyley knew of their presence is clear indication of the failure of the British to develop settlements. When he did find out about the invasion the British commander in chief D'Oyley lost no time in dealing with a situation which might otherwise have led to the Spanish recapture of Jamaica. It took him seven days at sea to reach the shores of Ocho Rios from his headquarters on the cay and on 23 October he won a substantial victory over the Spaniards a few miles from his place of landing. The Spaniards lost about 120 dead in the battle for a stockade and left many wounded prisoners on the ground. Triumphantly, for the first time since the capture of 1655 an English commander could write from Jamaica: 'The King of Spain's affairs do very much fail in these parts, and his trade is brought almost to nothing, by the many private men of war of English and French and ours still abroad to annoy them'. The king of Spain had not given up. On 8 May 1658 another invasion force arrived from Cuba in Rio Nuevo Bay, about 9 miles east of the site of the battle of Las Chorreras of the year before. Three days later this force was discovered by patrolling English ships. D'Oyley, who had sailed from Port Royal, once again offered Ysassi an opportunity to surrender but on receipt of a polite refusal from the Spanish governor he led his soldiers to the rear of a Spanish fort and breached it. About 300 Spaniards were slain and 100 taken prisoner, approximately 50 per cent of the total Spanish force. D'Oyley's superior generalship in these two battles on the north coast made it plain to the Spaniards that the British soldiers could achieve victories in the Indies if properly led. The battle of Rio Nuevo may be taken as a decisive turning point in the history of Jamaica under the English, since it was now clear that British superiority at sea made it impossible for the Spaniards to land and maintain troops in sufficient numbers to dislodge the British. Guerillas and snipers could still cause losses but Jamaica would remain British. There was no fear of retaliation from Spain after Blake's successful blockade of the Spanish coasts in the winter of 1656-57.

It is ironic that Cromwell never heard of D'Oyley's triumph for the good reason that he was already dead and no longer concerned with fighting any more of the Lord's battles on earth. He had died on 3 September 1658. Earlier that year Charles Sparke had written to his kinsman 'Mr Henery Williamson' in Thames Street, near the Customs House in London. The letter gave his address as 'Jemeicho' and was dated 16 March 1658. He desired Williamson 'for Christ Jesus sake ... the greatest Boone and favour ... as many of my fellow soldier friends had done for them to get My Lord Protector's hand for me to go home ... for God knows my condition heare is very sadd, for God sake move my mother and brother and the rest of my friends to send me some reliefe, for clothes I want, with victualls and drinke, for I have neither clothes victualls nor any sustenance from the State. Therefore good cosen for God sake help me'. The cry of Charles Sparke has power after so many centuries to make one realise how much individual unhappiness had been caused to thousands of English soldiers who had been enrolled in Cromwell's war to the death against the Spanish Babylon. Cromwell's Western Design benefited very few of its participants. One thing only is certain: that but for its failure today's Jamaica would have been quite a different place.

From the Restoration to the French Invasion

In attempting to recapture Jamaica from the English Spain had to rely on armed expeditions mounted from Cuba and Mexico because at home her resources had been severely reduced by the requirements of a war that was being waged at the same time against France and England. In October 1655 England signed a treaty with France which put a stop to confrontation of their ships at sea and made it possible for a joint Anglo-French expedition to be sent against the Spanish Netherlands. By 1658 Spain was ready to sue for peace, and by the Treaty of the Pyrenees in the following year England received Dunkirk from Spain while France got a part of the Netherlands. Although the Spanish empire was to endure well into the nineteenth century, the struggle for power in Europe after 1659 took the form of a rivalry between the new empires of France and England.

In the midst of his European preoccupations and increasingly occupied with internal political and financial problems, Oliver Cromwell had turned to Britons overseas for help in securing Jamaica as a British base in the Caribbean sea. He sent letters from England inviting Britons who had settled in New England, Bermuda, Barbados and other islands of the East Caribbean to take advantage of the new lands which had become available on Jamaica. Several hundreds from Nevis responded to his invitation and smaller numbers went from Bermuda, but the successful Puritans of New England saw no good reason to abandon their temperate and burgeoning settlements for a tropical island which the Spaniards had been unable to develop satisfactorily, despite nearly 150 years of residence. The masters of New England ships which supplied the English in Jamaica with food, lumber and beasts of burden were more reliable guides to conditions on the island than Cromwell's civil servants, and they had reported accurately the discontent amongst Cromwell's unpaid troops, the absence of civil administration and courts of justice on Jamaica and the subordination of all resident Britons to the decrees of the senior military commander. Only people trying to escape imprisonment for debt, or anxious to improve their fortunes by cultivation of virgin soils, were likely to choose Jamaica voluntarily until civil government was established there.

That Jamaica survived as an English possession during the years of the Protectorate was due primarily to the weakness of Spanish power, to the gradual acclimatisation of Cromwell's soldiers, to the food and other necessities sent from England and New England, and to the efforts which some of the troops made to grow food on plantations. Yet none of these factors would have been adequate for the consolidation of British power on the island unless backed by the ability of British sailors to keep the Jamaican shoreline safe from enemy attacks. Ashore there were no forts or other military defences capable of repulsing a powerful invasion by Spaniards or international sea rovers.

Had Cromwell sent his very best soldiers from England against Hispaniola in 1655 it is likely that victory might have been achieved over the Spaniards there, but it is doubtful whether such troops would have found it any easier to consolidate their hold over Hispaniola. What tropical colonies a long distance from home needed in the seventeenth century were seasoned settlers, experienced in techniques of survival. Soldiers, especially 'soldiers of the Lord' like Cromwell's, were in no way accustomed to live off the land and not even in England were they easy to keep in order.

George Monk had given excellent advice to Richard Cromwell when he told him to reduce the size of the army in England soon after he had inherited the title of Protector from his father. Above all he had warned him only to keep in command those officers who could be trusted to support the Protectorate. Richard did not follow Monk's advice and by 25 May 1659 he was forced to relinquish his title and to accept a re-established Commonwealth which had once more come under the control of the Long or Rump Parliament. So long as the army's leaders were divided and afraid of the rank-and-file the Long Parliament retained power in England, but Lambert's victory over some Royalist rebels encouraged the army to draw up stiffly worded petitions which expressed strong disapproval of their political rulers. The next step was for Lambert's soldiers to occupy Westminster and guard the Houses of Parliament, but nothing decisive was achieved until George Monk led his army into the City of London and lodged most of his soldiers there. Encouraged by the Londoners' welcome Monk quickly came to terms with those Members of Parliament who had been excluded by Pride's Purge in 1648, and with support of a Parliament strengthened by their presence he established contact with Charles II and persuaded him to return to England on 25 May 1660.

By coincidence Charles returned as king in the very month that the last detachment of Spanish guerillas finally abandoned Jamaica.

Charles during his exile had promised to return Jamaica to the Spanish king in return for Spanish assistance in regaining his throne. Some Spaniards may have hoped that he would return Jamaica in 1660, but Charles was in no position to distribute portions of his restored kingdom, especially since he had regained it without any Spanish help. Earlier, soon after Oliver Cromwell's death, the Spaniards had renewed their efforts to recapture Jamaica. Mexican troops were sent across from Cuba under command of an experienced officer, Juan de Tovar. But Spanish hopes were shattered soon after when Tyson, the British colonel commanding the Guanaboa Regiment, accidentally stumbled upon their major source of food supply, a 200-acre plantation at Lluidas Vale on the northern side of the mountains which separated their camp from the northern shores of Jamaica. From this secret food bowl the Spanish guerillas and their negro allies had been getting regular supplies ever since the British had landed. Its discovery became more serious for the Spaniards through defection of the negro leader, Juan Lubolo, who was in charge of the plantation. Tyson won him over by promising that he would be recognised as 'governor' of Lluidas Vale and that all the negroes on the plantation would be recognised as free men by the British authorities. Lubolo then helped Tyson to find a trail in the forest which led beyond the Moneague basin to a Spanish camp established close to where Shaw Park Hotel is now situated on the north coast. Tyson overwhelmed the Spanish forces there, but Ysassi escaped and held out for some months longer until in early May 1660 he fled from near Oracabessa in a boat which took him to Cuba. On that island he continued to do all that he could to encourage the Spanish recapture of the island on which he had courageously resisted the British occupation for five long years.

When in 1663 the first English civil government was established on Jamaica, eight years after the conquest, Tyson's promise of freedom to Lubolo's men was upheld and every negro was made eligible for a grant of 30 acres of land. Lubolo was made colonel of the militia and appointed chief magistrate for the district, but died soon afterwards in a skirmish with negro rebels who had not been set free. Lubolo's name in the form of Juan de Bolas is given still to one high mountain and two rivers of Jamaica. Negroes who remained loyal to the Spaniards and hostile to the English rallied under the leadership of one of their fellows, Juan de Serras. He led them away from their stronghold of Vermejales to a place which is marked on today's maps as Vera Ma Hollis. In 1670 their attacks on settlements became so frequent that the government officially described them as outlaws and offered rewards to persons who killed any of their leaders. For many decades more they continued to harass Jamaicans by raids on plantations and their strongholds in the mountains became refuges for negroes who ran away from their masters to join the outlaws who were later described as maroons. In a letter dated 20 February 1659 Charles Sparke gives an indication of early trading arrangements on the island, which reflect how progress was being made from full military control towards a system of private enterprise. Charles Sparke tells his brother in London that he is still very anxious to return to England and prays him, if he cannot get him a licence to come back home, at least to send him over to Jamaica a 'considerable cargo', which he will return 'in goods to both our profits'. He requested a shipment of brandy 'most valuable here . . . flower . . . if well conditioned . . . oyle . . . a good commodity . . . some good butter butt not mutch . . . some few shoose and good worsted stockings, cheese if goode', and notes that 'packinge cloth sutch as you make hopp baggs of will goe off well for cotton baggs'. In return for these goods Charles Sparke proposed to send over cotton grown in Jamaica. He asked his brother 'what price good cotton bares ready ginned?'

We learn from another letter sent later from Captain Barrington's house at 'Pointe Cagaway' that Charles 'never had the happiness to receive any answer' from his brother, but his efforts to enter the world of commerce while still enrolled as a soldier illustrates how complex was the business of survival in a colony supposedly dependent on instructions from authorities at home. The men on the spot had to improvise or stagnate. The years between Cromwell's death in 1658 and the receipt by D'Oyley in May 1661 of his first commission as royal governor were especially difficult. D'Oyley's government, if government it can be called in this extremely critical period when rebellious army leaders and lawless buccaneers were threatening to take over Jamaica, was in danger of becoming anarchy. Unpaid soldiers and sailors made difficult citizens who were not easily controlled by a commander who rarely received any instructions from England and had no authority to repatriate men who had survived the horrors of settling an island fertile in disease, liable to wild natural explosions and under constant threat of invasion by enemies at sea.

Apart from repeated Spanish invasions D'Oyley had to deal with an insurrection led by Lieutenant Colonel Raymond who persuaded farmer soldiers of Tyson's Guanaboa Regiment that the time had come for Jamaica 'to be settled in colonies' with 'constables and civil officers'. Only by having recourse to a court martial which resulted in the shooting of Colonels Tyson and Raymond did D'Oyley succeed in preventing the establishment of a military independent republican regime of Jamaica.

When towards the end of May 1661 D'Oyley received instructions from the Home government requiring him to take advice from an elected council of 12 persons the nucleus of a civil society was laid. Eleven of these councillors were to be chosen by as many of the army officers, planters and inhabitants as could conveniently 'gather together'. It would have been strange indeed if a majority of councillors were not selected from the leading army officers and landowners closest to the governor. D'Oyley's estimate of the forces under his command in the middle of 1661, other than sailors, was approximately 2,000 officers and men.

Old statistical papers show that by 1662 the English were cultivating 2,908 acres on Jamaica, chiefly in the plains of Guanaboa and Liguanea (1,249) and in the lowlands of Port Morant and Yallahs (819). Of a resident population of 5,728 about 1,181 lived in the Liguanea plains and 1,040 on Cagway (Port Royal).

Detachments of 1,523 men were spread around ten districts, 300 each at Liguanea and Port Royal, 230 around Guanaboa and other groups ranging between 150 and 72 at Clarendon, Port Morant, Old Harbour, Villa de la Vega (Spanish Town) Morant Bay, Yallahs and Angels. The most highly developed lands in the combined districts of Morant and Yallahs had been cultivated by settlers from Nevis, while the 700 acres at Guanaboa Vale had been planted by soldiers. On his way to take over from D'Oyley as governor, Lord Windsor made a halt at Barbados in 1662 and made himself unpopular there by issuing promises to persons willing to settle in Jamaica. Such an appeal seemed necessary to Windsor because he had been ordered to disband the army in Jamaica except for 400 infantry and 150 cavalry. The authorities in England allowed Windsor to preside over the first Jamaica Assembly which met in 1664, but replaced him the next year by Sir Thomas Modyford, a successful Barbadian planter who persuaded 800 of his fellow countrymen to come over and apply their agricultural knowledge for the benefit of Jamaica's economic growth. Modyford also encouraged a former Barbadian bond-servant, Henry Morgan, who took over leadership of the buccaneers in Port Royal after the death of Mansvelt. The occupation of Jamaica had been timely for the English buccaneers who had been driven out of Tortuga by the Spaniards in 1654. The cay which later developed into Port Royal was an ideal place for refitting vessels and provided ample opportunity for disposal of booty or spending of treasure. In 1659 Christopher Myngs gave a great fillip to buccaneering by capturing booty from the Spanish mainland valued at one and a half million pieces of eight. Edward Long the Jamaican historian who wrote in 1774 possibly reflected views which Modyford and other respectable settlers and officials held about the buccaneers. They were, he wrote, 'the principle supporters of the colony by the torrents of money which they poured in to the enriching of merchants and planters'. So thoroughly were the buccaneers integrated into the mainstream of Jamaican life in the first decades of British occupation that Long could write: 'when privateering was in its most flourishing state during the government of Sir Thomas Modyford and Sir Thomas Lynch, as many men were engaged on board these vessels as there were on shore in the island'. Morgan was a great leader of men but he was base, treacherous and cruel, as anyone can learn from reading John Esquemeling's account which was first published in 1678. Long was undoubtedly right in saying that privateering was actively encouraged by English officials at a time when there was no fleet to protect the settlers from Spaniards who were determined to recapture Jamaica. By sacking Spanish towns on other islands and the mainland the buccaneers undoubtedly kept the Spaniards busy defending other American possessions which they did not want to lose. The increasing ferocity of the buccaneers had alarmed the authorities in Spain so much that a treaty was signed in 1670 (the Treaty of Madrid) under the terms of which Spain, for the first time since Columbus' discovery, recognised the rights of other European countries besides Portugal to hold possessions in the Indies.

Jamaica and other islands which had been settled by Englishmen were now recognised by this treaty as rightful possessions of the English Crown. The English therefore had no further excuse for supporting illegal assaults upon Spanish towns and when Morgan returned from sacking Panama in 1671 he was soon after sent to England for trial. Modyford had also been recalled earlier to give an account of his stewardship. He stoutly maintained that encouragement of privateering 'could not have been avoided without the manifest ruin' of Jamaica.

Modyford's contribution to Jamaican development was ended, but Morgan was sent back as lieutenant governor in 1675 to assist Lord Vaughan. An entry in Hans Sloane's diary describes him in 1688 as aged 'about 45, lean, sallow coloured, his eyes a little yellowish and belly a little jutting out or prominent'. After bouts of intemperance 'his belly swelled so as not to be contained in his coat'. He tried several doctors but died soon after, racked by a cough.

By 1668 the population of the cay which became Port Royal had reached 8,000. The Governor had a residence there and there were altogether about 800 houses. About this time the channel between the cay and the Palisadoes was filled in, Fort Charles was enlarged and new forts built. By day business was transacted in warehouses stacked high with goods from Europe and North America, but by night whenever the buccaneer fleet was in port vice occupied the streets. The society, which had been protected by buccaneers from Spanish invasion and provided with Spanish money for spending, was one corrupted by gambling, prostitutes and drink, as the case histories in Hans Sloane's *A Voyage to the Islands* attest. So prolific were the numbers of taverns in the town that some persons complained that 'there were not now resident on this place ten men to every house that selleth liquors'.

Money ran like water through the buccaneers' hands. 'Being arrived' in Port Royal, Esquemeling wrote in 1678, with 250,000 pieces of eight and rich merchandizes 'they passed here sometimes in all sorts of vices and debauchery, according to their common manner of doing, spending with huge prodigality what others had gained with no small labour and toil'. He gives an instance of the cruelty of Morgan's men during the expedition against Panama. To gain information from a poor wretch caught wearing his master's breeches they 'inhumanely disjointed his arms. After this they twisted a cord around his forehead, which they wrung so hard that his eyes appeared as big as eggs and were ready to fall out of his skull ... afterwards they cut off his nose and ears and singed his face with burning straw, till he could speak nor lament his misery no longer. Then losing all hopes of hearing any confession from his mouth, they commanded a negro to run him through with a lance which put an end to his life ... as to religious persons and priests, they granted them less quarter than to others, unless they could produce a considerable sum of money.... Women themselves were no better used and Captain Morgan, their leader and commander gave them no good example in this point'. The buccaneers' ships at Port Royal not only disgorged riches to encourage the vices of the town but attracted some servants from the plantations. It is unlikely that there were sufficient slaves to replace men who joined the buccaneers or who died of fevers until the war against the Dutch (1665-67) ended with the Treaty of Breda.

Yet progress was being made with land development, for by 1670, about 209,000 acres were being cultivated and the island's population had grown to 15,000 inclusive of slaves. At the same time the rise of 'King Sugar' began to foreshadow the eclipse of the small yeomen who might have taken root in the island even though it was plagued by sudden deaths from epidemics and convulsions of Nature. The race to obtain great wealth and resettle in England was nourished in Jamaica by climatic as well as other factors. Yet there was no great evacuation, the population continued to grow, and besides sugar and indigo, harvested cocoa and tended herds of cattle. Under English rule the island was becoming more self-sufficient than it had been since the early decades of Spanish settlement.

The weakness of the Spanish economy under the Hapsburgs had made it possible for Dutch, French and Spanish intruders to establish strongholds within an American empire, which between 1516 and 1700 had been strictly reserved by Spanish monarchs as a patrimony for Castile. Settlers on trading posts or plantations readily welcomed 'protection' against Spanish reprisals which was offered by men operating as pirates, privateers or buccaneers from bases established during the seventeenth century on French Tortuga, Dutch Curaçao and British Jamaica. Traders of these three nations had as early as 1630 begun to supply goods to Spanish colonists who were never able to obtain adequate supplies from Spain. Illicit trade also flourished between Spanish American towns especially by means of fairs held in Acapulco, Porto Bello and Buenos Aires. So great was the expansion of colonial contraband trade that it was estimated in 1686 to have represented two-thirds of all Spanish American commerce. The British hold on Jamaica, which had been secured by buccaneering attacks on Spanish strongholds and reinforced by intermittent British naval presences, gave the island many favourable opportunities to supply Spanish American demands for goods and slaves. Spain itself had, by the second half of the seventeenth century become so dependent upon English and Dutch traders for goods shipped to the Indies from Spanish ports, that privileged Dutch and English merchants were allowed to reside in major centres like Seville, Cadiz and Malaga. Infiltration into the highly protected trading system of Castile had followed from the generous terms which the Dutch had wrested from their former Spanish masters through the Treaty of Munster (1648). France also obtained valuable trade concessions later from Spain when the Peace of the Pyrenees was signed in 1659. It was England's turn to gain wide entry for her goods in 1667 when Eminente's agreement resulted from changed diplomatic attitudes in England.

With the exception of Catalonia, where Barcelona was beginning to take the initiatives that helped to transform Spanish growth in the sixteenth century, the economy of Spain suffered violent changes between 1664 and 1680, a year of complete collapse. The rise of Jamaica as a British trading post, advantageously placed to exploit Spanish difficulties, to some extent came about through the inefficiency of Hapsburg policies in Spain. When the House of Bourbon eventually succeeded to the Spanish throne in 1700 new energies were released, which were only overcome by the superior naval forces of a new imperialist Greater Britain.

England during the first two decades which followed the Restoration of 1660 was beset by too many internal problems and preoccupations in Europe to do more than attempt to tidy up administration in order to gain the maximum advantage from the possession of its overseas territories. Clarendon, in accordance with the wishes of influential merchants in London had persuaded Charles II to create two special councils, one for 'trade' and the other for 'plantations'. Whatever might have been the opinions of overseas English settlers, who considered themselves to be no less English for living outside the boundaries of England, the authorities at home were convinced that the purpose of colonies was for the use and benefit of England. Merchants, office holders, statesmen and royal personages all agreed that the chief purpose of plantations was to increase the revenues of the Mother Country. Parliament supported these aims by passing Navigation Acts which confirmed and elaborated upon the Commonwealth's protective legislation of 1651,

3. *(above)* Oliver Cromwell by Samuel Cooper.
4. *(below)* The Reverend William Knibb, abolitionist, by Baxter.

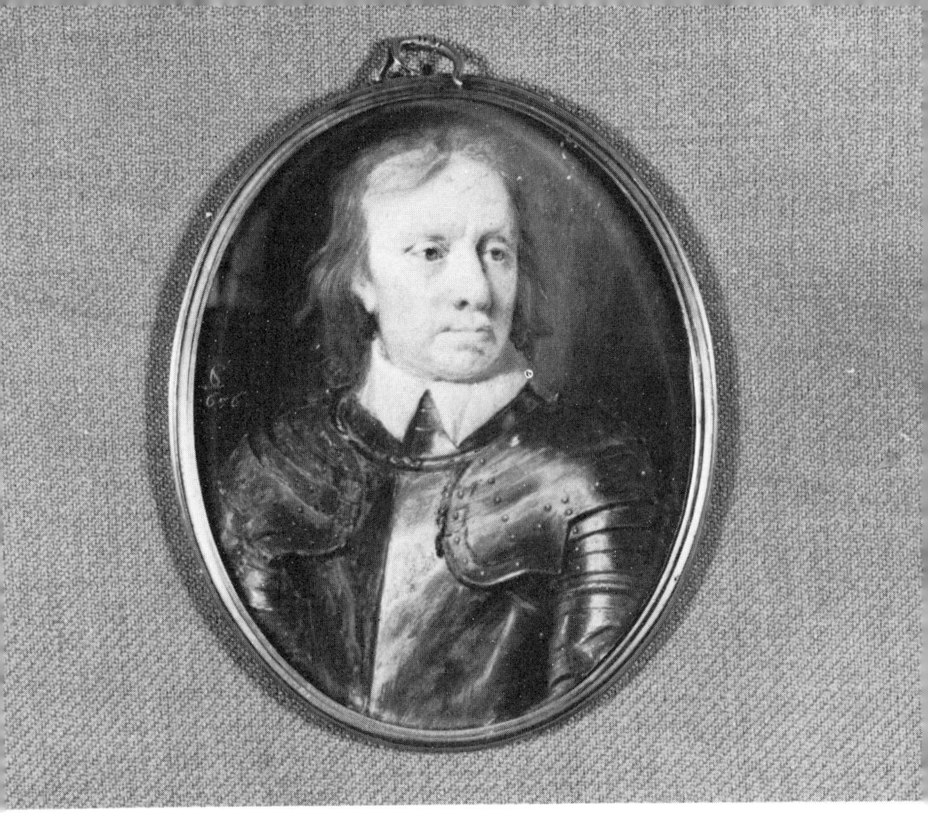

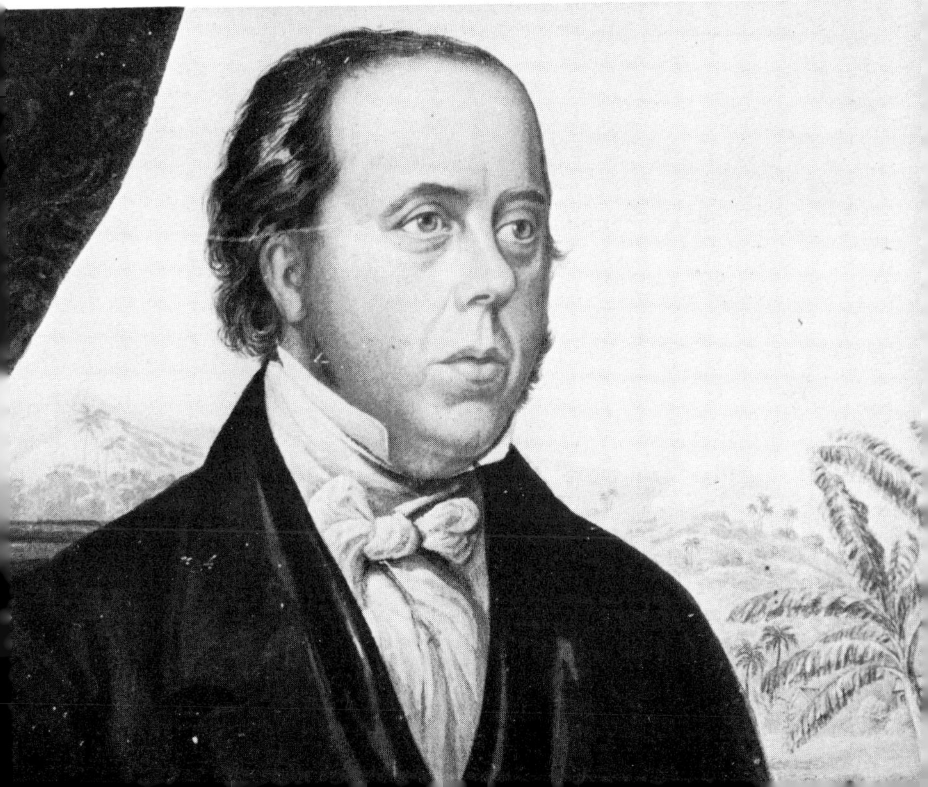

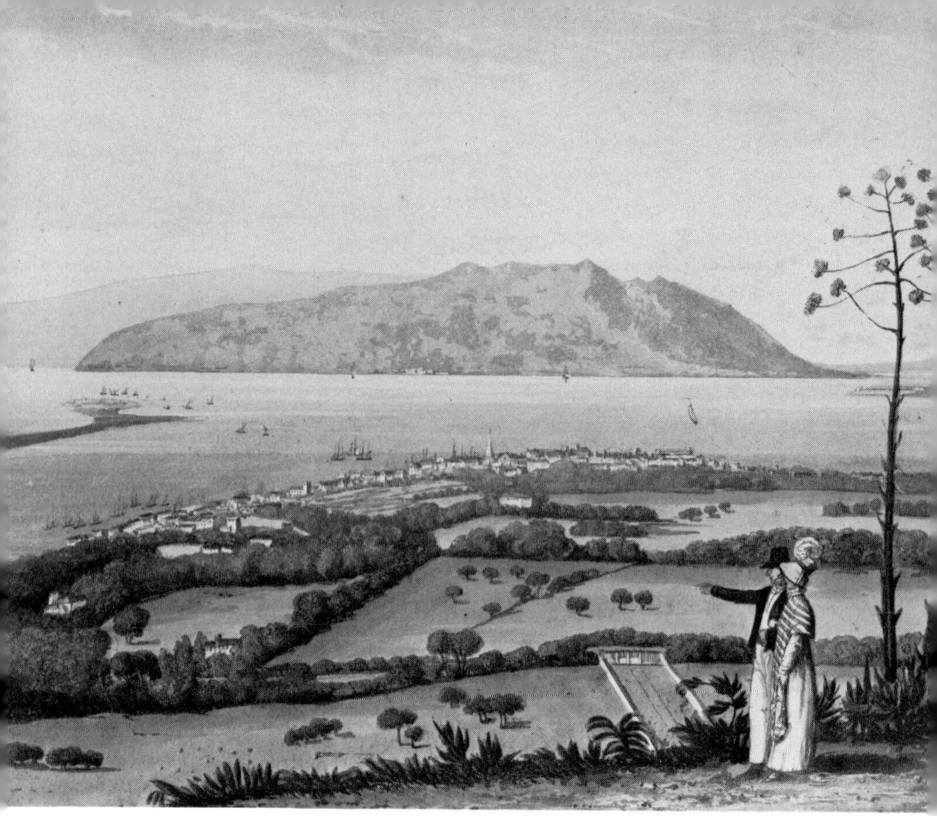

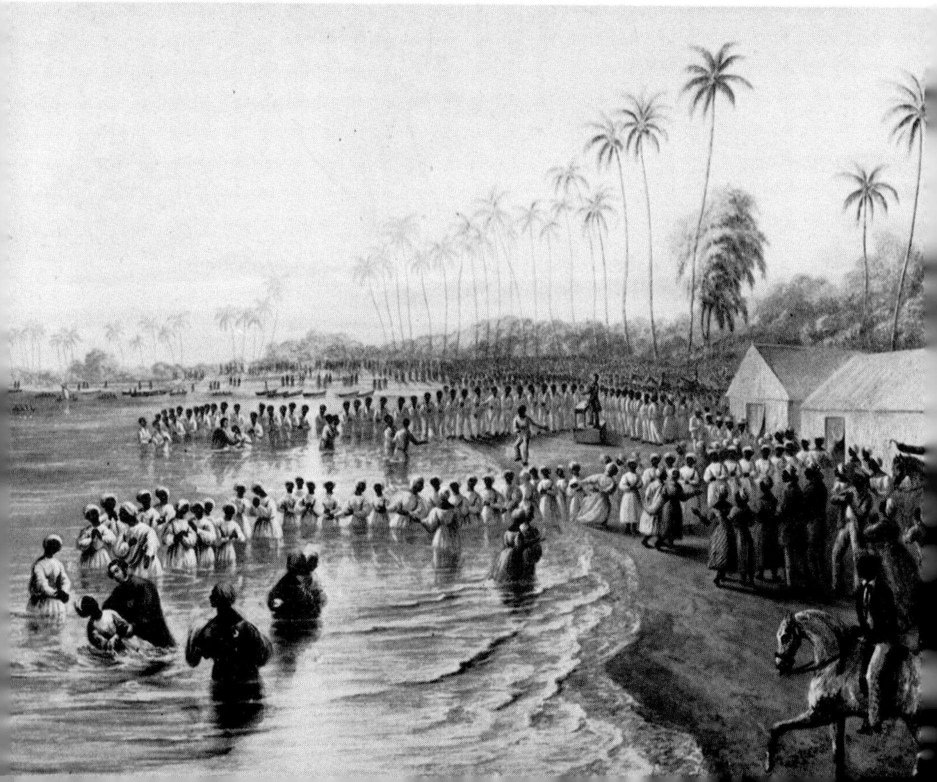

which had caused open war with the Dutch.

The intention of the men who wielded power in England was spelt out precisely in 'An Act for the Encouragement of Trade' which was passed by Parliament in 1663. Among its objects were maintenance of 'a greater correspondence between the Plantations peopled by the King's subjects and the Kingdom of England'. This centralising policy was intended to keep the plantations in a 'firmer dependence' upon England and to make them 'more beneficial and advantageous unto it in the further employment and increase of English shipping, vent of English woolen and other manufactures and commodities'. Above everything else the Act aimed to make England 'a staple not only of the commodities of Plantations but also of commodities of other countries and places'. Difficulties of enforcing English mercantilist legislation in places far distant from London led ten years later to an Act requiring captains of ships to pay duty at colonial ports of clearance unless certificates could be shown that bonds had been taken out in England to carry cargoes directly back to the home country. As a result of this law royal customs officials were appointed by the commissioners of customs in England to collect English rates of duty in colonial ports. While tightening these controls from London, England was also engaged in its third war of trade with the Dutch in the years 1672-74.

Jamaica does not appear to have been too greatly affected by the centralising of colonial policies which followed the Restoration because it was still very much a pioneer settlement only just emerging from the grip of lawless buccaneers and their supporters. The King had knighted Morgan in 1674 and sent him back to Jamaica as lieutenant governor, but he quickly undermined Lord Vaughan's authority by carousing and gambling in the taverns of Port Royal and encouraged privateering. Not until 1683 was he removed from office. English tolerance of Jamaica in its formative decades probably stemmed from hopes of gain which were entertained by royal and other shareholders in the Royal Africa Company which did profi-

5. *(above)* Kingston and Port Royal from Windsor Farm, from James Hakewill's *Picturesque Tour of the Island of Jamaica, 1825.*
6. *(below)* Mass baptism by Missionaries near Brown's Town, 1842.

table business with Spaniards in the slave market at Port Royal. At the same time the Stuart Kings Charles II and James II could not permit their subjects in any settlements overseas to believe that the king's authority was limited by the seas. Accordingly a rebellious Jamaican House of Assembly was presented by the Earl of Carlisle in 1678 with 37 laws already passed under the great seal of England. The English in Jamaica however refused to recognise the right of England to legislate for them in the same way as was done for the Irish to whom Poyning's Law of 1495 then applied. Thanks largely to the arguments of Colonel Long, chief justice of Jamaica, Charles II realised that the capture of Jamaica from Spain did not invalidate rights which had been granted to Englishmen in Jamaica and he agreed in 1680 that the laws of Jamaica should thereafter follow the precedent set in Barbados where laws were enacted by the governor, council and assembly.

This early constitutional quarrel with England was fought out during a period when Jamaicans were frequently threatened by attack from roving French ships. In 1679 martial law had to be proclaimed when a French fleet was observed in Jamaican waters. Jamaicans also regretted the absence of buccaneers in Port Royal when the Spanish *guardacostas* arrested their ships. In 1678 they joined with other Western plantations in a petition to England against 'the intolerable injuries, unheard of cruelties, innumerable depredations and bloody murders committed by the Spaniards ... in the West Indies ever since the Peace with Spain of July 1670'. Jamaican fishermen also suffered so many attacks from French privateers operating from ports on the west coast of Hispaniola that Governor Lynch had to authorise the construction of a 50-oared galley to be used against them. Threats from pirates and the likelihood of Jamaicans returning to piracy was exacerbated in 1685 by a revolt of slaves who fled to the mountains after killing a number of settlers on plantations. Once again martial law had to be declared. Governor Molesworth about this time experienced great difficulty from a House of Assembly which was led by

Roger Elletson, a friend of Sir Henry Morgan. Molesworth dissolved the House, saying bluntly that 'all things have been carried not by strength of argument or reason, but by noise and number of voices, led by malice and followed by ignorance'. Molesworth's attempts to arouse Jamaican oligarchs to a sense of responsibility were soon nullified by the second Duke of Albemarle whose father had been one of the lords proprietors of the Bahamas. The Duke supported Morgan, whose love of liquor he shared, and permitted a new assembly under control of Elletson as speaker to pursue policies directly opposed to those formulated or approved in London. Albemarle died in November 1688 and his policies were reversed, but Jamaica next year experienced another slave revolt. Fresh troubles followed in 1691 when women and children had to be brought from the north coast to Port Royal to avoid assaults from French privateers who were sent over from Hispaniola by an energetic buccaneer-governor Jean du Casse. Port Royal proved to be a poor haven for the refugees. On 7 June 1692 Jamaica experienced a terrible earthquake. According to an account written some days after, 'the wharf next to the harbour giving way, all the houses thereon run down with the land into the sea. Ours with divers others near two fathom under, and in other parts of the Point, the ground opened and the sea gushed up a wonderful height, so that in a moment almost all the place was under water, there being very little spot left, and that in heaps, cracks and gullies. It is thought two-thirds of the people were lost; some sunk into the earth, some knocked on the head by houses, some cut in pieces by timber floating and some drowned.' The earthquake, which had taken at least 2,000 lives, was followed by an epidemic which carried off 3,000 more persons. As if nature had not done enough to harry the Jamaicans, French privateers under orders from du Casse now renewed their raids. In October 1693 the governor reported to London that 'the enemy daily infests our coasts'. In December, finding English sentries asleep, French raiders captured 370 slaves and much booty. Thoroughly alarmed by this time the Jamaican governor and council abandoned defences on the northern and eastern shores and took women and children into Port Royal which at the time was being rebuilt. The council also published a decree that any slave killing a French invader would be made free. Towards the end of May 1694 some Englishmen who escaped from a prison in Hispaniola brought news to Port Royal that du Casse had assembled a fleet of some 20 ships and over 3,000 men to invade Jamaica. A landing of 800 men was made from ships anchored in Cow Bay on 27 June. The French forces were unable to capture Port Royal, but they wreaked havoc on persons whom they encountered on their road march to Port Morant. According to a report which is preserved in the Calendar of State Papers 'more inhuman barbarities were never committed by Turk or infidel', than during this march. The French fleet made Port Morant their headquarters for one month and then landed at Carlisle Bay, 35 miles west of Port Royal. After looting and destroying undefended property the fleet gave up the attempt to capture the island and set sail for Petit Goave on Hispaniola on 3 August. The official English losses during the invasion were about 100 killed and wounded. More than 1,000 slaves were taken away, while 50 sugar works and 200 houses were burnt down. Great hardships were later experienced as a consequence of the widespread destruction of fruit trees, food crops and livestock. Worse, there was another slave revolt at the end of the year.

Despite ruthless hammering of the north shores of Hispaniola by a combined Anglo-Spanish force in 1695, Governor Beeston was still complaining in July 1696 of 'frequent depredations of the French on the outparts of the Island, where, there being no strength to repel them, few weeks pass without the robbing and burning of houses in some of the remote settlements'. Matters were further aggravated by the departures from the island of 'all our privateers and seamen ... by the harassing and ill-using of the men of war, who have frightened away not only our own people but also those of the northern colonies from bringing us provisions'. Improvement of the situation was made towards the end of 1696 when an English Order in Council ruled that men should only be impressed by authority of the Governor.

The Treaty of Ryswick (September 1697) decided that the French should have the western part of Hispaniola which they called St Domingue. This new development led the English to station a fleet at Port Royal for the defence of Jamaica. The vice-admiral in charge, John Benbow, later died there of wounds received during a naval engagement off Santa Marta and was buried in the parish church of Kingston.

Jamaicans in the Eighteenth Century

The English decision to banish Spanish-hating buccaneers from Port Royal had been taken in some measure because influential groups in England expected to gain greatly from trading arrangements for the supply of slaves to Spanish settlements overseas. Port Royal was very suitably situated for a slave mart and in 1672 the Royal Africa Company obtained extensive grants of West African lands from which regular supplies of slaves could be obtained. Indeed a steady traffic in Africans developed so quickly in Port Royal that a Spanish agent, James Castillo, was appointed in 1684 to buy slaves there for Spanish-American settlements. Castillo apparently paid Governor Molesworth substantial sums to ensure that the very best available slaves were reserved for the Spanish plantations. Molesworth went so far as to arrange for Castillo to be registered as a naturalised British subject a year after arrival. The Jamaican planters resented Castillo's privileged position as a slave buyer and in 1688 obtained consent of the Duke of Albemarle, who succeeded Molesworth, for a petition to be sent to James II alleging that few slaves, 'and those refuse too', had fallen to their share over a period of six years. Castillo was temporarily disgraced, for reasons connected with Catholic religious intrigues between Spanish and English ecclesiastics, but later visited the English court and not only was recognised by the king as Spanish commissary general for supplying slaves to the Spanish West Indies but received the accolade of knighthood. Sir James returned to Jamaica where he lived on the Windward Road on the site of today's Harbour View in such style that the main fort and out-buildings on his estate could be used during the first decade of the eighteenth century for the accommodation of 200 soldiers. When the earthquake temporarily closed the mart at Port Royal in 1692 Sir James allotted £300,000 to be spent on obtaining slaves from the Dutch West Indian islands.

After 1689 English people realised that ultimate control of the realm and its colonies was the responsibility of the men who controlled Parliament, but until 1765 at least Parliament left the king and privy council to look after colonial affairs. King and council alone could give sanction to recommendations of the board of trade which continued to sit for 86 years after its formation in 1696, and was concerned primarily to see that the plantations provided a favourable balance of trade for the English realm. Colonial administration was never organised within that period as something apart from the regular government of the realm and no special files were set aside for the West Indies or America. Entries affecting the plantations were made in regular books or bundles employed by the admiralty, treasury, war office, customs house, post office or high court of admiralty. Greatest contact with the colonies was maintained by the admiralty which had to shoulder the burden of colonial defence. Among its duties were the despatch of squadrons, correspondence with naval officers and governors, the supply of frigates for patrol, the provision of men-of-war for convoying ships, finding transport for soldiers, the issue of letters of marque and reprisals and the arrangement of packet services to the West Indies. Comprehensive as these burdens or duties might appear on paper, there was in fact relatively little real protection, either military or naval, which England could give its colonies before 1756. The English victory of Barfleur and La Hogue (1692) had prevented French control of the English Channel and England's capture of Gibraltar (1704) and Minorca (1708) also limited the effectiveness of combined Spanish and French armadas, but England did not have full command of the sea until much later. Even when, in the years 1707-08, 24

British warships were cruising in West Indian waters, hostile privateers still prevented the operations of normal commerce. A report from Jamaica in 1708 summed up the position in a statement; 'trade in general seems at a stand and nothing on foot but privateering'. While trade was being ruined for the merchants and planters, profits could be made by English adventurers who took prizes at sea or attacked the coastal cities of Spanish America. Commodore Wager, for example, in an encounter off Carthagena deprived the Spaniards of galleons estimated to be worth many millions of pounds in today's currencies.

One consequence of parliamentary supremacy in England after 1689 was the encouragement it gave to upholders of parliamentary supremacy in colonies. In 1703 Governor Handasyde reported that most of the members of the Jamaican house of assembly were Creolians 'at great variance with those born in England, as if they themselves were not descended from English parents'. The root of the quarrel was based on the unwillingness of the Jamaican representatives to pay for the cost of English troops stationed at Jamaica for purposes of defence. The truculence of Jamaica's house of assembly increased with the emergence of prosperous planting and trading families who were in no way inclined to submit to dictation from the representatives of English planting and trading families in England. The father of the speaker of the House in 1710, Beckford, owned 22 plantations and nearly 4,000 slaves and his property was valued at over £1,000,000 when he died. From this fortune his son built Fonthill in Wiltshire and filled its 'gothic abbey' with a splendid collection of art and books.

When the king sent an instruction in 1718 to the effect that the Council of Jamaica 'had as much to do in passing bills for raising and granting of money as the Assembly has', there was great opposition from the Lower House. A tug of war ensued between assembly and governor and council until a compromise was reached in 1728, when, in return for the Crown's consent that the island should enjoy all such laws and statutes as had been 'at any time esteemed, introduced, accepted or received' there, the assembly passed a permanent Revenue Act. By 1752, according to a report from Governor Knowles who was especially disliked for moving the archives from Spanish Town to Kingston, the assembly had made itself the preponderant element in the government of Jamaica. By 1766 the House took the view that the time had come to declare itself as sole competent judge of its privileges, 'a birthright inherent in his Majesty's most loyal and dutiful subjects of the Commons of Jamaica and founded in the law of Parliament, which is part of the common law of England'. To make quite clear what was intended by this high-sounding claim, members of the House recorded their opinions that the House 'has all the privileges of the House of Commons in England and no instructions from King or ministers can either abridge or annihilate the privileges of the representative body of the people of this island'.

The English had supported an Austrian king for Spain against a French king because they feared the trade rivalry of a France in control of Spanish wealth obtainable from her American possessions. One of the first acts indeed of Philip V, when he became king of Spain, was to transfer the *Assiento* or contract for supplying slaves to Spanish colonies from the Portuguese to the French. The Tory ministry which signed the Treaty of Utrecht in 1713 had stipulated for an Assiento from Spain together with the right to send one trading ship every year to their fair at Portobello. Whether intentional or not, the consequence of this Assiento was to encourage smuggling of British manufactures into Spanish ports at a time when the seas of the Caribbean were already teeming with pirates. Far from helping to rid the sea of these menaces to legitimate trade, captains of naval vessels were themselves making money from smuggling. The Duke of Rutland, governor of Jamaica in 1724 reported to London that 'the behaviour of all the Captains of men-of-war from the first to the last, if strictly inquired into, is not to be justified'. His complaint seems extremely well founded in view of the fact that Governor Sir Nicholas Lawes had previously reported in

1720 that 'we are daily robbed and plundered by vessels fitted out from Trinidado on Cuba'. Clearly, legitimate traders were not getting the protection they wanted. Some progress had been made earlier when pirates surrendered to the authorities in Jamaica and Bermuda as a consequence of a royal proclamation of 1717. The two notorious women pirates, Anne Bonney and Mary Read, had been sentenced to death in Jamaica in June 1721, but their sentences were suspended because they were 'quick with child'. John Rackham and Charles Vane were hanged, however, and in the following year 41 men who were taken in a single ship suffered penalties of death.

If the Court of Spain had attempted to suppress the guardacostas as energetically as the British had tried to suppress their pirates in the years which followed the Peace of Utrecht, the war of 1739 might never have been fought. Instead, by using the guardacostas to prevent illicit trade with her colonies, Spain gave them the opportunity to interfere with the normal trade which England was conducting with Jamaica and her other overseas settlements.

Walpole's reluctance to fight against the Bourbons, who had a vested interest in the restoration of the Stuarts to the English throne, seems reasonable enough in view of the fact that the Young Pretender was able to keep his flag flying for a year on British soil until his defeat at Culloden. But the mood of the country, whose merchants had been encouraged by propagandists to believe in the possibility of revolutions in Spanish-American territories forced the renewal of conflict with Spain and the despatch of punitive naval and military expeditions against Spanish America.

The importance of Jamaica as a supplier of goods to Spanish America loomed greatly at the time of the war of 1739-48 because there had been a depression in the West Indian sugar industry after the Treaty of Utrecht (1713). The sugar plantations of the French and Dutch from that time were able to put sugar on the European market at prices much lower than those quoted by English planters, who were accordingly inclined to rely more on the English home market to protect their investments in the re-export trade from England to Europe.

The Molasses Act of 1733 was brought about by West Indian interests in Parliament in an effort to prevent North American purchase of French West Indian rum and molasses. English sugar producers hoped from this Act to keep the price of their sugar profitably high. In 1739 a further Act of Parliament permitted direct export of sugar from West Indies to Southern Europe, yet another attempt by powerful West Indian interests in Parliament to raise sugar prices in England. Sugar estates in Jamaica had increased in number from 57 in 1673 to about 430 in 1739, requiring over 100,000 slaves to make them productive. Too few rich men then owned too much land, said Robert Hunter, who governed Jamaica after doing similar tours of duty in New York and New Jersey and they were indolent and inactive. Not only did they refuse to stand for election to the House of Assembly, but they gave their interest for 'the choice of such as are recommended to them by their lawyers, and those who make that interest are for the most part men of low fortunes and desperate circumstances and want personal protection'.

In the first quarter of the eighteenth century Jamaica had to suffer other hardships besides frequent interference from Spanish guardacostas, pirates or falling demand for sugar. Epidemics were common, and in 1727 yellow fever killed 4,000 seamen in just a few months. In August 1722 a terrible hurricane had caused nearly 400 persons to lose their lives and swamped most of the ships riding in Port Royal harbour. But not everything was gloom. In 1717 Governor Lawes had approved the setting up of Jamaica's first printing press and eleven years later he grew coffee for the first time on his estate, Temple Hall, thereby helping to diversify the agriculture of the island and reduce its dependence on fickle sugar.

Jamaica by this time had become the largest producer of sugar in the British islands, as well as headquarters of the British illicit trade with Spanish America. Its harbour at Port

Royal was also the main point for occasional British expeditions sent against Spanish America. From Jamaica, ships of the navy would set out to take rich Spanish prizes as their contributions to the disruption of Spanish trade and its replacement by the trading ships which the navy protected by convoy into Spanish American ports. Because of this intensive patrolling of the Caribbean only one treasure fleet reached Spain during the nine years of the war (1739-48) and no galleons or flotas were able to set out from Spain. In the eyes of traders, whether in Jamaica or England, the nine-years war against Spain was justified alone for having increased British trade with Spanish colonies in America.

The maroons, descended from Africans who had fled to the mountains, had been conducting intermittent raids on Jamaican plantations ever since 1665 and no effective reprisals appeared to be possible. In 1720 a suggestion was adopted for hunting them with Indians imported from the Moskito coast on the American mainland, but the maroons persisted in their raids. Despatch of two regiments from England helped very little, nor were the local Jamaican militia capable of consolidating the occasional capture of maroon towns. Resistance of the maroons during the Spanish war has been attributed by some historians to supply of arms brought in by Spaniards or by profiteers resident in Jamaica. Hostilities involving 200 sailors, who were ambushed and murdered, 200 additional Moskito Indians, and some companies of free negroes and mulattos, eventually led to a negotiated peace with the leader of the maroons, Cudjoe, in 1739.

Colonel Guthrie on behalf of the Jamaican government exchanged hats under a silk cotton tree long known as Cudjoe's tree. The terms of the agreement provided that 1,500 acres of land be given to the maroons in the district between Trelawny Town and the Cockpits. Cudjoe was named chief commander in Trelawny Town and granted powers of punishment of criminals (exclusive of the death penalty). The agreement also called for two white men to live permanently amongst the maroons in their villages as representatives of the government. A year later Quaco, chief of the maroons in the Blue Mountains, also made peace with the authorities.

Colonel Trelawney, who had led a contingent of Jamaicans during Wentworth's abortive attack on Panama City in 1742, served 14 successful years as governor of Jamaica (1738-52). His worst experiences were during the hurricane of 1744 and the slave conspiracy of 1745. The hurricane and attendant earthquake nearly destroyed Port Royal completely, damaged the defensive fortifications at Mosquito Point, swept away wharves and warehouses at Kingston, Passage Fort and Old Harbour, and submerged more than 100 ships. The negro conspiracy was revealed by a nurse who passed information to the authorities so that the ringleaders could be executed or banished.

The disparity in population between negroes and whites had reached alarming proportions by 1741 when there were 100,000 slaves and only 10,000 whites. Edward Long, writing his history of Jamaica in 1774, made the point that imported Africans and not Creole blacks were the ringleaders of various seditions and mutinies on the plantations. Of imported negroes he blamed specifically the 'Coromantins', whom Jamaican planters bought more readily than French or other West Indian planters. According to Long the Coromantins did not like working on the land because of the 'martial ferocity of their disposition'. Long also paid tribute to the co-operation of the maroons who honoured their agreement made with Governor Trelawney and often helped Jamaican planters to recover escaped slaves. If Long's assessment is correct Jamaica stood in greatest peril in the year 1760 when 'almost all the Coromantin slaves' were involved in a conspiracy that was kept secret from the whites. The Coromantins had chosen the parish of St Mary because it was fruitful, full of woods and sparsely peopled by whites. Their intention was the 'entire extirpation of the white inhabitants, the enslaving of all such negroes as might refuse to join them, and the partition of the island into small principalities in the African mode, to be distributed among their leaders and head men'.

Tacky's Rebellion, as the outbreak in St Mary's was later called, began with a raid on Port Maria on Easter Sunday. Tacky's prowess as leader of the rising may have been bolstered by the support he received from an old Coromantin 'priest', who attributed to him powers to 'catch all bullets fired at him in his hand and hurl them back at his foes'. It is as likely that Tacky was an organiser of outstanding ability for there was scarcely a single parish, according to Long, to which the conspiracy did not extend. In Westmoreland great assistance to the rebels was given by a group of French negroes captured at Gaudeloupe in 1759. In Kingston the rebellion took the curious form of the proclamation as 'queen of Kingston' of a female slave, Cuba, who, until her capture, wore a robe on her shoulders and a crown on her head and sat in state under a canopy when the rebel Coromantins met to discuss their tactics.

Even after the shooting of Tacky and the killing of another leader called Jamaica, in an engagement with the maroons of Scot's Hall, the rebellion spread all over the island and it was not until 12 October 1761 that Lieutenant Governor Sir Henry Moore was able to tell the assembly of its 'total suppression' and to invite their support for measures which included erection of barracks and disposal of armed troops for the protection of the islanders. The year before Sir Henry Moore praised the ready assistance given by Rear Admiral Holmes in transporting troops and provisions, and in stationing ships where they could be of most service. He had also noted the improved status of the militia who had previously suffered from defects of a law which easily permitted avoidance of military service to those persons who paid an inconsiderable fine of ten shillings for non-appearance when called out. The assembly in 1761 resolved to double the deficiency tax which had earlier been imposed upon proprietors who lived outside Jamaica, on the grounds that their presence might have helped to dissuade their slaves from joining conspiracies and that greater contributions would help to pay for new burdens of defence expenditure.

A bill to impose a higher duty on all 'Fantin, Akim, Ashantee and Coromantin negros' imported and sold in Jamaica did not get the support of the assembly and Long attributed a fresh outbreak in Westmoreland a year later to lack of such legislation.

Despite slave uprisings, hurricanes and epidemics, the economy of Jamaica expanded considerably over the years 1729 to 1770. Exports to Great Britain, which averaged £542,648 in value during the war years of 1739-48, rose to an average value of £968,385 during the Seven Years War and in the years of peace 1764-70 reached an average of £1,185,979. Average value of imports from Great Britain into Jamaica also rose from £140,627 in the years 1729-38 to £463,426 in the years 1764-70. During the Seven Years War imports had risen to £479,071, but these figures probably included naval and military stores. There was considerable increase in imports of luxury goods over the period but Jamaican merchants were running up correspondingly higher debts with their suppliers in London. Apparent prosperity in terms of Jamaican trade which resulted from higher prices for their sugar and rum was reflected in England by the lavish spending of some absentee proprietors. English landed proprietors in the House of Commons did not welcome infiltration by Jamaican and other West Indian landowners as representatives of boroughs in Parliament. Beckford was usually jeered by members of the House whenever he spoke the word 'sugar'. Dislike of Jamaicans and other West Indian landowners who were spending their fortunes to acquire stakes in the Mother Country became so great that Pitt was prompted to defend them. 'The produce of the sugar colonies', he told native-born squires in the House of Commons, 'was the labour of our own people ... they are supplied with everything from hence .... They sent home all their produce and are the support of our marine', and he would 'ever consider the colonies as the landed interest of this Kingdom and it was a barbarism to consider them otherwise.' These friendly remarks of Pitt's were no more than repetitions of long-established beliefs as to the economic benefits of colonies, but after the remarkable British victories of 1759, new men in Britain began to express quite different views about Britons born at home and so-called Britons overseas. Pitt held on to an imperial vision which was fast being replaced by place and power seekers who accommodated themselves to new tides of public opinion. In his desire to crush the Bourbons of Spain and France absolutely Pitt seems to have foreseen dangers which later cost Britain dear when, in isolation, battle was joined against the rebels in her North American settlements. Giving back Havana and the valuable French sugar islands of Martinique and Guadeloupe to the Bourbons were natural consequences of a policy of appeasement which derived less from realistic appreciation of strategic factors than from the intensity of a new mood in Britain which represented the ambitions of nearly all except those who thrived by war.

Jamaicans had taken part in the joint expedition of British sea and land forces which left Barbados in April 1762 and brought about the surrender of Havana for the loss of 600 men. Their historians have since recorded with pride that a captured Jamaican slave named Cuffee earned his freedom by running away from the Cuban plantation on which he had been made to work for eight years, and enrolling as a volunteer in the 46th Regiment as soon as it reached Cuban soil.

Long in 1774 divided the inhabitants of Jamaica into Creoles or native whites, blacks, Indians and their varieties; Europeans and other whites; and imported or African blacks. The white Creoles who never left the island, he wrote, were in general of quick apprehension, brave, good-natured, affable, generous, temperate and sober. Their tables 'are covered with good cheer ... their hospitality is unlimited ... they affect gaiety and diversions ... cards, billiards, back-gammon, chess, horse-racing, hog-hunting, shooting, fishing, dancing and music'. Music was also much in favour with Creole blacks who 'are known to play twenty or thirty tunes, country-dances, minuets, airs and even sonatas on the violin; and catch with an astonishing readiness whatever they hear

7. An eighteenth-century map of Jamaica, showing the main ports and the colony's seal.

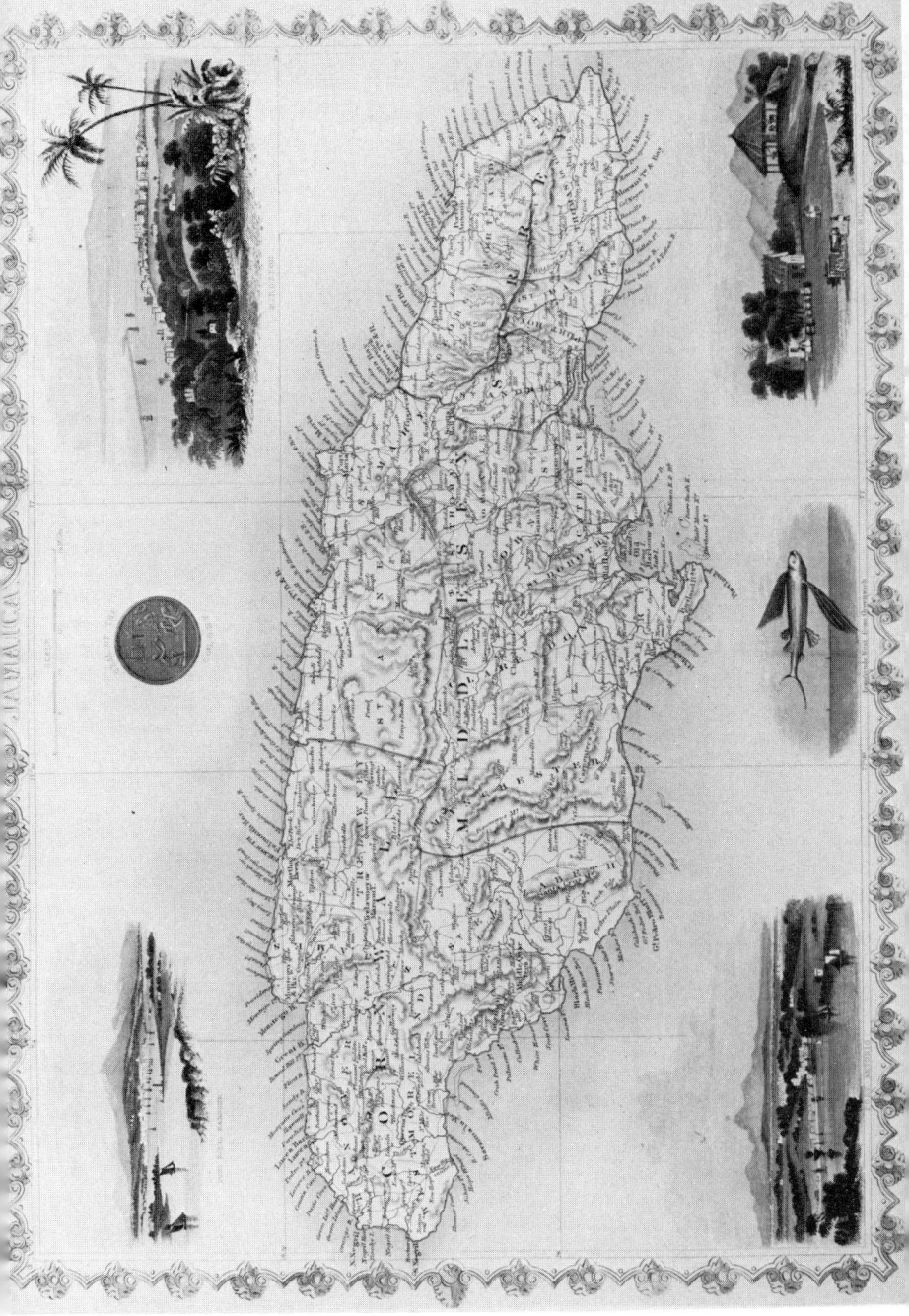

played or sung'. The Creoles also had foibles. 'They are possessed', wrote Long, 'with a degree of indolence and supineness in their affairs which renders them bad economists ... they are not always the most chaste and faithful of husbands ... they are too much addicted to expensive living, costly entertainments, dress and equipage. ... They are also fond of monopolising large tracts of land, buying up all around them, and attempting to settle new estates before the old one is cleared of debts .... It is a settled maxim that "you are not distinguished, nor of any note, unless you are in debt...." ' Most of the old Creole families were allied by intermarriages among their ancestors before the island was 'populously settled'. Long blamed Creole ladies for following the English custom of disdaining to suckle their offspring. Scarcely one of the negro or mulatto wet-nurses, he wrote, was not 'a common prostitute or who has not some latent taint of the venereal distemper. ... Another misfortune is the constant intercourse from their birth with negro domestics, whose drawling, dissonant gibberish they insensibly adopt, and with it no small tincture of their awkward carriage and vulgar manners.... We may see ... a very fine young woman awkwardly dangling her arms with the air of a Negro servant, lolling almost the whole day upon beds or settees, her head muffled up with two or three handkerchiefs, her dress loose and without stays. At noon we find her employed in gobbling pepper-pot, seated on the floor, with her sable hand-maids around her. In the afternoon she takes her siesta as usual, while two of these damsels refresh her face with the gentle breathings of the fan, and a third provokes the drowsy powers of Morpheus by delicious scratchings on the sole of either foot. When she rouses from slumber, her speech is whining, languid and childish.... Her ideas are narrowed to the ordinary subjects that pass before her, the business of the plantation, the tittle-tattle of the parish, the tricks, superstitions, diversions and profligate discourses of black servants, equally illiterate and unpolished.... Women often marry young and are mothers at twelve years of age.... The temperance of their

8. The Court House, Spanish Town, built 1819.

life carries them on, notwithstanding, to a good old age .... Intemperance and sensuality are the fatal instruments which ... have ... sent their heedless votaries in the prime of manhood, to an untimely grave ... young widows ... are greadily snapped up by distressed bachelors or rapacious widowers, as soon as the weeds are laid aside. Sir Nicholas Lawes, formerly governor of the island used to say that the female art of growing rich here in a short time, was comprised in two significant words *marry* and *bury!*'

Long blamed all the frailties and failings of Jamaican ladies upon defects of education. Elsewhere he praised them for being 'lively, of good natural genius, frank, affable, polite, generous, human and charitable ... faithful in their attachments, hearty in their friendships ... They are temperate and abstemious in their diet, rarely drinking any other liquor than water. They are remarkably expert at their needle ... religious in their lives and sentiments and chaste without prudery in their conversation. In horsemanship, dancing and music they are in general very accomplished. Their gaiety inclines them to be fond of dress, balls and company.'

Long asserted that the natives of Scotland and Ireland throve much better in Jamaica than the English. Nearly one third of the European inhabitants, he said, were either natives of North Britain or descendants from those who were. The lower order of white people were for the most part 'artificers, indented servants and refugees ... Overseers ... if they are sensible and thrifty ... enjoy very comfortable lives, and save enough out of their salaries to buy a settlement of their own ... subordinate to the overseers are the plantation bookkeepers, warehouse or store keepers, distillers, tradesmen, and drivers or sub-overseers (mostly Negros)'. Many inferior servants, said Long, had been supplied by the 'Crimp's' office. They were 'the very dregs of the three kingdoms. They have commonly more vices and much fewer good qualities than the slaves over whom they are set in authority, the better sort of which heartily despise them.... By their base familiarity with the worst-disposed among the slaves they do a very great injury to the plantations; causing disturbances, by seducing the Negro's wives, and bringing an odium upon the white people in general by their drunkenness and profligate actions.'

Some restrictions ('rather exemptions from burthen than privations of any benefit') were laid on Jews, but they were free to exercise their religion and customs and to hold landed property. They had no voice, however, in the legislature or courts of justice when Long wrote. They were divided by sects and by class. The 'Smouses have ... a distinct conventicle or meeting of their own at a private house where they vociferate to the great disturbance of the neighbourhood ... Among the chief men are several opulent planters and capital merchants, who are connected with great houses in the city of London. It has been a very striking remark that the multitude of them settled in this island, the purchases they are continually making both of houses and lands and the vast wealth they collectively have staked here are sure indications that they are delighted with the mildness and equity of the government and rest satisfied that their property is entirely safe and securely held'.

Quakers, principally from Barbados, had settled in Jamaica in some numbers but few remained in 1732 when a law entitled them to vote at elections after proving their qualifications by affirmation instead of oath.

Moravians had arrived in Jamaica in 1754 and 20 years later were chiefly confined to an estate in the parish of St Elizabeth. Long expressed concern about the effect their teachings might have upon the militia, but does not speak of any missions to the African slaves. He did note, however, that Moravians in Philadelphia at that time were very zealous in converting the Indians. Besides Jews, Quakers and Moravians, 'schismatics, publicly avowed in Jamaica', Long observed the presence of many 'Roman Catholics and dissenters, who enjoy their respective opinions in private, without seeking to form themselves into distinct congregations, or to put themselves to the expense of maintaining preachers or pastors'.

Of 3,700 free blacks and mulattos Long estimated that about 1,500 of them were 'sensible men, fit for able service in the militia'. In 1762 mulatto children had inherited from white parents four sugar estates, seven parks, 13 houses, and other lands. Long strongly disapproved of the effects these legacies were having upon Jamaican society. 'The Europeans', he wrote, 'who at home have always been used to greater purity and strictness of manners are too easily led aside to give a loose to every kind of sensual delight: on this account some black or yellow quasheba is fought for, by whom a tawny breed is produced. Many are the men, of every rank, quality and degree here, who would much rather riot in these goatish embraces than share the pure and lawful bliss derived from matrimonial, mutual love'. One result of sexual relationships between whites and non-whites was an aversion of their offspring towards 'relapse into the Negro . . . the opulent among them withdraw to England, where their influence, if they ever possessed any, ceases to be of any use'.

Long summarises the 'different distempers' of Africans newly imported into Jamaica. 'The Coromantins, and many others of the Gold Coast slaves, are haughty, ferocious and stubborn. The Minnahs, timid and desponding, apt to destroy themselves upon the least, and without any provocations. The Mundingo Negros are very subject to worm disorders, the Congos to dropsies. The Ebo men are lazy and averse to every laborious employment, the women performing almost all the work in their own country; these men are sullen and often make away with themselves, rather than submit to any drudgery; the Ebo women labour well but are often subjected to obstructions of the menstrua, often attended with sterility and incurable. The Congos, Papaws, Conchas, Whidahs and Angolas in general are good field labourers, but the last-mentioned are most stupid. The Negros brought from Senegal are of better understanding than the rest, and fitter for learning trades, and for menial domestic services. They are good commanders over other Negros, having a high spirit, and a tolerable share of fidelity: but they are unfit for hard work; their bodies are not robust, nor their constitution vigorous. The delicacy of their frame perhaps has some effect upon their minds, for they are easier disciplined than any other of the African Blacks. The Aradas are thought to excel all the rest in knowledge of agriculture, yet their skill is extremely incompetent. The Congos and Gold Coast Negros, in general, are good fishermen, and excel in making canoes'.

Right or wrong as these judgments may be they suggest that there was as great a variety among Africans imported into Jamaica as among the whites.

The arrival figures for Africans were however much higher. Long estimated that between January 1764 and July 1766 as many as 27,000 Africans were imported into Jamaica. These were exceptional figures, the average yearly import being 6,000. In 1768 the number of negros registered as being in Jamaica had risen to 166,904 of whom the majority were Creole blacks. Long, throughout his book, was better disposed to Creole blacks than imported Africans. He attributed this difference to the fact that Creole blacks were inured from their infancy 'to regular discipline'. Yet he found them 'in general irascible, conceited, proud, indolent, lascivious, credulous and very artful.... The Creole Blacks differ much from the Africans, not only in manners, but in beauty of shape, feature and complexion. They hold the Africans in the utmost contempt, styling them 'salt water Negros' and 'Guiney birds'.... Their master's character and repute casts, they think, a secondary light upon themselves.... Their attachment to the descendants of old families, the ancestors of which were the masters and friends of their own progenitors, is remarkably strong and affectionate. This veneration appears hereditary, like clanships in the Scotch Highlands ... some of these Negros have been known to possess from £50 to £200 at their deaths, and few among them that are at all industrious and frugal lay up less than £20 or £30. For in this island they have the greatest part of the small silver circulating among them, which they gain by sale of their hogs, poultry, fish, corn, fruits and other commodities, at the markets in town and country.... Creole

Blacks ... may with a very moderate instruction in the Christian rules be kept in good order without the whip. ... They love warmth in the night and never sleep without a fire in their hut. ... They dread rain upon their bare heads almost as much as the native Africans. ... The Negros use their heads, instead of their shoulders or backs, for carrying all sorts of burthens; with a dried plantain leaf they plait a circular pad, which they call a cotta; upon this the load rests ... the cotta serves likewise for another purpose; on the voluntary divorce of man and wife it is cut in two, and each party takes half. ... Diet consists generally of pulse, herbs, plantains, maize, yams, or other roots, prepared with pork and fish, fresh or salt; salted beef, herrings, jerked hog, or fowls. Salt fish they are extremely fond of, and the more it stinks the more dainty; they make likewise a kind of pudding, with pounded maize; and sometimes of the sweet potato, which they call a potato pone; their broths or pots ... are well seasoned with the country peppers; ochra is a principal ingredient ... cane rats are much in esteem, and, when roasted and stuffed are said to have a delicate flavour. ... The Creoles wash their mouths as soon as they awake in the morning ... about noon is their usual time of bathing, in some river open to the sun. ... They are all married (in their way) to a husband or wife, *pro tempore,* or have other family connections, in almost every parish throughout the island; so that one of them, perhaps, has six or more husbands or wives, in several different places; by this means they find support when their own lands fail them; and houses of call and refreshment whenever they are upon their travels ... most of them become intimately acquainted with all affairs of the white inhabitants, public as well as private. In their houses, they are many of them very neat and cleanly, piquing themselves on having tolerably good furniture and other conveniences. In their care for their children some are remarkably exemplary. ... They laugh at the idea of a marriage which ties two persons together indissolubly. Their notions of love are that it is free and transitory. This is well known to their white gallants. ... Murder is with most of them esteemed the highest impiety. Filial disobedience and insulting the ashes of the dead are placed next. But as for petty larcenies, affairs of gallantry, fornication, etc. they are reputed only peccadilloes, which are sufficiently punished in this world. They firmly believe in the apparition of spectres. Those of deceased friends are *duppies;* others of more hostile and tremendous aspect are called *bugaboos.* The most sensible among them fear the supernatural powers of the African obeah-men, or pretended conjurers, often ascribing those mortal effects to magic, which are only the natural operation of some poisonous juice or preparation, dexterously administered by these villains.... But the Creoles imagine that the virtue of baptism or making them Christians render their art wholly ineffectual; and for this reason only, many of them have desired to be baptized that they might be secured from obeah.... The Negros wear the teeth of wild cats and eat their flesh, as a charm for long life; for they hold the vulgar opinion that a cat has nine lives.... Bits of red rag, cat's teeth, parrots' feathers, egg shells and fish bones are frequently stuck up at the doors of their houses when they go from home ... to deter thieves ... Every funeral is a kind of festival, at which the greater part of the company assume an air of joy or unconcern; and together with their singing, dancing and musical instruments conspire to drown all sense of affliction in the minds of the real mourners.... The corpse being interred, the grave is but slightly overspread with earth. Some scratch up the loose mould, with their backs turned to the grave, and cast it behind them between their legs, after the manner of cats.... This, they say, is done to prevent the deceased person from following them home.

They have good ears for music; and their songs ... are generally impromptus ... instead of choosing panegyric for their subject matter they generally prefer one of derision, and not unfrequently at the expense of the overseer, if he happens to be near and listening.... The merry-wang is a favourite instrument, a rustic guitar of four strings. It is made with a calabash: a slice of which being taken off, a dried bladder or skin is scraped across the largest section; and this is fastened to a handle, which they take great pains in ornamenting with a sort of rude carved work, and ribbands. The goombah, another of their musical instruments is a hollow block of wood, covered with sheepskin stripped of its hair. The musician holds a little stick, of about six inches in length, sharpened at one end like the blade of a knife, in each hand. With one hand he rakes it over a notched piece of wood, fixed across the instrument, the whole length, and crosses with the other alternately, using both with a brisk motion, whilst a second performer beats with all his might on the sheep-skin, or tabor. Their tunes for dancing are usually brisk. . . . The female dancer is all languishing and easy in her motions; the man all action, fire and gesture. . . . In the towns during the Christmas holidays, they have several tall robust fellows dressed up in grotesque habits, and a pair of ox horns on their head, sprouting from the top of a horrid sort of vizor, or mask, which about the mouth is rendered very terrific with large boar-tusks. The masquerader, carrying a wooden sword in his hand, is followed with a numerous crowd of drunken women, who refresh him frequently with a sup of aniseed-water, whilst he dances at every door, bellowing out John Connu! with great vehemence; so that, what with the liquor and the exercise, most of them are thrown into dangerous fevers; and some examples have happened of their dying. This dance is probably an honourable memorial of John Conny, a celebrated cabocero at Tres Puntas, in Axim, on the Guiney coast; who flourished about the year 1720. He bore great authority among the Negros of that district. . . . In 1769 several new masks appeared; the Ebos, the Papaws, etc. having their respective Connus, male and female, who were dressed in a very laughable style.'

The laws of Jamaica required planters to do their best to convert their negroes and to have them baptised. But planters and clergymen often found 'insurmountable' difficulties in fulfilling the law's command. Long himself had no doubt that only good consequences could follow if the 'more sensible' part of the negroes were to be baptised and 'occasionally instructed, as far as they can be made to understand, in the morality and fundamental points of our holy faith'. He considered baptismal fees at £1. 3s. 9d per head 'enormously high'. A Popish missionary, he noted, would perform the ceremony gratis and be happy at the occasion, but 'in some other establishments we find that it is *no fee,* no holy water'. Long blames the severity of Jamaican negro regulations upon English *villeinage* laws which had come to the island by way of Barbados. These laws, he said, showed the abject slavery under which the common people of England formerly laboured. 'The Negros in our colonies', he said, 'might, perhaps, have fared better, if their masters had taken the Athenian slave code for their guide.... So soon as the African trade became a national concern, from its importance, the parliament in Britain fell in with the general idea, and considered Negros, purchased from that continent, as a lawful commercial property; and this in so strong a sense that the greatest oppression, under which our Negros in the islands at present labour, arises materially from the ordinance of that statute, which declares them to be as houses, lands, hereditaments, assets and personal estate, transferable and amenable to payment of debts due to the King or his subjects'. Long believed that the law of humanity called for the abolition of English laws which he thought would be changed by the English parliament 'if the provincial assemblies were ... to facilitate their concurrence, by substituting an equivalent security to the creditor'. The prosperity of the colonies also depended on a change of the law. For 'changing the property of labouring Negros from one owner to another, living in different places, obstructs the settlement of lands, turns those already settled into ruinate; lessens the number of planters, diminishes the stock of labouring Negros, and produces a certain loss to the community in various ways'. Long urged the gentlemen of Jamaica to set the example and raise their island to the 'same rank of superiority in the wisdom and mildness of its laws, as it already enjoys in its extent and opulence above the other British territories in the West Indies ... let them ... conciliate the attachment of their Negros by protection and encouragement, rather than seek to exact an involuntary obedience by austerity and terror ... if the native slaves in our colony can with safety be brought under an enlarged degree of protection, and secured by rational provisions from violence and barbarity; or be permitted to redeem themselves from perpetuity of servitude, with the fair and honest earnings of their private industry; it seems highly just, humane and politic to favour them ... after obtaining their freedom it still remains by legal regulations to enforce their employing themselves in some honest course of livelihood; they will then contribute largely not to the strength above, but to the wealth and prosperity of the island, and to the profits of Great Britain'.

The long-sighted views of Edward Long represented the new mood of enlightened self-interest which had taken root in England by the 1770's. Unfortunately humanitarianism, enlightenment and other consequences of England's industrial revolution were to be put into cold storage and in some instances reversed because of reactions to unexpected cataclysms like the American Rebellion, the French Revolution and the war against Napoleon's empire.

The Decline of Sugar and End of Slavery

The year 1750 was especially significant in the history of Jamaica because Spanish contractors then replaced Britons as authorised suppliers of slaves to Spanish-American settlements. From that year, too, Cuba began to increase its output of sugar which over a 50-year period rose 13 times to reach 650,000 quintales in 1800. Had Britain retained Cuba under the terms of the Treaty of Paris, Jamaican sugar growers would undoubtedly have been tempted to take their skills to its more fertile lands as sugar growers from Barbados, Nevis and Surinam had in the seventeenth-century sought the more fertile lands of Jamaica. As it happened, Spanish retention of Cuba ensured that Cuba's slave-grown sugar could be produced during most of the nineteenth century at prices far below what was possible for Jamaica and other West Indian islands. Competition from French sugar-producing islands was also building up in the decades which preceded the French Revolution and was particularly keen on St Domingue which by 1783 was producing almost as much sugar as all the British West Indian islands combined.

Jamaica after the end of the Seven Years War (1763) was also forbidden by the authorities in England to continue trading with Cuba and Puerto Rico. The order given to the British naval commanders in Port Royal was to suppress all illegal commerce with the Spaniards. 'Not a Spanish vessel', a correspondent wrote in the *Gentleman's Magazine* of July 1764 'can now come with money to this island, but what is seized by officers either under the Admiral or Governor. . . .

They now carry their money to the French and Dutch islands, which would otherwise have centred with us.' Competition from other sugar-producing islands, shortages of white indentured servants and soaring costs of negro slaves encouraged Jamaican landowners to introduce new crops on their estates. Between 1763 and 1775 yields of coffee beans rose spectacularly and cacao was also extensively planted. Efforts to reduce the costs of slave labour were also being made by hirings of gangs organised by local suppliers who charged between £8 and £12 per head annually. It is possible that this practice contributed to the frequency of slave uprisings during this period. Hopes of revived trade with Spanish American territories did not materialise from the Act of 1766 which established Jamaican freeports, and the act became invalid eight years later.

Jamaicans had been thoroughly alarmed when the American Continental Congress decided to close their ports to British West Indian produce from 1 December 1774 and to put an embargo on all American exports after 10 September 1775. A radical group of Jamaican merchants who were members of the Assembly waited until rural members had left St Iago de la Vega (Spanish Town) for their plantations and then passed a petition which requested the British sovereign to overrule his Parliament and to give justice to his American subjects. Depriving colonials of their rights as Englishmen abroad, was, in the opinion of the petitioners, tantamount to dissolution of their dependence upon the Mother Country. Sentiments similar to these were expressed by other West Indian legislatures while the House of Commons heard from members who were West Indian merchants or landowners that British property valued at £30 million was endangered and that benefits arising from British trade with the islands might be lost unless the North American colonies continued to supply them with customary and necessary goods.

War between Britain and the rebellious American colonies justified Jamaican fears. Shortages increased because of the activities of privateers, while prices of essential commodities rose astronomically. Rice, which before the war was available at 13s. 9d. to 20s. reached between 40 and 80 shillings during hostilities. Freight rates and insurance charges also rose sharply. Only when an occasional American cargo ship was taken and brought into Port Royal was any relief experienced. For a short period in 1778 Spanish American ports were open to British traders, but were closed when Spain declared war on Britain that year. The home government attempted to relieve West Indian sufferings by permitting goods and provisions to be sent from Ireland. Some benefits were received from this change of policy and production of local food was intensified. French and Spanish trade ceased altogether after 1778 and the islands were exposed to attacks by enemy fleets and privateers. Jamaica benefited by the presence of British ships in its harbours when they were not absent on expeditions. Nelson took part in 1780 when his ship the *Hinchinbrooke* left Port Royal to escort transports to Nicaragua, where assaults upon forts were intended to prepare the way for British advance landwards to the Pacific coast. A letter from Nelson, whose residence at Port Royal is commemorated by a marble tablet there, mentions how, on another occasion Jamaica was 'turned upside down' to meet a threatened attack from joint French and Spanish forces who had assembled on neighbouring St Domingue: 5,000 men were placed under canvas between the Ferry and Kingston, 1,000 at Fort Augusta and 300 at the Apostle's Battery. New defensive structures had also been erected on hillsides, old forts were repaired and trees put across roads as obstacles to invaders. But when an invasion of Jamaica did come on 3 October it was not an invasion by human beings, but by one of the most horrifying hurricanes ever to have swept through the West Indies. It hurt particularly the south-western part of Jamaica. In his report to London, Governor Dalling wrote that the sea suddenly broke in upon Savanna-la-Mar and, 'on its retreat, swept everything away with it, so as not to leave the smallest vestige of Man, Beast or House behind – This most dreadful catastrophe was succeeded by the most terrible hurricane that ever was felt in this country with repeated shocks of an Earthquake, which has almost totally demolished every building in the parishes of Westmoreland, Hanover, part of St. James and some part of St Elizabeth's'. Crops were destoyed and famine and disease followed.

Hard times were still being experienced in August 1781 when another violent hurricane struck Jamaica, driving ships ashore and destroying newly-planted fields of provisions. Successive flooding of croplands caused great losses among slaves. As many as 15,000 were thought to have died between 1780 and 1787. However the year 1782 was to be for many islanders a year of great rejoicing. On 12 April in the waters between Martinique and Guadeloupe, Rodney, near the Isles des Saintes, took advantage of a shift of wind and broke the French line of ships under command of the Comte de Grasse. When Rodney brought de Grasse and his captured flagship *Ville de Paris* into harbour the islanders released their suppressed joy in victory celebrations that went on for weeks. Their gratitude to Rodney later took the form of a marble statue which was sculpted by the Englishman John Bacon. It stands today at the centre of Spanish Town. Jamaicans still honour Rodney for saving them from almost certain subjection by French authorities; some remember with gratitude that he introduced the mango seedlings which were taken from a French ship on its way from Mauritius to French West Indian islands. Earlier in 1778 the ackee, Jamaica's national dish, had been introduced from a slave-ship, and before the century was out, in 1793 the first breadfruit plant was introduced by Captain Bligh, and successfully propagated in the Botanical Gardens at Bath. For 50 years it was the food of pigs!

English sugar refiners during the war with the American colonists had to reduce their output because of shortages of raw sugar and accordingly started a campaign to lower the duty on foreign sugar entering Britain. The Society of West Indian Merchants in London were quick to resist the 'most fatal consequences' which would in such an event 'ensure to the sugar colonies, and to the navigation, commerce, revenue and manufacture of Great Britain thereon dependent'. Stephen Fuller, Jamaica's agent in London presented his own petition to the House of Commons and joint West Indian opposition in Parliament forced refineries to work a three-day week from 30 June 1781. By the time that peace was established in 1783 renewed supplies were reaching London in sufficient quantities to satisfy the refiners.

Americans and West Indians alike wanted resumption of normal trade after cessation of American hostilities. The Council of Jamaica urged that liberal commercial relations with the United States should be established: the Society of Planters and Merchants in London did not think any arguments were necessary to support the proposition that American ships should take their produce to the sugar islands and take away island produce as freely as ever. John Adams, writing from Paris in 1783 summed up American attitudes by saying that 'the commerce of the West Indian islands is a part of the American system of commerce' and warned of possible combinations between the islands and the continent if injudicious regulation 'was made'. In England, however, there was great objection to the American and West Indian views. Lord Sheffield in particular objected that American participation in West Indian trade would make it unprofitable for Great Britain to retain the West Indian sugar islands. He suggested that Loyalists in Nova Scotia and Canada and agriculturalists in Bermuda could supply all West Indian requirements, even though the islanders might have to pay more. Sugar growers, argued Sheffield, should not complain about paying higher prices for imports because their prosperity stemmed from high prices paid in Britain for their sugar. 'The Navigation Act', said Sheffield, 'the basis of our great power at sea, gave us the trade of the world. If we alter that Act, by permitting any State to trade with our islands ... we desert the Navigation Act and sacrifice the marine of England.'

Jamaican property owners Bryan Edwards and Edward Long rushed to support arguments which the Society of Planters and Merchants in London used in order to destroy

Sheffield's case. Nevertheless it was Sheffield who proved to be more representative of a changed British public opinion, so free commercial relationships were not reopened between the United States and the British West Indies. The star of the planters' interest in England was plainly on the wane.

One immediate consequence of the prohibition on legal American commerce with the islands was the growth of illicit trade. In a Jamaican report of 1784 it was stated: 'There is every reason to believe that the fraudulent importation from the United States is very considerable ... probably equal to that which is imported legally.' Smuggling did not, however, produce prosperous conditions. A petition of the council and assembly of Jamaica in 1784 referred to debts incurred by property owners for defence of the island and of prospects of ruin. Conditions were not improved by a succession of hurricanes (in 1784, 1785 and 1786) and Lieutenant-Governor Clare had to open Jamaican ports to avert a food shortage between August 1784 and January 1785. This action was too late to prevent death from starvation or disease of about 15,000 slaves!

The changing pattern of the Jamaican economy in the decade which followed the grant of American independence is reflected in the changed condition of the sugar planters. By 1791 only 451 of 767 sugar estates were owned by old proprietors, and 177 had been sold for debt. Perhaps the most hopeful occurrence of these distressing years was the arrival from Charlestown of 3,891 Loyalists, of whom 2,613 were negro. They brought new skills to Jamaica even though they added to the number of mouths which had to be filled.

Revolution in St Domingue, where by 1790 there were 792 sugar estates, 2,810 coffee plantations, 705 cotton fields and over 3,000 indigo plots gave a fillip to the economies of Jamaica and other British islands. The Jamaican assembly, regretting the 'principal' cause of a rise in prices for the island's produce, informed the king in a message that 'only such accidental and temporary increase in the value of our staples could have saved this island from absolute bankruptcy'. High prices in London were not welcomed

9. *(above)* Holy Cross church near Half Way Tree in Kingston.
10. *(below)* A ministerial residence, Vale Royal, St Andrew.

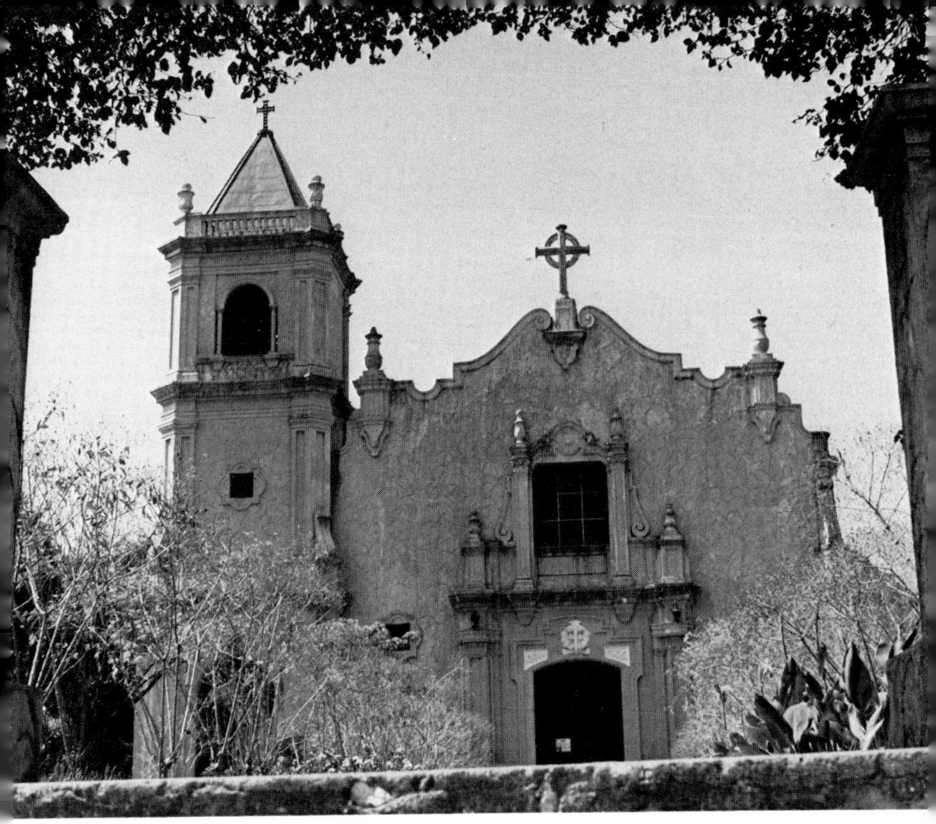

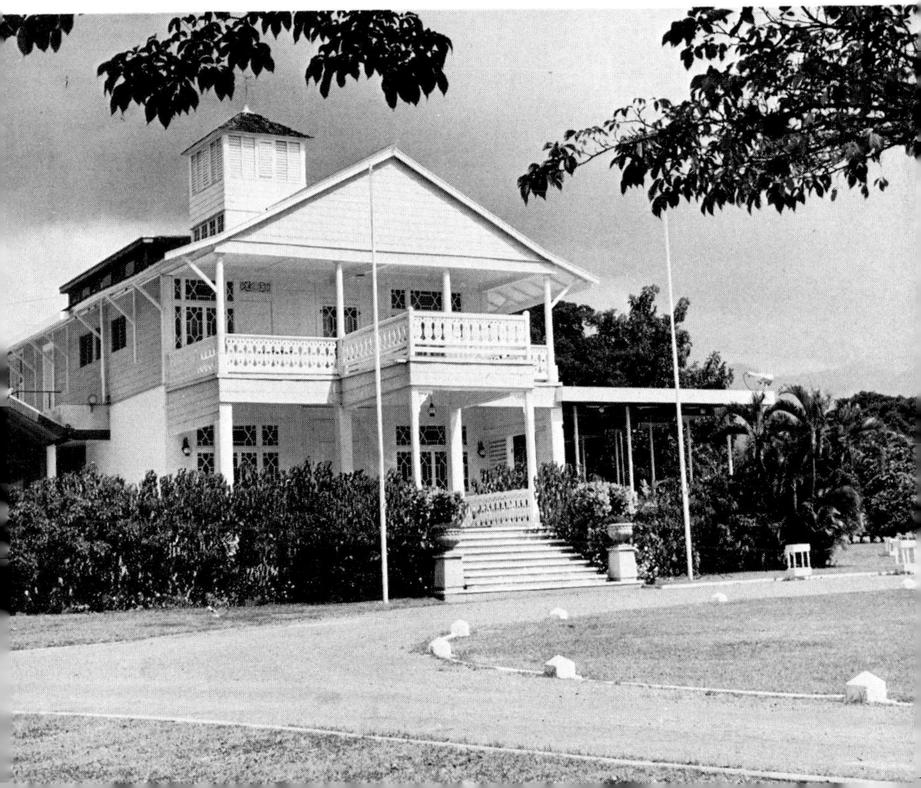

however by the refiners who now began to clamour for admission of sugar from the East Indies. Despite West Indian protests Parliament passed an act which controlled the price of sugar reaching England from the Caribbean islands. At the same time encouragement was given to the authorities to step up imports of East Indian sugar, which in the ten years ending in 1800 reached a value in excess of £2½ million.

Competition from the East and the opportunities provided by the collapse of St Domingue's economy encouraged planters to modernise the Jamaican sugar industry. In 1796 Dr Higgins was sent to Jamaica by the Society of Planters and Merchants with the specific intention to improve manufacturing processes following upon the introduction of higher yielding cane plants. In the years 1799 to 1801 exports of Jamaican muscovado sugar averaged over 100,000 hogsheads annually and exports of coffee rose from 40,736 cwt in 1791 to over 34 million pounds in 1814.

Once war had been declared between Great Britain and revolutionary France there was no reason why the British should not attempt to reduce St Domingue. An expedition including a former member of the legislature of St Domingue left Jamaica in September 1793 and established strong bridgeheads on the island. More than 12,000 soldiers out of 18,000 who were sent there died of yellow fever in the years 1795-96. Such losses forced General Maitland in 1798 to agree with Toussaint L'Ouverture that British forces should be completely withdrawn. The high cost in human life and the preferential access which French sugar planters had been temporarily given to the English sugar markets were attacked by some West Indian propagandists like Bryan Edwards. Others were more preoccupied with the effect that L'Ouverture's achievement of power might have upon the negro population throughout the West Indian islands. Their alarm was considerably increased when in 1801 L'Ouverture's forces captured the Spanish city of San Domingo and gained control of the whole island of Hispaniola. Such power in the hands of a negro so close to Jamaica was frightening to men long accustomed to slave uprisings and maroon

11. *(above)* The Court House, Lucea.
12. *(below)* Rose Hall great house, St James.

guerilla activities. Fears of negro uprising had been responsible in 1795 for the unusually severe repression of a maroon revolt. A hundred bloodhounds were brought over from Cuba and proved more effective than the soldiers in forcing the rebels to submit. When it proved impossible for them to surrender on the appointed day the lieutenant governor, the Earl of Balcarres rounded them up when they eventually came in and deported 600 of their leaders to Nova Scotia.

Surrounded by majorities of slaves in their islands, British West Indians had been horrified by Victor Hugo's proclamation of emancipation in 1794 and by the subsequent enrolment of West Indian blacks in French military forces. Their fears were further inflamed by the arrival of numbers of French Royalists who fled from the revolutionary Jacobin governments which were quickly set up in French West Indian islands. As early as 1793 51 French families with their servants were given permission to settle in Jamaica and many more took refuge there when the British forces withdrew from St Domingue in 1798. Only about 200 of these refugees were permitted to remain in Jamaica. They contributed greatly to the expansion of the coffee industry and to the general improvement of horticulture, especially on the outskirts of Kingston.

For most of the duration of the war between Great Britain and revolutionary France the regulating Act of 1788 restricting American West Indian trade was temporarily suspended by West Indian governors who later obtained Acts of indemnification from the British parliament. When in 1800, however, heavy shipments of sugar were made from Jamaica to the United States, the Earl of Balcarres was sharply rebuked by the English authorities for granting permission. Administration of colonies in this period was difficult. The home secretary had been made responsible for war and the colonies in 1782 as well as for running the internal affairs of the British Isles. It was not until 1794 that the home office was relieved of war and the colonies which were both then transferred to the war office. Some idea of the neglect which colonies were receiving in these years may be gained from the fact that not *one* person moved from the home office to the war office when colonial business was transferred. The Duke of Portland who 'handled' colonial affairs for nearly seven years until 1801 was remarkable for the mediocrity of his intellect, and his successors were preoccupied with the serious problems arising from renewed hostilities with Napoleon's France in 1803. It was not until Robert Peel became under-secretary of state in 1810 that improved techniques in handling colonial business were introduced. Further progress was made by his successor, Henry Goulburn who served under the Earl of Bathurst, the man who has been described as the 'real founder of the colonial office'. It should be noted, however, that in 1814 the colonial department which was responsible for all British overséas territories outside the Mediterranean was still staffed only by one under-secretary, nine clerks and two extra clerks. It was not until 1822 that systematic annual reports or blue books from colonies were required in London. Two years later the 'empire' was divided by the colonial department into four geographical areas: Eastern Colonies, North America, Mediterranean and Africa, and West Indies.

In 1824 a chaplain general for the colonies was appointed in the person of the Reverend Anthony Hamilton, secretary of the Society for the Propagation of the Gospel in Foreign Parts. Under his leadership a society was incorporated in the British West Indian islands for the conversion and religious instruction and education of the negro slaves, two West Indian bishoprics were created and two bishops and 20 clergymen sent to the West Indies. An exceptional turn was given to West Indian administration in 1825 when Henry Taylor was appointed head of the West Indian department, a post which he continued to hold for 47 years!

Whereas the British government had disallowed in 1774 an Act of the Jamaica legislature designed to discourage importation of negroes, influential public opinion in England had changed so considerably by 1804 that the House of Commons passed by a large majority in that year a Bill for the abolition of the slave trade. Because of parliamentary delays a new Abolition Act had to be passed through both Houses and did not receive the king's assent until 25 March 1807. Britain was later that year to pass through a serious economic crisis which by the winter was causing panic and depression. The trouble arose from the simultaneous closing of continental and United States markets which together represented three-fifths of British exports. Economic salvation only came when in May 1808 Spain, in a state of rebellion against her French king, renewed trade with England. Trade was opened at the same time with Spanish America and Britain gained as well access to the markets of Portugal and Brazil. The condition of England remained critical, however, and worsened considerably when trade with Northern Europe and North America contracted. Industrial failures and bankruptcies were followed by the so-called 'Luddite riots' which indicated how frustrated were the workers who had benefited greatly from England's earlier industrial revolution. A futile and tragic war with the United States in 1812 added to the sombre conditions. In the winter of 1811-12 the young Whig politician Henry Brougham organised protests mainly supported by the middle class merchants and industrialists in affected areas like the West Riding, Birmingham and Leicester. They campaigned especially against the Orders in Council which had failed to re-open trade with the Continent and which had been responsible for the war with the United States. It is significant of the changing trends within British society that support for the Orders was backed by West Indian and Canadian merchants as well as by London and Bristol businessmen, shipowners and some industrialists in Liverpool, Birmingham and Glasgow. Similar divergences of interest were to be revived when a Reformed Parliament prepared to banish slavery from the boundaries of the British empire.

A Virginian slave, James Somerset, freed from a ship sailing to Jamaica and rescued by a writ of habeas corpus obtained by Granville Sharp, was the first person known to have achieved freedom in England by setting foot on British soil. So ruled Chief Justice Mansfield, thereby liberating all unfree negroes in England and preparing the way for the emancipation of all British slaves which followed in 1833. One desirable consequence of abolition of the slave trade had been a decrease in the number of slaves manumitted on West Indian plantations, an unexpected development which roused the ardour of British philanthropists and missionaries who were determined to resist every effort and every argument in favour of slavery until the foul blot of traffic in human beings was erased from the pages of Britain overseas. Attempts like those of the Jamaican legislature to imprison Wesleyans led to disavowal of colonial acts by the imperial legislature, proof if ever it was needed of the merits of association with a Mother of Parliaments. The great reforming work of preparing for the abolition of slavery depended on the supervisory agencies available at the heart of empire. The gospel of Mammon which was the legacy of the age of European mercantilism had permitted no ray of hope to shine for the descendants of Africans transported into the Americas with the sole aim of making profits for those who could afford to purchase them as property. Not even Lord Byron's dear friend Matt Lewis, a most enlightened absentee proprietor of inherited Jamaican estates, could envisage abolition of slavery. 'Every man of humanity', he wrote in 1817, 'must wish that slavery, even in its best and most mitigated form, had never found a legal sanction, and must regret that its system is now so incorporated with the welfare of Great Britain as well as of Jamaica, as to make its extirpation an impossibility, without the certainty of producing worse mischiefs than the one which we annihilate.'

In England, however, new winds of change were blowing which were to sweep away from people's minds concern for problems which could arise even from good actions. After the Allied victory at Waterloo in 1815 the arguments of Ricardo, Malthus, James Mill and J. R. McCulloch persuaded many English traders that colonial monopoly should not be their objective. Their views seemed plausible enough in view of the fact that the value of Britain's exports to the United States had increased by seven times the value they had attained before the outbreak of the American Rebellion. Britain was not the only country which could practise trade restrictions. The United States Congress in 1818 passed a Navigation Act which closed the ports of the United States to British ships arriving from a colony that was closed to United States vessels and British vessels sailing from United States ports were put on bond not to land them in any colony closed to American ships. In 1820 Congress passed a still more drastic Act. American antagonism to British trade restrictions had been greatest in 1806, the year in which James Stephen championed West Indian interests and persuaded Britain to put an end to American undercutting of British sugar growers through transport in American ships of sugar grown in the French West Indies to European markets. About this time, however, another threat to British sugar growers was growing on the European continent where sugar from beet was being encouraged as a substitute for sugar from cane. By 1807 Jamaican sugar was being sold in London below the cost of production and between 1799 and 1807 65 Jamaican plantations were abandoned, 32 had been sold to meet claims and lawsuits were pending against 115 more! Everything seemed to be going wrong for the West Indian sugar growers at the precise moment when they were compulsorily deprived of fresh supplies of slave labour.

The high cost of sugar production in Jamaica and other West Indian islands was aggravated by the increased output from Cuba and Brazil where soils were deep and rich. Shipments to Europe from Cuba rose from 206,487 cases, in the years 1811 to 1814, to 300,211 cases in the single year of 1823. An act of the Westminster Parliament passed in 1822 promised a restoration of trade between the West Indian islands and the United States, but produced little real benefit. Instead, it led to increased attacks from the Liverpool East India Association who were anxious to profit from sugar grown in Hindustan. In the battle between East and West Indian interests, the West Indian interest was temporarily victorious, but the arguments put forward by

Ricardo, Wilberforce, Zachary Macaulay and others were to prove eventually disastrous for West Indian sugar growers when their British preferential tariff was lowered in 1846. Russell explained his government's action by saying at the time that the admission of slave-grown sugar was necessary 'in order to lower the price of sugar for the benefit of the working classes at home'. Twenty-three years earlier the advocates of equalised East Indian and West Indian sugar duties had argued that more English people would in consequence of equalisation be able to use sugar; that revenues would rise from such consumption; that Britain would be able to sell more manufactures in the East; that sugar could be carried as ballast on return journeys to England; and that 120 million inhabitants of India would benefit as against less than one million specially favoured West Indians. West Indian sugar growers probably triumphed over East Indians in the early stages of the battle for survival by arguing that preferential treatment was only an indemnification for abolition of the slave trade, which had made their sugar uncompetitive with sugar produced by slaves in Cuba and Brazil. Once their preferential treatment was removed, distress would end in ruin and slaves would suffer worse misfortunes than ever before.

The first crack in the inevitable collapse of the protected West Indian sugar edifice appeared in 1825, when Parliament equalised the duty on West Indian and Mauritian sugar and conferred on Mauritian growers rights of direct export to Europe, which had been previously granted only to West Indians. A West Indian company formed in 1825 and led by Jamaican landowners William Manning and George Hibbert, proved inadequate to cope with depressed financial conditions in the islands, and not even the end of restrictions on American trade was able to restore a prosperity which was to finish spectacularly for all planters when emancipation was finally decreed by the parliament at Westminster. An organised movement to free all negro slaves within the empire was started in London in January 1823 and by 1824 as many as 750 petitions for emancipation had been presented to Parliament. Far from welcoming overtures for amelioration put forward by Earl Bathurst, after consultation with leading members of the West Indian body in London, West Indian legislatures protested vigorously against what was considered to be unwarranted interference by the home government in their internal affairs. The Jamaican House of Assembly advocated 'the most firm, strong, constitutional measures to resist such attempt, and to preserve to the inhabitants of this Colony those rights which have been transmitted to them from their ancestors'. They only passed one of Bathurst's suggested measures, which was designed to protect female slaves from attacks upon their persons. It was not until 1831, the year of a final slave rebellion, that an unsmiling legislature bowed to the reforming edict. Some Jamaican historians have emphasised the importance of the 1831 rebellion in the chain of events which led to emancipation. Certainly it was significant, if only because more than 100 negroes were hanged and property losses amounted to the then considerable sum of over £1 million sterling!

The emancipation project which became law on 1 August 1834 abolished bondage and converted slaves into apprentices for maximum periods of six years in the case of field hands and of four years for all others. Sunday labour was forbidden and the normal week's work was set at 45 hours. Compensation given to owners by the home government was less than ten shillings in the pound and shortage of capital among estate owners made the end of the planters as a ruling class inevitable.

From Emancipation to Modern Times

A Britain torn by social conflicts and in urgent need of great sums of money to pay the huge bill of £830 million incurred withstanding French attacks upon her Empire, was not a Britain well equipped to solve the problems of primary concern to former trading posts or overseas plantations. The rising middle classes of England then saw greater opportunities for themselves in the new markets which had been opened to them through the rebellion of Spain's former American colonies, than ever seemed likely to recur in sugar islands which had long since ceased to be major sources of wealth. Far from being considered the essential foundations of a prosperous economy, as they had seemed to be in the age of mercantilism, tropical colonies appeared to the trendsetters of free trade as burdens, useful only perhaps as dumping grounds for Britons who had failed at home or had to be kept in prisons or workhouses. Bentham and Adam Smith dismissed colonies in general as unprofitable. Only a relatively small number of philanthropists, Christian missionaries and imperialist visionaries cared much about the people in them and these more often turned their thoughts to residents of North America, Asia, Africa and the Mediterranean. Jamaica, like the rest of the West Indies had become of very little concern to the élites who were then engaged in the exciting tasks of challenging an established aristocracy and appropriating some of its power.

Abolition of slavery was followed four years later on 1 August 1838 by the end of the apprenticeship system, which meant in Jamaica that 311,000 black and coloured people ceased to be the responsibility of 'temporary' masters and were free to do as they pleased. Parliament showed its concern for those who might come before magistrates of the small planting community by passing a bill under the terms of which the governor in Jamaica was given direct responsibility for the management of the prisons.

This interference in the internal affairs of Jamaica, after apprenticeship had ended, is indicative of the new temper of a Reformed Parliament which had little tolerance for West Indian planters as a class. Sir James Stephen, who was the chief architect of colonial policy as under-secretary of state from 1836-47, had, in a memorandum written in 1831 before slavery was abolished, summed up majority opinion in England when he described West Indian landowners as 'unconscious of the rapid progress of that day' and condemned their lives as 'passed in a contracted circle amidst petty feuds and pecuniary embarrassments. There is no civilised society on earth so entirely destitute of learned leisure, of literary and scientific intercourse and even of liberal recreations', he wrote. It was unlikely that the resident planters on Jamaica, who had been compelled to free their slaves and to end the period of apprenticeship earlier than they expected, would feel much inclination for higher learning or such liberal recreations as Sir James considered to be the hallmark of a civilised society. Their feelings had no cultural overtones. They were simply hopping mad with the continuous interference of a parliament whose members showed no understanding whatever of their difficulties. How were they to grow canes and make sugar in competition with slave-grown economies without an adequate labour force? So inflamed did the members of the house of assembly become that Sir Lionel Smith, a governor with a high record of achievement in the Windward islands and Barbados, was obliged to report to the secretary of state in 1838 that it was 'impossible for anyone to answer for the conduct of the House of Assembly'. There were 'many in the island', he said, 'who would be delighted to get up an insurrection for the pleasure of destroying the negros and missionaries. They are in fact mad'. This balanced judgment of Sir Lionel Smith is of considerable importance, because it reminds us that relations between landowners and workers expressed in racial terms of whites and blacks were far from cordial. There had been a long history of slave insurrections in Jamaica and these had left a legacy of ill-will between the haves and have-nots, expressed most unhappily in terms of colour. The sparks which erupted in blazing flames of hatred in 1865 had been smouldering for decades before and after emancipation.

Jamaican recalcitrance and refusal to accept the British Prison Act compelled the governor to dissolve the assembly. In England, although the Tories exploited the Jamaican situation in their own interest and successfully caused a resignation of the government, the Whigs soon returned to office and sent a second Jamaican Bill out to the island, where a new governor, Sir Charles Metcalfe, proved much more tactful than his predecessor in obtaining cooperation from the legislature.

Sir Charles could see that the planters had lost most of a year's crop and that only a small acreage had been planted or prepared for 1839. Many negroes, with no one to stop them, had refused to work and took to growing their own simple requirements of food in the hills or on Crown lands, where they squatted. A natural reluctance to work on the part of people who had been forced to labour most of their lives, was aggravated by the behaviour of some landowners who charged exorbitant rents for huts and plots of ground while offering very low wages to those who were induced to go on working. Some planters also earned ill-will by turning away old dependants in the hope of receiving substitute white workers from overseas. On the whole relations between owners and ex-slaves in Jamaica were bad from the beginning. Determined to see what was happening for himself Governor Metcalfe rode through the island on horseback. His conclusions were practical. Whatever the rights or wrongs of the situation it was obvious to anyone who took the trouble to look at the fertility of Jamaica that no ex-slave needed to work for anyone else. Land was there in abundance to feed whoever tilled it. Metcalfe disapproved, however, of the activities of Baptist missionaries whom he accused of deliberately fomenting 'discontent' among the negroes by encouraging them to avoid work on the plantations. An Act was passed in 1840 to cope with the conditions which Governor Metcalfe had found. It encouraged the importation of African workers. In the midsummer of 1841 a ship arrived in Port Royal, bringing 200 Africans 'liberated' from slave ships and 88 volunteers from Sierra Leone. In the following year about 1,800 more Africans arrived of whom 400 had been brought over from St Helena. In the view of the planters, whose estimates of a satisfactory labour force varied from 15,000 to 50,000, the new arrivals were insufficient to put the sugar industry back on its feet.

Jamaica's problems in the critical decades preceding and following the emancipation of slaves should be set against the background of continuous changes in the mother country. There rulers were faced by a new mass of disorganised people whose clamour for improved living conditions was challenging the fixed liberties, charters and privileges of an old-established order. The challenges were taking place at a time when the social fabrics of European, near-Eastern and Mediterranean countries were being torn apart, and when repressive measures were the natural reactions of those in the seats of power. These decades also saw the rise of a new school of economists who preached the remedy of *laissez-faire* as the only way to spread prosperity among the greatest number of human beings. Their goal was the abolition of restrictive trade practices everywhere: trade should be permitted to develop by the laws of the market place. Even before slavery had been abolished British ministers had shown enthusiasm for the new doctrine and had begun putting it into effect. The monopoly of the East India Company was abolished, tariffs were removed on trade between Britain and Ireland and duties were to be whittled down to 20 per cent. An Act of 1825 had given Britain its first modern tariff by repealing more than 1,000 statutes. Some regard was still paid, however, to the maintenance of an imperial trading system which reserved privileges for British shipowners and gave preferences to Australian wool-producers, Canadian log-cutters and West Indian sugar cane planters.

An imperial vision was, nonetheless, blurred when in 1832 the Cabinet, by resisting King and Lords to support the first Reform Act, visibly demonstrated the passing of political power to a House of Commons which now saw its strength rooted in a rising new middle class. Although somewhat less in number than 250,000, the new voters represented the aspirations of manufacturers, professional farmers and artisans to share with landowners a partnership in running the political machine. Aristocracy, as such, was not sent packing – it remained firmly in the saddle until 1867 – but the radical opinions of new élites, who resented the earlier intrusion through purchase of seats of Indian nabobs and West Indian planters on the parliamentary scene, limited the power of aristocrats. Reform was a plant of slow growth in Britain where only one third of the workers could write their names. It would have been extraordinary indeed if its pace had been quickened in Jamaica, where less than 2,000 voters appointed the House of Assembly and which saw its major concern as the maintenance of the privileges of a minority. Jamaica was a long way distant from the savage strikes and revolutionary dogmas which men like Engels and Marx were then disseminating in Europe. Their problems did not include wars against China and Afghanistan, Chartist agitation, high wheat prices or alarms of invasion from France. Faced by these and many similar serious situations the rulers of Britain in these turbulent years had little time to spare for Jamaican or other West Indian problems which to them seemed trivial by comparison. If Jamaican interests went counter to the interests of the people in Britain then Jamaican interests would have to yield. Once Peel had removed protection for the English corn producers in 1846 in order to satisy the clamour of the English middle and working classes for cheaper food, the way was open for further concessions. The great hunger in Ireland caused by the potato blight had not prevented the export of corn from Ireland to England in 1846. So what resistance could the Jamaican sugar growers make to the Sugar Duties Act of 1846 which offered the English cheaper sugar from countries employing slave labour, at the expense of Jamaica and other British cane growers? Times had indeed changed and the West Indian lobby in Parliament was powerless to resist pressures from new powerful quarters. Terrible economic conditions in Ireland may have seemed to offer hope of attracting a labour force from Ireland to the West Indies, but O'Connell had denounced an earlier emigration scheme in 1841, as a system of 'white slavery'. When the Irish started to stream across the Atlantic (in 1846 over 100,000; in 1847 over 200,000; and between 1849 and 1852 over 200,000 yearly), they went to the United States, not to the West Indies. Although the Irish gave Jamaica a wide berth several thousand African workers continued to arrive until the summer of 1849 when the House of Assembly decided that no more money could be provided for the transportation of new immigrants. Jamaica was not only feeling the effects of the lowering of duties on slave-grown sugar entering England, but the English commercial depression of 1847 had caused the failure of some merchant houses which had been in the habit of financing Jamaican planters.

As though a stagnant economy was not enough, the spread of cholera throughout Jamaica in 1850 further depressed conditions. No less than 10,000 persons died of the disease within three months and before the epidemic ended around 32,000 persons had succumbed. Shortages of field labourers on the plantations, increased by death and recession, became more critical when time-expired workers refused to renew contracts and took to wandering the countryside instead. Efforts to remedy conditions were made in London by the West India Committee who appointed William Beckford, Edward Thompson and Henry Westmoreland to see the secretary of state for war and the colonies. They asked him to agree to the continued despatch of immigrant African workers to Jamaica at the expense of the imperial government, but the decision had already been taken to stop this subsidy before the end of 1851. From the years of emancipation until 1849, when lack of funds caused the suspension of imported free African labourers, it is estimated that 7,500 new workers were brought in to help in the growth of cane and production of sugar. They were not enough, and they did not for the most part remain on plantations, but they did contribute enormously to the maintenance of the sugar industry at a time of great need for Jamaica. The initiative for obtaining immigrant labourers had been taken by the Jamaican House of Assembly and efforts were maintained until 1854 when under a new constitution, the executive committee, of which the governor was chairman, took over responsibility for government. Since the governor represented the government of the United Kingdom it was henceforth Britain's policy for supplying immigrants into Jamaica that mattered. Between 1852 and 1859 there was no supply of Africans, although there was a trickle of immigrants from other countries. When in 1860 contract labourers were once more brought to Jamaica, they came for the most part from India.

Writing in the 30's of this century a Jamaican governor, Lord Olivier, complained that for half a century nothing at all was attempted in island state policy to promote the direct interests and progressive capacities of some hundred thousand food growers and their families. Nothing, he said, was attempted officially for the health, the agriculture or the education of the country working people, and he quotes Dr Maxwell, president of the Metcalfe Agricultural Society of 1848, as saying that 'they have been cast adrift, and like gulf-weeds float hither and thither without any fixed governing principle or acknowledged plan to ameliorate their condition'. Yet Lord Olivier himself admits in his book *Jamaica: The Blessed Island* that the white community of Jamaica had been ruined in 1850 and that the black mountain people were impoverished.

The truth of the matter is that, as W. J. Gardner wrote in his *History of Jamaica* (1873), new laws and institutions suited to a state of general freedom had to be given priority in Jamaica. The mere list of laws passed during Metcalfe's administration was enough, Gardner noted, to fill several pages. Large sums of money were spent on courts of justice, jails and the established church: the police cost upward of £40,000 per annum while £15,000 was spent on the militia. It was during Metcalfe's term of office and at the instigation of General Sir W. Gomm that barracks for European troops were established at Newcastle, thereby reducing the mortality of troops. The peasantry, according to Gardner, was relatively the most prosperous and independent segment of the Jamaican community at the time. He invited attention to the formation of agricultural societies in these post-emancipation years and to the direct encouragement by the house of assembly of the cultivation of indigo, cocoa, divi-divi and tea. Efforts were also made to produce silk and to grow cotton.

During Lord Elgin's administration which followed that of Metcalfe, further improvements were made, despite the severe losses caused by the Kingston fire of 1843 and the fiasco of imported coolies who were 'the sweepings of the streets of Madras'. A railway between Spanish Town and Kingston was completed and a waterworks established in Kingston. The Royal Agricultural Society fostered local agricultural societies, and new methods of cultivation, improved machinery and new breeds of cattle were introduced. Even irrigation was studied. A mutual life assurance society and friendly societies were formed. Other advances included enlargement of hospital accommodation, consolidation of laws and investigations into the conduct of charities. The regime of Sir Charles Grey from late 1846 until late 1853 coincided with the worst years of Jamaica. Sugar planters had for good reason not responded to the secretary of state, Earl Grey's suggestion in his 'colonial policy', that the 'more a negro earned the less he worked'. Their problem was not the wages paid to sugar workers but the absence of sugar workers to whom wages might be paid. From the beginning of his first meeting with the assembly on 16

13. Francis Williams, the eighteenth-century scholar, painted about 1735.

February 1847 Sir Charles faced animosity from assemblymen, whose clamour was for retrenchment. Nor did he improve his relationships with the planters by spreading a rumour to the effect that the Americans might be tempted to capture Jamaica and to reintroduce slavery. Sir Charles had found a deficiency of £64,000 in the island's finances in 1846. By 1851 the public debt had increased to £680,000, while public buildings were falling into disrepair and roads were impassable in places. Public meetings were held throughout Jamaica and resolutions were passed requesting the home government to take remedial measures. A delegation was sent to England in 1852, and a petition from Jamaican clergymen and missionaries was presented to the House of Commons. No help was forthcoming from the Reformed Parliament, which was dedicated to Free Trade and to the gradual equalisation of the duties on free and slave-grown sugar, which happened in 1854.

Under Sir Henry Barkley, who took over from Grey as governor in October 1853, a form of responsible government through an executive committee of governor's advisers was introduced, in return for a loan of £500,000 from the imperial government in London. At the same time a new Jamaican privy council was formed from members of the legislative council, the assembly and chief government officers. For a time there was a compromise between the executive government and the assemblymen, the first serious difficulty arising in 1860 from an excess of expenditure by the government on much-needed improvements to roads. Disputes as to where responsibility for government measures lay eventually led to a majority vote in the assembly to the effect that responsibility for the proper control of public affairs was clearly established by the Act of 1854 for the better government of the island. In 1861 Jamaicans were given a brief opportunity to forget their internal troubles and to demonstrate their loyalty to the British throne during a visit to the island as a midshipman on board HMS *St George* of Queen Victoria's son Prince Alfred. 'Banners, evergreens, flowers and fruit almost hid many of the houses in Kingston',

14. Linstead Market.

wrote Gardner; 'triumphal arches were abundant, but most wonderful of all was the immense concourse of people ... temporary platforms were prepared on which upwards of two thousand Sunday school children were gathered, singing, as the prince approached, the well known strains of the National Anthem.'

But beneath the surface the condition of Jamaican society was gradually being undermined. The acting governor Eyre who had won a reputation as friend of the Australian aborigines found great opposition in the assembly to the executive committee he had been bequeathed by Governor Darling on his departure in 1862. Prorogation of the assembly only infuriated the assemblymen whose views were not challenged by the executive committee. Attempts were made to have Eyre recalled to London, but failed because the acting governor was supported by missionaries and others interested in the social advancement of Jamaica. This body warmly approved a document known as the 'morality proclamation' in which Eyre announced that in future no person would be put on the list of applicants for public appointments unless he was able to transmit a certificate from a minister of religion, or other trustworthy person of position and responsibility stating that he was strictly honest, sober and moral in his conduct and habits. Promotion was also to be barred to persons in public life found to be leading intemperate or immoral lives. Eyre's conduct made him many enemies, but approval of his morality proclamation found favour with some assemblymen and their protests against their colleagues who sought Eyre's recall, together with resolutions passed by the upholders of religion and social improvement, encouraged the authorities in London to promote the acting governor to the office vacated by Governor Darling.

Gardner, who went to Jamaica as a missionary of the Congregational Church in 1849 and remained there until his death, records the occurrence of a great religious revival in 1861, a year in which the price of food began to rise steeply in Jamaica as a consequence of the loss of imports from the war-torn United States. 'Many thousands of marriages were celebrated', he wrote, 'evil habits were abandoned. The rum shops were forsaken by multitudes, and thousands were added to the different congregations, of whom many became communicants and have remained faithful.' In the eastern districts of the island, however, Gardner considered the influence of the native Baptists: 'one of the greatest drawbacks to the advancement of the people ... their leaders were men of no education'. To their influence and teaching he attributed the deplorable events which overtook Governor Eyre and finally led to his recall to the United Kingdom, where his behaviour was championed or opposed by some of the most powerful and influential people of the time. Gardner took the view that Eyre's lot was cast in 'evil times, for never, since the day of emancipation, had the island been in circumstances of greater peril. The house of assembly was generally felt to be a barrier in the way of all progress, and in no proper sense of the word could it be regarded as a representative body. Jamaica, with a population of upwards of half a million, was divided into 23 parishes or electoral districts, returning 47 members in all. But in 1864, the united registries showed only 1,903 persons qualified to vote, and at the last general election, held that year, only 1,457 persons exercised their privilege ... 32 members, who were at this time elected, had less than 50 votes each, and 25 of these had less than 30 ... in the county of Cornwall, containing five parishes and a third of the entire population of the island, there were only 246 voters, 162 of whom returned ten members to the assembly.... For the past 20 years the character of the house had been gradually deteriorating, and its deliberations were often painfully interrupted by scenes of confusion and strife. The appointment of the executive committee had led to no permanent improvement, for after the first few years, a constant struggle for place and power was maintained, and partisanship became more bitter than before. The violent language so often used in the house was not without influence on the people at large. At public meetings expressions of a very seditious character were commonly employed and a turbulent spirit exhibited itself in many parts of the island. The community had grave reasons for complaint, for while the assembly was wasting time in wrangling about its so-called privileges and rights, glaring abuses in almost all public institutions were unredressed, and very little was done to promote the social elevation or true prosperity of the country.'

A letter addressed by Dr Underhill (one of the secretaries of the Baptist Missionary Society who had visited Jamaica in 1861) to Secretary of State for Colonies Cardwell in 1865 precipitated the terrible events of that year. Underhill had suggested ways of improving the depressed conditions of the people on the island and Governor Eyre had circulated a copy of his letter to leading persons of the community for comment and discussion. What he had apparently not anticipated was the use his enemies would make of a document which might be interpreted as a criticism of his own administration. According to Gardner, 'the greatest mischief was done in St Thomas in the East, where an inflammatory address drawn up by Mr G. W. Gordon was distributed, and meetings of a seditious character held'. Gardner describes Gordon as a great planting attorney, whose mother was a woman of colour. 'In early life he kept a store in Kingston, and even then attracted attention by his peculiarities. In course of time he became possessed with a perfect mania for the acquisition of land and bought properties in several parts of the island. They never paid under his management, and at the time of his death they were all mortgaged!... In his dealings with the labourers and others in his employ his conduct was often called into question, and most certainly it was not of such a character as to justify the position he assumed as friend of the people.... Mr Gordon was fond of power. Unfortunately neither in his relations to the churches he was first connected with, nor in his public life were his conduct and ability such as to secure it. He had been for many years a member of the house of assembly, then he was unseated, and for a considerable time he was unable to resume that position: he was, however, a member for St

Thomas in the East at the time of the outbreak . . . he was also magistrate in six or seven parishes. It would be impossible to assign him a clearly defined position in the political circle of the colony. He certainly had not the confidence of those gentlemen of colour who took a leading part in the discussions of the assembly. . . .'

According to Gardner, some months before the outbreak at St Thomas in the East, Gordon had been deprived by the governor of all commissions held as justice of the peace in consequence of unsubstantiated accusations he had made against a brother magistrate. He was also being challenged by the custos of the parish, Baron von Ketelhodt, a close friend of Governor Eyre, as to his qualification to fill the office of church-warden in the Anglican Church, of which he was no longer a member. At public meetings which were supported by native Baptists, and especially by the deacon, Paul Bogle, whom Gordon had appointed, very strong language was used. A friend of Gordon's was so alarmed by his speeches that he prepared an article in his defence, aimed, as a Royal Commission reported later, to shield Gordon and his supporters 'from the charge of anarchy and tumult, which in a short time must follow these fearful demonstrations'.

Although it is easy to understand why in today's Jamaica, Gordon and Bogle can both be revered as early champions of the rights of non-white Jamaicans, in the context of the political realities of the time it is also easy to understand why he was then considered to be subversive of established order and institutions. The report of the Royal Commission is full of statements like 'don't kill him, we have orders to kill no black, only white. . .we don't want the women now, only kill the white man, we have the house to live in ourselves. . . .' Under such circumstances, cool and impartial judgment was improbable. Eighteen people, inclusive of the custos, had been killed on 11 October in the disturbance at Morant Bay, provoked by the march of Bogle and his associates to the court house. About thirty more were seriously wounded. Yet, as the Royal Commission reported, Bogle gave thanks in his chapel at Stoney Court 'that God has succeeded him in his work'. He made preparations for defence in case 'the enemy came' and told the men he drilled that 'this country would belong to them; that it had long been theirs' and 'they must keep it wholly in possession'. If these were the attitudes of Bogle and his followers, and Bogle was Gordon's man, no governor could be expected to take a lenient view of Gordon's behaviour. 'All this has come of Mr Gordon's agitation', Eyre told the secretary of the Jamaican government, Edward Jordon, when he heard of the outbreak, and later in a despatch to the secretary of state for the colonies he wrote that Gordon 'had not only been mixed up with the matter, but was himself, through his misrepresentations and seditious language addressed to the ignorant black people, the chief cause and origin of the whole rebellion'.

So far Eyre had acted with restraint. When martial law was declared in the county of Cornwall (but not Kingston), on 13 October, the decision had been taken by 30 men of all parties, inclusive of the governor, the privy council, members of the house of assembly and military and naval officers. Subsequently acts were committed by members of the forces engaged in putting down the rebellion which were reprobated by the Royal Commissioners, but the governor's behaviour in listening to the advice of his council of war was, in their opinion, justified.

It is almost impossible for persons who have not experienced a riot in a multi-racial community to understand how quickly dormant racial antipathies can be stirred by agitators and fanned into flame by panic, nor how, in time of panic, reprisals can spread beyond reasonable suppression and become excessive. It is equally difficult for those who have not lived through such a time of trouble to appreciate how quickly responsible opinion is eager to find a scapegoat on whom blame may be fixed for rupture of the social fabric. Something had in fact gone very wrong between the year 1859, when Trollope visited Jamaica, and the year 1865, when the whole political machine of Jamaica sputtered to a standstill and had to go into reverse.

Whatever went wrong originated partly from the antipathy which Governor Eyre allowed himself to feel for Gordon, and partly from the unrestrained abuse which Gordon used about the Queen's representative. Trollope, (author of *The West Indies and the Spanish Main*), had met coloured men at the governor's table; 'they sat in the House of Assembly; they cannot be refused admittance to state parties or even to large assemblies; they have forced themselves forwards and must be recognised as being in the van ... they do make money and enjoy it, they practise as statesmen, as lawyers and as doctors in the colony ... they have been or are judges, attorneys-general, prime ministers, leaders of the opposition'. As for the old-fashioned Jamaican planter, the 'true aristocrat of the West Indies', his day was done, but no men, Trollope wrote, were 'fonder of the country to which they belong, or prouder of the name of Great Britain than these Jamaicans.... They would fain dispense altogether with their legislature and be governed altogether from home'.

Knowing such Jamaican planters and liking them, fearful of the consequences of the American Civil War, in which Southerners very similar in outlook to the old Jamaican planters, were being hunted, mindful of the ferocity of the Maori war, recollecting the atrocities of the Indian Mutiny, did the devoted Anglican Governor Eyre see himself as an anointed defender of the British way of life in Jamaica? Was this why he circulated in June 1865 50,000 copies of the Queen's Letter in which Jamaican workers had been invited to work 'for wages, not uncertainly or capriciously, but steadily and continuously at the time when their labour is wanted, and for so long as it is wanted', and emphasising that it 'was from their own industry and prudence ... and not from any such schemes as have been suggested to them that they must look for an improvement in their conditions?' This letter was a classic vindication of the long held, and not yet eradicated belief of persons who, like Trollope, maintained that 'the negro's idea of emancipation was and is, emancipation not from slavery but from work'. In his lonely vigil as upholder of the time-honoured biblical tradition of earning one's bread by the sweat of the brow, Eyre must have been greatly uplifted by the confidence which he had received from his superiors in London. He needed such comfort for Gordon had been most offensive in the House of Assembly where he said: 'When a Governor becomes a dictator, when he becomes despotic, it is time for the people to dethrone him.... I have never seen an animal more voracious for cruelty and power than the present governor of Jamaica ... if the law is to be disregarded it will lead to anarchy and bloodshed ... if we are to be governed by such a governor much longer, the people will have to fly to arms and to become self-governing.'

Eyre would not have been Eyre if he had not felt the contempt in these verbal whiplashes which came from a man for whom he had little respect or sympathy. He saw Gordon as the 'instigator of all the evils' and by consenting to his arrest and transportation to Morant Bay for trial by court martial must have imagined, as the reporter in the *Colonial Standard* actually wrote, 'the hand of retributive justice that doomed him to meet his death on the very spot of his vile machinations'. Eyre never doubted that he had acted rightly. However defective, he said before leaving Jamaica, his action may have been in 'a strictly legal point of view', Mr Gordon was the 'proximate occasion of the insurrection, and of the cruel massacre of particular individuals whom he regarded as his personal enemies, and that therefore he suffered justly.'

Unfortunately for Eyre's peace of mind his view of the Morant Bay rebellion was not shared by a vocal influential body of persons in England. 'The Eyre controversy' raged in England for years, with Victorian scientists and men of letters joining with members of Parliament, clergymen, radicals and others in a determined effort to see Eyre either as a 'saviour of society' or as a near monster who was responsible for a month-long reign of terror, during which nearly 500 negroes were killed, more were flogged and tortured, and 1,000 homes burnt. Several literary Victorians, Carlyle, Ruskin, Tennyson, Dickens and Kingsley among others helped Eyre with money or in other ways, while men of science, Charles Darwin, Huxley, Lyell, Herbert Spencer, rallied behind the Jamaica Committee, whose most active champion was J. S. Mill. Huxley called the case of Governor Eyre 'one of the most important constitutional battles in which Englishmen have for many years been engaged', while Mill wanted to know 'who are to be our masters; the Queen's judges and a jury of our own countrymen, administering the laws of England or three military and naval officers, two of them boys, administering as the Chancellor of the Exchequer tells us, no law at all?'

The official view of Eyre was expressed by the Earl of Carnarvon, secretary of state for the colonies in a speech to the House of Lords on 2 August 1866: 'Promptitude, courage, fearlessness of responsibility, if not accompanied by a sound judgment on the part of the person who possesses them, become faults rather than virtues.... The first attribute demanded of a Governor is not only justice but perfect impartiality and the power of rising above panic and the apprehensions of the moment. It is to the fatal want of this quality in Mr Eyre that we may trace at least half of the mischief which arose after the outbreak....' Carnarvon's judgment was supported by Gardner when he wrote about Eyre in his *History*: 'The unfortunate animus he displayed towards those he regarded as opponents did a great deal to prevent justice being done to the painful circumstances in which he was placed, or to the promptitude with which he dealt with the outbreak in its first stages.'

One consequence of the Morant Bay rebellion could not have been anticipated by those who were responsible for the uprising. On 10 January 1866, as Gardner noted, 'the history of representative institutions in Jamaica terminated for a season, after having existed for two hundred and two years'. On 11 June an Order in Council was passed in London, establishing a legislative council in Jamaica, consisting in the first instance of the officer in command of the troops, the colonial secretary, the attorney general, the financial secretary, the director of roads, and the collector of customs, together with a few non-official members. On 16 October the first legislative council was convened.

Personal animosity against Gordon had led Eyre into paths which could not be supported by English authorities. He was recalled, but not before he had the satisfaction of seeing pure Crown Colony government instituted in Jamaica. Under this system it was possible for a great reforming governor, Sir John Peter Grant, to lay the foundations of modern Jamaica in response to a growing imperial concern for the human condition of the majority of British subjects throughout the empire. Twenty years after the Morant Bay rebellion Joseph Chamberlain, who was to become the greatest of all colonial secretaries, said at Warrington: 'Now that we have a government of the people by the people ... of course it is socialism. The Poor Law is socialism. The Education Act is socialism. The greater part of municipal work is socialism, and every kindly act of legislation by which the community has sought to discharge its responsibilities and its obligation to the poor is socialism, but it is none the worse for that. Our object is the elevation of the poor.'

Sir John Peter Grant, who ruled Jamaica from 1866 until 1874, undoubtedly saw his role as an executor of overdue social reforms. His first acts had been directed to improve local administration: parishes were reduced to 14 in number and parochial boards formed to replace the old vestries. A police force was created, district courts were set up, and the machinery of justice reformed. Beginnings were made in a state health service, including better quarantine arrangements, and supplies of drinking water were improved. Some progress was made with educational services, the Institute of Jamaica was founded and botanical gardens were laid out. After the transfer of the seat of government from Spanish Town to Kingston in 1872, the City's water supply was improved, a fire brigade was established, and general amenities, like the Parade Gardens and Victoria Market and Pier, provided. New progressive attitudes were also extended to immigrants and a special department was organised to protect imported East Indian labourers. Coolie labour, as Gardner called it, was thought necessary because the majority of the black population had become freeholders, who were self supporting. In 1870 the Rio Cobre Irrigation Works was started to provide water for dry lands near Spanish Town, thereby initiating a significant change from ancient agricultural practices. A beginning was also made in 1866 with the export of bananas. The first shipments were made from Oracabessa and Port Antonio by Captain George Busch, who sold them in Boston. Four years later Captain Lorenzo Dow Baker began a commercial development which was to prove of lasting benefit to the island. Repeal of old laws permitted aliens to acquire property in Jamaica and encouraged a 'very considerable number of enterprising Cubans and others' to purchase land and buildings. A government savings bank was established in 1870 and postal services greatly improved. A new lease of life was injected into the Church of England in Jamaica by the decision taken in 1870 for its disestablishment. Sir John Peter Grant had found finances in a deplorable condition and a debt in excess of three quarters of a million pounds. By 1872 the income of the colony was in excess of expenditure and regulated, as Gardner wrote, on 'sound principles of equity and economy'. 'Never', Gardner contended, 'since the abolition of the sugar duties in 1846 have the inhabitants generally been in a more prosperous or contented state: and never, at any former period, has the prosperity that is enjoyed rested on a sounder basis'. In 1870 sugar exports were the highest for 19 years, the coffee crop the largest since 1838. More rum was made than before; a considerable fruit trade had sprung up with America; Cuban settlers were cultivating excellent tobacco; cocoa was resuming its place among the products of the colony. Jamaica's population had by then passed the half million mark of whom a little over 13,000 were white, 100,000 coloured and nearly 400,000 black persons.

In the final paragraphs of his history Gardner expressed sentiments which reflected the views of the new imperialists who were then coming into prominence in England and elsewhere: 'The discontent which once characterised so many of the people is now rarely witnessed. Taxes are more cheerfully paid, because it is known that they will be carefully expended for legitimate purposes. Education is extending, and Christian churches are flourishing. Crime is under control. Industrious habits are stimulated by the prospect of success, while the commercial and agricultural condition of the island alike indicate steady but real progress.' Prospects of material advancement and spiritual progress were accompanied by an awareness of British power. At the Crystal Palace in 1872 Disraeli talked of 'a great country, an imperial country ... commanding the respect of the world'. This was before the scramble for Africa and other places of economic and strategic importance was started by some advanced European and other powerful nations.

Between 1875 and 1900 the area of the British Empire had increased by approximately 5 million square miles. Expansion was the new theme of the economists who were encouraged by a volume of world trade that, in the years between 1850 and 1870, rose by 270 per cent. Just as Jamaica had shared to some extent in increased world prosperity, so it was to experience in some measure the decline in impetus of world trade volume which only rose 170 per cent in the 30 years between 1880 and 1913. In a changing world the contribution of its agricultural products was still appreciated, but as a market for British exports Jamaica and other West Indian islands were relatively unimportant in comparison with the United States, Canada, Australia, New Zealand, Argentina, Uruguay and South Africa. By 1870 a third of British capital exports were going to these and other countries and by 1913 the volume had increased by yet another third.

Late in the year 1883 the Colonial Secretary, Lord Derby, writing from London to Governor Sir Henry Norman, announced his intention of making representation in the legislative council 'really popular', provided that this could be done without placing the 'selection of the representatives in the hands of a large class of illiterate or ignorant voters'. To prevent this he suggested the appointment of a Royal Commission to ascertain and report on what 'franchise or combination of franchises would constitute a reasonably large body of electors qualified by knowledge and education to form an intelligent judgment on public affairs, and so ensure the fair representation of all interests'. A ninth member had been added in 1881 to the original six of the legislative council. An Order in Council of 18 May 1884 and an Amending Order of 3 October 1895 increased numbers and allowed for the election of 14 members. This new constitution which endured until 20 November 1944 was noteworthy for giving nine elected members power to veto any financial measure; it also provided that the unanimous vote of the 14 elected members could only be overridden by other votes if the Governor declared that such a decision was of paramount importance in the public interest. Jamaica's council of a governor plus five officials, ten nominated and 14 elected members gave rise to the comment that the government of Jamaica, to run smoothly, depended upon a 'series of successful efforts to avoid a contest between the Governor and an unknown nine out of 14 men!'

Competition with bounty-fed European beet sugar had brought the West Indian sugar industry to the verge of collapse by 1897, when a Royal Commission reported that the industry was in danger of 'practical extinction'. Jamaican exports had fallen from a value of £910,000 in 1882 to about £300,000 in 1897. The government of this period had taken energetic measures to diversify the economy, spending more than £100,000 to encourage new industries based on agriculture. Sir Henry Blake had founded the Jamaican Agricultural Society in 1895 and George Douet, its first secretary and John Barclay had promoted the making of Jippa-Jappa (Panama) hats from local straw.

Agriculture, however, suffered generally from the shortages of rainfall recorded during the two decades of 1870 and 1890, while 'fire-stick' cultivation was progressively damaging soils and forcing squatters further and further into the interior of the island. Labour shortages, too, aggravated the critical situation of sugar factories. The Royal Commissioners had reported that, if the expensive factories, which alone could afford to produce the class of sugar demanded by modern markets, were to be operated, they must have a nucleus of reliable labour. Skilled workers were also needed on the banana estates which were giving a timely prop to the economy at a time when the cultivation of middle grade coffee was also diminishing because of competition from Brazil.

During the regime of Sir Anthony Musgrave, a beginning was made with the bridging of rivers along the north coast of Portland. Under Sir Henry Blake, who was governor from 1888 until 1898, many improvements were made to roads and new roads built into the interior, including some requiring bridges. Money was also borrowed to construct hotels required by visitors who came to Jamaica in 1891 for the Great Exhibition which was opened by the royal prince who later ascended the throne as King George V.

When the governor was popular the Crown Colony administration of Jamaica worked for the general advancement of the people. An unpopular governor instead brought to the surface latent criticism of a government which was effectively carried on by instructions from London. Under Sir Augustus Hemming who had succeeded Blake, citizens of Kingston made strong protests at a public meeting against arbitrary and 'premeditated attacks upon representative institutions'. Resurgence of discontent against government by remote control was encouraged by negroes like Dr Robert Love. He helped the first negro candidate to be elected to the legislative council and was elected himself in 1906. In less than 20 years from that date negro members eclipsed white in number and by the 'thirties nearly monopolised membership.

Writing in 1913 the great Jamaican journalist and author, H. G. de Lisser took stock of the society which had resulted from Lord Derby's attempt to secure the 'fair representation of all interests' in the law-making process. He found that the natives then filled most of the positions formerly held by men from the United Kingdom. Yet the life of the country bore the 'indelible impress of English influences; the language is English, the literature is English, the religion is English, the sentiments of the people are more English than anything else, and Jamaicans are proud of their connection with the British Empire'. De Lisser praised the government in the first decade of the twentieth century for standing out as the 'leading influence in a dozen different movements all making for the amelioration of conditions in Jamaica, and for the betterment of the common people'. At the same time he was at pains to point out that 'the pioneers in education, the teachers of morality, the sworn friends of the friendless, the downtrodden, the unconsidered' had been for many decades the missionaries and the ministers. He was particularly lavish in his praise of the archbishop of the West Indies, Enos Nuttall, whom he called an 'Englishman of Englishmen', and a 'Jamaican of Jamaicans'. Through his activity, the Anglican church in Jamaica, 'once without influence and not deserving it, once the Church of a few wealthy, contemptuous, dissolute persons' had become as much the church of the poor as the 'most democratic non conformist body'. De Lisser also praised the Jesuits who were led by an American bishop, for their achievement in becoming entirely associated with the people of Jamaica.

Despite the advantages Jamaica had obtained from several reforming governors, civil servants, clergy and teachers, another current of political life was opening new channels which flowed away from paternalism in the direction of greater Jamaican participation in government. In 1909 the franchise was lowered and women were allowed to vote ten years later. When, however, the future Lord Halifax, as Major Wood, visited Jamaica in 1921, he discovered that whereas an elected or nominated member of the legislative council might act as a 'unit' of criticism against government, there was no organised opposition party. There was instead 'a complete divorce of 14 elected members from responsibility'. He found no demand for responsible government and took the view that the only effect of granting it then, might be to 'entrench in power a financial oligarchy which would entirely dominate the colony and use their position for the sole purpose of benefiting one class instead of the community as a whole'. He considered that the first step to be taken was to associate people directly with the task of their own government. But the Crown was a 'responsible trustee' and could not divest itself until 'satisfied that it can delegate the change to hands of not less certain impartiality or integrity than its own'.

Events were building up, however, in the 'twenties which were to shatter earlier hopeful concepts of a regenerated West Indies moving slowly perhaps, but steadily, to better things. Even before the great American Depression of 1929, there was sufficient squalor and discontent in Jamaica to point out the lessons which the Jamaican founder of the Universal Negro Improvement Association of the United States, Marcus Garvey, began to teach as soon as he returned to his native land in 1927. Garvey, who is today especially honoured in Jamaica as a hero, encouraged negroes to be proud of their race. His message also raised hopes of economic advancement during a period of general world recession. The Jamaican economy was then being propped up largely by the cultivation of bananas which by 1890 had replaced sugar as the main export and by 1930 was accounting for 57 per cent of total domestic exports. Employment in agriculture was also falling, from 67 per cent of the labour force in 1880 to 54 per cent in 1930. However, there had been a steady increase in the local consumption of agricultural produce, which rose from around 29 per cent in 1832 to approximately 61 per cent in 1930. The years 1934-48 were years of severe economic depression in Jamaica. Emigration outlets for workers in Panama and Cuba had closed and unsettled world conditions were not at all conducive to investment in untried enterprises. Social disturbances were widespread throughout the West Indies in these years and in 1938 at Frome in Westmoreland a strike of sugar workers had ended in bloodshed. Disorders soon spread to Kingston and other parts of Jamaica.

15. (*above*) Bamboo grove and stream in Irwin Botanic Gardens near Montego Bay.
16. (*below*) Rafting on the Martha Brae near Falmouth.

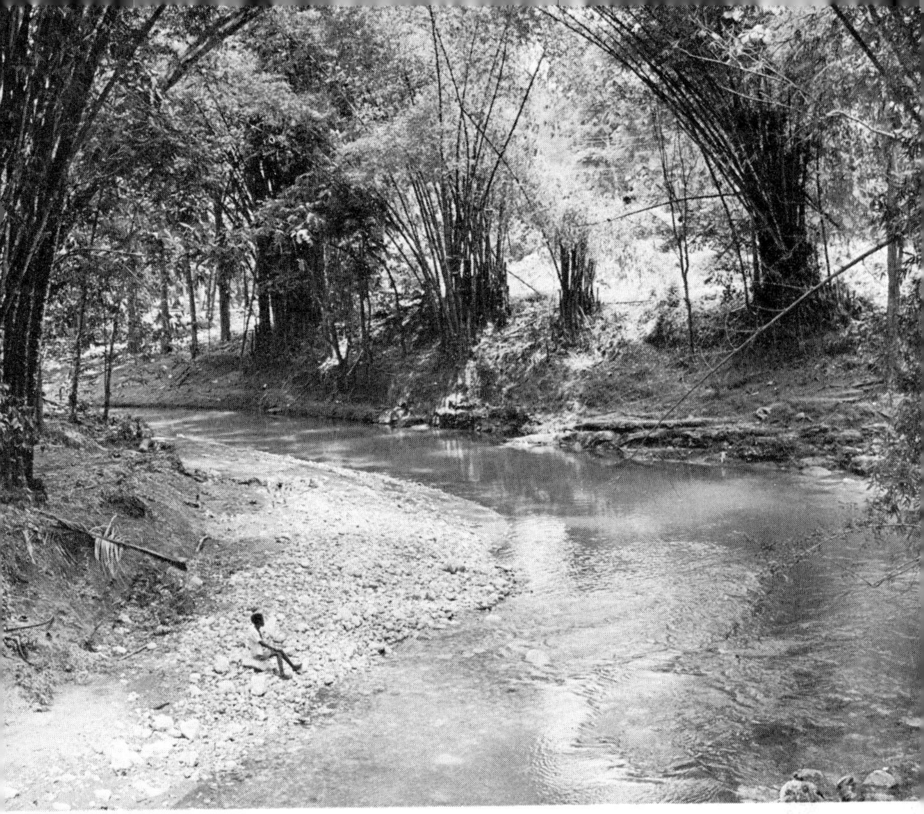

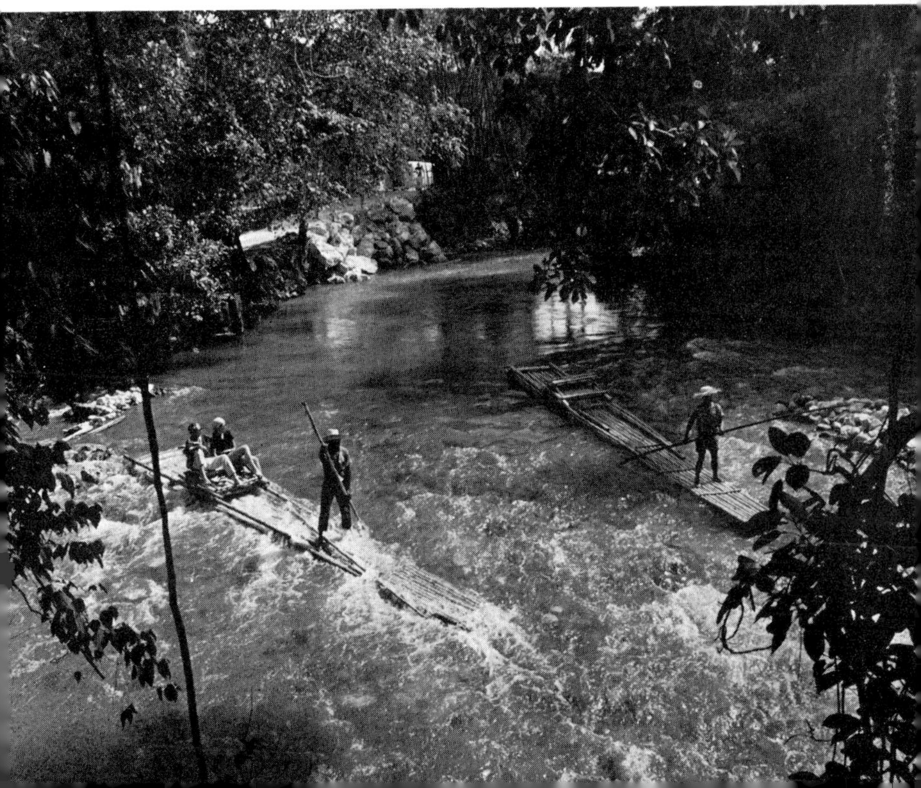

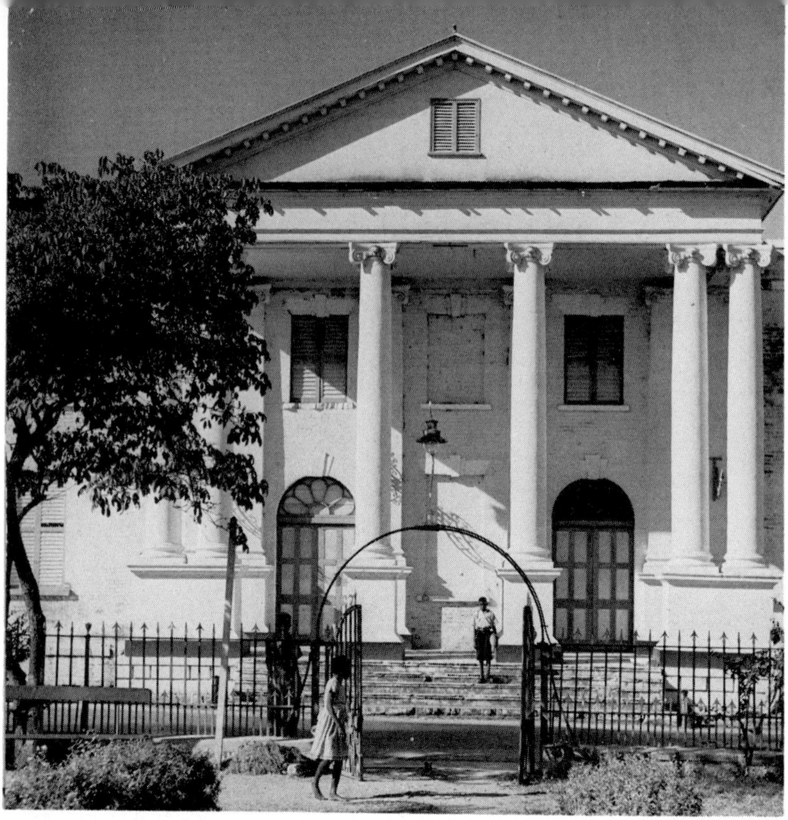

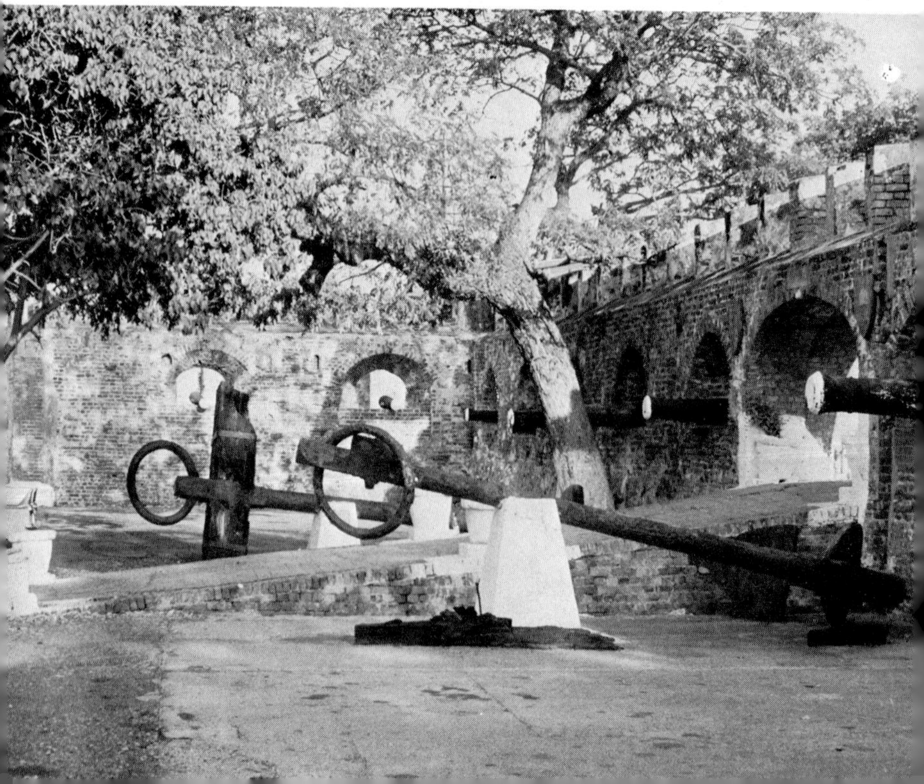

Workers' discontent provided Alexander Bustamante with an opportunity to organise his Industrial Trade Union. Dockers, and those engaged on banana and sugar plantations joined his movement, which was given increased impetus when Bustamante was arrested and imprisoned for a brief period. The governor of the day, who later became Lord Milverton, was quickly persuaded to release Bustamante in the belief that his leadership of working men would be more beneficial for Jamaica than a new socialist movement associated with his cousin Norman Manley, a Queen's Counsel and friend of Sir Stafford Cripps. Bustamante was later knighted by the Queen, but Manley's People's National Party was to put down very deep roots, which have shaped today's Jamaica. Where Bustamante triumphed most conspicuously over his cousin was in winning the referendum which took Jamaica out of the ill-starred federation over which Norman Manley had persuaded the reluctant Grantley Adams of Barbados to preside as first and only Prime Minister. Manley's disappointment was great, for he had been hailed widely as the chief architect of federation.

The Jamaican cousins each founded trade unions which later became the foundations of their respective political parties (the Jamaican Labour Party and the P.N.P.).

A thoroughly aroused Jamaican people was ready to ask for political changes as well as higher wages, so Jamaica was included in the comprehensive investigations of a Royal Commission, whose report had to be delayed because of the outbreak of World War Two. The colonial office did not drag its feet, however, and in 1940 the British parliament passed its first Colonial Development and Welfare Act. A development and welfare organisation was established in Barbados to supervise expenditure of 'pump-priming' money in the West Indies and in 1942 an Anglo-American Caribbean Commission was established to deal with urgent specific problems then affecting the Caribbean area as a consequence of German hostilities. Unemployment had provoked fresh disturbances in Jamaica in June and July 1942, as opportunities for work in the Canal zone came to an end. By April

17. (*above*) The Palladian façade of the Old King's House, Spanish Town.
18. (*below*) Fort Charles, Port Royal.

1943 some relief was given when over 8,000 Jamaicans were recruited as farmworkers in 16 American states. Agriculture was also encouraged and in July of that year Governor Sir John Huggins announced that over 200,000 acres of land were under food crops. In these critical years of war Jamaican manufacture of copra was increased so that the island produced enough soap, cooking oil and margarine for its own use and even had surpluses for export. Cassava and banana flour were also produced locally and a new yeast food, torula.

On 23 February 1943 the British government announced a new constitution for Jamaica. This provided for a privy council, an executive council, a legislative council and a House of Representatives. The island was divided into 32 single-member constituencies and on 14 December 1944, under adult franchise, the Jamaican Labour Party gained 22 seats, the P.N.P. five, and independents five.

The first telegraph cable had been laid as far back as 1870. Toward the end of 1941 scheduled air services were operating from Jamaica to Miami, Cuba, Haiti, Aruba and Colombia. A public health training centre was started in 1942 and the improved health of the community was to be reflected in the decline in infant mortality rate from 78.3 per 1,000 in 1950 to 34.7 in 1968. In the 'fifties and early 'sixties Jamaica lost considerable numbers of its people through emigration. In the 18 years between 1950 and 1968 emigration equalled over 30 per cent of the national growth of population. Of the emigrants, 85 per cent went to the United Kingdom in the years between 1953-64.

Between 1950 and 1968 Jamaica's gross domestic product rose at an annual rate of 6.7 per cent, increasing by 221 per cent from $171 million in 1950 to $549.2 million in 1968. Nevertheless unemployment remained high and in 1967 was reliably estimated to be 20.2 per cent of the working population. New avenues of emigration were found in the United States and Canada and a small trickle of persons continued to reach the United Kingdom, but Jamaica's problem was how to reconcile an input of 20,000 persons annually into the labour force with a net new-job creation of no more than 5,000.

Agriculture in Jamaica suffered greatly from emigration. As much as 34 per cent of those who emigrated in the years 1954-61 had been employed in the agricultural sector, which in 1960 was still accounting for 39 per cent of the employed labour force. Rationalisation of the sugar industry had led to the reduction from 134 sugar factories in 1897 to 24 in 1950, and 15 in 1969. Improved technology in factories and fields had resulted in a threefold output of sugar for the years 1945 and 1969. In 1965 the yield of sugar exceeded half a million tons and independent cane farmers were responsible for 50 per cent of the canes harvested. Improved conditions in the sugar industry were timely because there was a sad decline in the banana trade. Great losses were incurred in the hurricane of 1951 and by 1968 bananas were accounting for no more than 7.7 per cent of visible exports. Coffee and cocoa declined as exports, but the value of citrus exported rose from $2.2 million in 1950-52 to $5.5 million in 1966-68. By 1964 Jamaica was producing 25 million pounds of beef and 37 million quarts of milk, but idle or underdeveloped land was still estimated to be half a million acres. Over the years 1946-68 the government of Jamaica had spent $56.4 million on agricultural development, but this represented at best 18 per cent of its total expenditure on development.

The prevailing climate of economic opinion had been in favour of industrialisation. The Textile Industry Encouragement Act of 1947 was the beginning of special incentive legislation. It was followed in 1948 by the Cement Industry Law and in 1949 by the Pioneer Industries Encouragement Law. In 1952, the year in which the cement factory began operating, an industrial development corporation was appointed. In 1956 outright tax holidays were introduced by the Industrial Incentives Law, and a law was also enacted to encourage export industries. In 1959 a development finance corporation was created to enable more rapid extension of industries. By the end of 1968 there were 179 enterprises operating under the incentive laws and employment had been created for about 26,000 persons, or just 1,000 above the yearly accretion of the labour force. A year later it was established that at least 39 industrial operations were being carried on in rural areas, giving employment to 3,800 persons.

The most revolutionary development in Jamaica occurred when in the years 1950-51 the Strategic Material Division of Economic Cooperation Administration in the United States made a contract with Reynolds Jamaica Mines (a subsidiary of Reynolds Metal Company) to assist development of bauxite deposits in Jamaica. Funds were also made available about the same time to Jamaica Bauxite Ltd. (now Alcan (Jamaica) Ltd.) for the same purpose. A Bauxite and Alumina Industries (Encouragement) Law had been passed in 1950 and mining operations began in 1952. Between 1953 and 1968 gross domestic product from mining advanced by around 1,300 per cent, contributions rising from $5.2 million in 1953 to $72.4 million in 1968. By 1968 about 5,000 persons were engaged in mining operations. Unskilled workers were in the enviable position of earning nearly five times as much as agricultural workers and three times more than workers in manufacturing industries such as cement and clay products, textiles, metal products, food, beverages, furniture and fixtures. Exports of bauxite and alumina in 1968 accounted for 49.5 per cent of Jamaica's total domestic exports.

Bauxite mining was not the only industry to achieve special prominence in modern Jamaica. Before the war nearly one million dollars had been spent by more than 65,000 tourists. In 1944 a Hotels Aid Law was passed, and accommodations increased by three times between 1945-69. In the latter year 95 hotels were equipped with over 4,000 rooms and over 400,000 visitors took holidays in the island. Tourism was particularly encouraged as a welcome contributor to foreign exchange earnings. The industrial and tourist development of Jamaica was accompanied by greater use of the island's roads. Motor cars registered rose from 13,040 in 1950 to 69,886 in 1969. The subsidised railway which the government had taken over from a private company in 1896 was maintained not only for the use of private travellers but for the carriage of bananas and bauxite. There were 205 route miles of railway and 2,700 miles of road by 1968. The bauxite companies had added five ports, bringing the total of those in regular use to 15.

The years of uncertainty for the West Indian federation witnessed a growth rate in Jamaica of only 2.8 per cent per annum. Jamaica became independent in 1962, but despite acceleration of pace after 1964 it cannot be claimed that the economy has yet undergone the rapid structural transformation which is required to satisfy the expectations of all its people. Development has tended to widen the gap between country and towns, while the educational system has not been able to produce sufficient skills for the island's needs. A major handicap which has to be overcome is the high percentage of illiteracy that persists despite large expenditure on mass education.

Kingston, Port Royal and Blue Mountains

Jamaica is an island of 2,823,174 acres, or 4,411 square miles. In shape something like a turtle, it lies in the Caribbean Sea, between latitude 17.43 N and 18.32 N, 100 miles west of Haiti, 90 miles south of Cuba, and 445 miles north of Carthagena. Its shortest breadth between Kingston and Annotto Bay, is 22¼ miles; its greatest 52 miles. The longest stretch on Jamaica is 148 miles.

A mountainous island, Jamaica has only 891 square miles of flat land, 26 peaks or spurs rise to heights between 1,500 and 6,000 feet. The highest of them all is in the Blue Mountains, at a point 7,402 feet above sea level. Many rivers and springs have their sources in the central mountain ranges which rise like a backbone from east to west across the island. Waters from them run downwards, sometimes in magnificent torrents and falls on to the northern or southern shores of the island. Few rivers are navigable. The largest are the Black River (44 miles), the Rio Minho, the Rio Cobre, the White Garden River, the Plantain Garden River and the Rio Grande. The natural vegetation of the island is woodland or forest except around swamps, ponds, rivers and the seashore. Rainfall varies from 35 inches in some of the dry coastal areas to over 200 inches in the Blue Mountains.

When Christopher Columbus landed in 1494 the only breaks in the green of the primeval forest were clearings made by Indians. The forests were then thick with splendid trees, mahogany, cedar, bulletwood, mahoe, braziletto, fiddlewood and others but there were no coconut palms, no bananas, no sugar cane, no coffee, no logwood, no ackee, no bamboo and no tamarind trees. Today's fertile coastal plains and the foothills of Portland and St Mary were once dense dark woods with streams. Iguanas used to roam the thickets and woodlands of the south which is still called, after them, the Liguanea Plain. Thousands of birds frequented the lagoons and pools of the marshes. Petrels made their nests on the slopes of the Blue Mountains, while macaws, goat suckers and snakes had not yet become rare.

The English in 1758 divided Jamaica into three counties which they named after famous counties in England. Cornwall in the west comprises 1,565 square miles, Middlesex 2,026 and Surrey 820. Kingston (which includes Port Royal), St Andrew, St Thomas and Portland are parishes of Surrey; St Catherine, St Mary, Clarendon, St Ann, and Manchester of Middlesex; and St Elizabeth, Trelawny, St James, Hanover and Westmoreland of Cornwall.

Kingston, which was first designed in 1693 to replace Port Royal as a commercial centre, extends for more than ten square miles on the Liguanea Plain and has a population of about 120,000. It did not become the island's administrative capital until 1872 when the centuries-old seat of government was moved there from Spanish Town. Roads from the north, east and west lead into Kingston, which is also the terminus for the railway that runs across the island to Montego Bay and to Port Antonio.

Kingston Harbour has about eight square miles of navigable sea, and an area twice as large. Vessels are berthed under supervision in shipping complexes at Newport West and Newport East. The harbour is almost enclosed by a seven-mile neck of land called the Palisadoes. On this neck, which leads across to Port Royal, is located Kingston's Norman Manley International Airport. Because Kingston expanded by land the former parishes of Kingston and St Andrew were amalgamated in 1923 into the Kingston and St Andrew Corporation. The combined population of this corporate area exceeds half a million. In recent years a development called New Kingston has provided a modern complex of hotels, banks, shops, supermarkets and business houses which have arisen on the site of the former Knutsford Park Race Course. Throughout Jamaica there is a great variety of climate. In Kingston the mean temperature is 78.7. It rises to 87.6 during the day and falls to 71 in the early morning. The temperature falls by one degree every 300 feet of ascent into the hills. Heavy periodic rainfalls usually occur in May, June, September, October and November in most parts of the island. In the north-eastern part of Jamaica heavy rainfall is also common at the end of the year and light rains are frequent in March.

Kingston is not one of the world's loveliest cities, but it has greatly improved since Trollope saw it near the end of the fifties of the last century. Then he saw houses 'mostly of wood, unpainted disjointed and going to ruin'. The streets he described as 'beds of sand' in dry weather, and as water-courses when it rained. As for omnibuses, they were as difficult to catch as mosquitoes, running from no given point to another but meandering about through slush and sand. Kingston, as Trollope knew it, was not lighted at all, its buildings were ugly and hardly any Europeans or white Creoles lived in it, 'because they hated it'.

If it were possible for Trollope to see Kingston today he would find streams of large motor cars, omnibuses and other vehicles flowing sometimes speedily, sometimes slowly through wide well-paved streets. Instead of neglected wooden houses he would see an assortment of buildings in many architectural styles embracing many shapes and many degrees of ugliness, comfort, beauty and luxury. Away from the harbour area where vast changes are still being made he would discover avenues of tree-lined homes which were laid out several decades after his visit. Most of modern Kingston would be new to him because many buildings were con-structed of concrete and stone after the earthquake of 1907.

If there is any truth in the Jamaican expression that 'Jamaica is an island to the south of the North Coast' then Kingston is without doubt the capital of that island. It is for the Jamaican what London is for the English, Paris for the French and New York for the American. It is where everything Jamaican is centred, the Gun Court, the University, the cathedrals, the big race course, the sky-scrapers, the theatres, the restaurants, the parliament and ministerial buildings and the headquarters of industry, finance and commerce. It is where the strong heart of Jamaica beats and where its diversity of peoples may be seen in relationships with themselves and others. It is not, except perhaps from the air or from a high building or mountain peak, recognisable as a beautiful city. But it is, as de Lisser said of it long ago, interesting. It is that and much more. For it is a city which reflects many external influences yet remains distinctively Jamaican. Of all the West Indian capitals which have been moulded by the British Raj it is the one which shows least sign of tutelage. There are many Jamaicas, but one Kingston. The traveller who only wants to escape from cities and to get close to Nature will not nor-mally choose a town for a vacation, but many of those who fly thousands of miles to visit new countries want to spend at least one day in a major city. In New Kingston there is such good and plentiful accommodation that the journey to the island's heart can be as productive of enjoyment as a stay in the more remote exclusive resorts. Besides modern swimming pools within smart hotel precincts, as brown a tan can be acquired in Kingston as on any north coast beach.

On a quick visit there will perhaps be only time for a brief look at Port Royal, and perhaps Devon House, the Royal Botanic Gardens, the University grounds at Mona and the National Stadium or Casa Monte. For those with several days or a week in hand there is time to see much more. A good starting point for sightseeing is the Institute of Jamaica on East Street near the Harbour. In addition to its excellent library it houses a natural history museum and puts on frequent exhibitions of paintings and other arts. There are specimens of the now almost extinct conies and of iguana lizards, a hawksbill turtle, a mongoose and several Jamaican birds. Perhaps the most interesting possession of the Institute is a tortoiseshell comb and case which is thought to have been made in 1671 for the governor's wife, Lady Lynch.

Most popular and more widely publicised are 'The Shark's Papers', a packet of German letters discovered by Lieutenant Fitton in the mouth of a shark that was caught off the shore of Haiti in 1799. Discovery of the papers led to the arrest of a Baltimore brig for illicit trading. According to Frank Cundall, a former secretary of the Institute, the shark's head was sent to the United Services Institution in London.

Kingston Parish Church at the south end of what was once called the Parade Ground was rebuilt after the earthquake of 1907. Three of its memorials were sculpted by John Bacon. Near the chancel rail is buried Admiral John Benbow, who died at Port Royal in 1702 after a four-day battle at sea against the French Admiral du Casse. In the graveyard lies Janet Scott, sister of Michael, the author of *Tom Cringle's Log*. Scott who first visited the West Indies in 1806 lived for some years in the Blue Mountains. In *Tom Cringle's Log*, which was first published in book form in Paris in 1836, Scott described the two-storied houses in Kingston as looking as though they were built of cards, 'most of them being surrounded with piazzas from ten to fourteen feet wide, gaily painted green and white ... on the ground floor these piazzas are open and in the lower part of the town where the houses are built contiguous to each other they form a covered way, affording a most grateful shelter for the sun, on each side of the streets, which last are unpaved and more like dry river courses than thoroughfares in a Christian town'.

Modern Gordon House on Duke Street is the meeting place of the Jamaican House of Representatives and the Senate. Headquarters House in Duke Street was once used by the legislative council. It used to be known as Hibbert's House in memory of Thomas Hibbert, one of Jamaica's wealthy traders of the eighteenth century. From 1814 to 1872 it was used as an army headquarters. The Ward Theatre nearby on North Parade was presented to Kingston by a custos of Kingston in 1911. It is named for the donor, Colonel Charles Ward, whose wealth derived in part from the manufacture of rum.

Shaare Shalom, the synagogue of the Ashkenazi and

Sephardic Jewish communities of Kingston is situated at the corner of Duke and Charles Streets. There is a Jewish Institute in Charles Street. Jewish disabilities in Jamaica were abolished in 1831; from 1845 to 1900 congregations also existed at Port Royal, Spanish Town and Montego Bay.

The large Roman Catholic Cathedral of the Holy Trinity on North Street was built after the earthquake of 1907. Its splendid dome is one of the landmarks of Kingston, but when I tried to explore inside one Friday I found its gates securely locked. The Prime Minister's office and several other important ministries are located near King George VI Memorial Park where the heroes of Jamaica are especially honoured. Northwards along Marescaux Road is the splendid verandahed building of Mico College. This famous teacher-training college owes its name to a bountiful Lady Mico, who left money in 1670 to be used for paying the ransoms of Christians who had been captured and enslaved by pirates operating from North African bases. The interest which accrued was later applied to the development of educational institutions in the West Indies.

Besides the Ward Theatre, where lavish Jamaican folk musicals are produced during a four-month season beginning on Boxing Night (26 December), Kingston has two other theatres. One of these, the Barn, is on Norwood Road in the Belmont area not far from the Artists Gallery and the Liguanean Golf Club. The theatre is a converted barn and the Barn Theatre Company is a group of semi-professional performers. Visiting players sometimes appear at the Barn, where plays are performed for a great part of the year. The Little Theatre, on Tom Redcam Avenue close to the Kingston and St Andrew Parish Library, is a modern building where productions are staged by the National Dance Theatre Company for periods of four weeks during July and August, and at stated times between November and February. Under the leadership of Rex Nettleford, the National Dance Theatre Company has established an international reputation. The Little Theatre is also used by the Jamaica Playhouse, a group of players who perform plays which have sometimes been successful in major cities of the world. The Creative Arts Centre at Mona is also regularly used by Jamaican players other than the University Drama Society. Some of the plays of the National Theatre Trust are performed there as well as at the Ward Theatre. Other famous Jamaicans who perform in Kingston, throughout Jamaica and abroad, are the Eddie Thomas Dancers and the Jamaica Folk Singers. In recent years a new group, the Tivoli Touring Troupe, have emerged from the Tivoli Gardens, a former depressed area. Backed by the West Kingston Trust and the Institute of Jamaica the Troupe has taken part in folklore cabaret performances and in the Monday entertainments of 'Duppy Night at Devon House'. The Tivoli folklore show takes place in the west patio of Devon House, a magnificent restored building which stands in well-tended grounds near the junction of Waterloo and Hope Roads. There, Jamaican dishes are served daily by attractively dressed Jamaican waitresses in an outdoor restaurant beside an old stable. A towering mahogany tree with climbing vines provides welcome shade in an atmosphere of simple elegance. Indoors are exhibitions of painting and furniture which reproduce the atmosphere of 'English Jamaica'. A splendid staircase leads to an upper floor where besides poster beds, warming pans, baby's cradle and sewing table are displayed a large assortment of famous Jamaican prints of earlier times. Further along Hope Road is Jamaica House, the modern residence of the Prime Minister which is at the southern end of the parkland in which King's House, the governor general's home also stands. Originally King's House and its 170 acres was the official residence of the Anglican bishop of Jamaica. The building is large but is not one of the most beautiful of West Indian governor generals' residences. The grounds are well laid out.

The Hope Road eventually joins the Old Hope Road and leads to the Royal Botanical Gardens about six miles north-east of Kingston. The gardens were formerly part of the Hope Estate which passed through marriage to the 3rd Duke of Buckingham. In 1850 the Buckingham family sold about 600 acres to the Kingston Water Works Company. The property was transferred to the government, which acquired the remaining acres in 1913. In recent years a small zoo has been added to gardens which are renowned throughout the West Indies for their many coloured bougainvilleas, their ferns, orchids, lofty palms, flowering vines, lily ponds and gay tropical shrubs and flowering plants. In the middle of the eighteenth century, when sugar was made on the Hope estate, aqueducts were installed to bring water from the Hope River to waterwheels which drove the mills that crushed the cane. Sections of the aqueducts have been preserved on the site of the University College of the West Indies, established on the other side of Hope Road against a background of the Long Mountain which rises to over one thousand feet. Few universities of the world can boast of more beautiful surroundings. The college hospital is regularly used by people from the surrounding districts and from Kingston which is six miles distant. The college at Mona has been active since 1948. The university also has colleges in Barbados and Trinidad. Its first Chancellor was Princess Alice, Countess of Athlone, and until 1962 its degrees were awarded by the University of London.

Beyond Hope Gardens the road to Buff Bay climbs steeply along twisting curves to Newcastle, which was first employed in the mid-nineteenth century as a health station for British troops. Trollope, who made three visits to Newcastle, wrote in 1859 that 'one would almost enlist as a full private in one of Her Majesty's regiments of the line if one were sure of being quartered for ever at Newcastle'. He found there a 'goodly village in which live colonels and majors and chaplains and surgeons and purveyors, all in a state of bliss – as it were in a second Eden. It is a military paradise in which war is spoken of, and dinners and dancing abound!' James Anthony Froude, writing in 1887, painted a very different picture. An hour's ride from Gordon's Town brought him to the lowest range of houses which were 4,000 feet above the sea. The hillside he described as 'bare, and the slope so steep that there was no standing on it, save where it had been flattened by the spade; and in this extraordinary place were 400 young Englishmen of the common type of which soldiers are made, with nothing to do and nothing to enjoy. . . . Every other day they can see nothing, save each other's forms and faces in the fog; for fine and bright as the air may be below, the moisture in the air is condensed into cloud by the chill rock and soil of the high ranges . . . healthy the camp is at any rate. The temperature never rises above 70 nor sinks often below 60. They require charcoal fires to keep the damp out and blankets to sleep under; and when they see the sun it is an agreeable change and something to talk about'. Newcastle is still used as a training depot and hill station for Jamaican soldiers from military headquarters at Up Park Camp, which lies between Mountain View Avenue and Old Hope Road close to the National Stadium. Its 'necklace of twinkling lights' is clearly visible from Kingston on mist-free evenings. The organisers of a three-hour sightseeing tour from Kingston justifiably commend the panoramic view which may be had from Newcastle of Kingston and its harbour. They also increase the appeal of the journey by hinting at 'the cool drink or a cup of Blue Mountain coffee' which may be enjoyed at Bamboo Lodge in the gardens where Horatio Nelson is said to have slept some time in 1770.

Trollope praised the Blue Mountain range of hills saying that 'nothing can be grander, either in colour or grouping'. For him the finest view in the island was to be had from Raymond Lodge, where Jamaicans believe that *Tom Cringle's Log* may have been written. He had less praise for Blue Mountain Peak, to climb which he provided himself with a companion, who in turn provided him with 'five negros, a supply of beef, bread and water, some wine and brandy and what appeared to me to be about ten gallons of rum'. He has nothing remarkable to tell about the ascent. 'We soon', he wrote, 'got into a cloud, and never got out of it . . . we were soon wet through up to our middles . . . every now and then we regaled the negros with rum . . . and every now and then we regaled ourselves with brandy and water'. At the

Blue Mountain Peak they built a hut and made a fire. 'Slowly and mournfully', wrote Trollope, 'we dried ourselves at the fire, or rather did not dry ourselves, but scorched our clothes and burnt our boots in a vain endeavour to do so. . . . Mournfully, we turned ourselves before the fire – slowly, like badly roasted joints of meat; and the result was exactly that; we were badly roasted and raw at the same time. And then we crept into our hut and made one of those wretched repasts in which the collops of food slip down and get sat upon. . . . Having looked to our fire and smoked a sad cigar, we put ourselves to bed in the hut. The operation consisted in huddling on all the clothes we had. But even with this the cold prevented us from sleeping. The chill damp air penetrated through two shirts, two coats, two pairs of trousers. It was impossible to believe that we were in the tropics. . . . And so the morning came . . . but as for sunrise – ! The sun may rise for those who get up decently from their beds in the plains below, but there is no sun rising on Helvellyn, or Righi, or the Blue Mountain Peak. Nothing rises there; but mists and clouds are for ever falling.'

Those who live in the neighbourhood of the Blue Mountain Peak claim that there are bright periods without mist for some part of each day (other than the season of rains), but no one can guarantee clear vision at a particular hour of the day. Fortunate adventurers beyond the Portland Gap (5,600 feet) have been able to get a glimpse of Cuba 100 miles to the north, while others who reach the peak when the sun is shining have been rewarded by the sight of Cuba and Hispaniola in the distance.

The ideal way to visit Port Royal is by motor boat from Kingston Harbour, but most people go there by way of the Windward Road which leads to Morant Bay and the eastern shores. At Rockfort, under Long Mountain, the Caribbean cement factory is a landmark to Jamaica's industrial revolution as well as the generator of particles of dust which are blown in all directions by the wind. Both Rockfort and Harbour View a mile further along were important in the defence plans for Jamaica in earlier centuries.

Kingston Harbour is excellent for yacht racing and serious sailors will probably arrive with an introduction to the Royal Jamaica Yacht Club which is situated to the right of Palisadoes International Airport not far from Palisadoes Park and Gunboat Beach. At the far end of the Palisadoes narrow, five-mile peninsula, 15 miles by road from Kingston on the outskirts of Port Royal, is Morgan's Harbour, the water-sports centre of Jamaica's south coast. The beach resort complex there offers marina with full facilities and charters modern vessels for deep-sea fishing or sea excursions.

By sea Morgan's Harbour is only three miles from Kingston and the crossing can be done by a water taxi in ten minutes. A ferry leaves the Crafts Market, Kingston for Morgan Harbour twice daily.

Lime Cay, a favourite picnic spot on the southern side of the peninsula, is ideal for skin diving and swimming and easily accessible from Morgan's Harbour. On days of good visibility the mountains behind Kingston appear more green than blue to the visitor in Port Royal and scattered houses can be clearly seen stretched against clusters of dark green trees. Nothing in today's Port Royal recalls the wickedness of the pirate's city which was sucked under the sea in the terrible earthquake of 1692. On the contrary, the first building to be seen is the church of St Peter's, whose walls are ornamented by tablets which record the names of many British sailors whose lives were untimely snuffed out by the deadly yellow fever which rampaged through the Caribbean islands for more than a century. Inside the town many of today's buildings are used by Jamaican policemen attached to the training school. Signs indicating 'courtesy pays' are liberally sprinkled everywhere and the young policemen march about smartly, fully conscious of their roles as special representatives of modern Jamaica. The backdrop for this parade of young constables is the old low lying Fort Charles, conspicuous for its squat turretted wall and several cannons mounted in arched windows. Children during schoolbreaks sip cool drinks and munch sweet cakes or bread under the leafy trees facing the entrance and are so keen to have their 'picture' taken that they will actually run to take up gun positions. Nowhere in the West Indies have I seen such delightful friendly children, who are living testimonials to the oft expressed invitation of the Jamaican police to 'wear the badge of citizenship'.

A tombstone in St Peter's churchyard, originally erected across the harbour at Green Bay near Port Henderson, commemorates a Frenchman, Lewis Galdy, who was 'miraculously saved by swimming' during the earthquake of 1692, and who lived in new Port Royal until his death in December 1739. Most of the town which this French refugee from Montpellier had known before the earthquake still lies under the sea around the peninsula of Palisadoes. Old Port Royal, where Morgan and many other pirates indulged their grossly sensual appetites, should not be confused with the more respectable naval station and forts where British fighting men upheld mastery of the Atlantic waves for more than one hundred years. Nelson is the most famous of all those who trod the 'quarterdeck' of Fort Charles which was built by Lilley after 1692. Not until 1836 did the last British admiral pull up anchor and set sail from a port whose dockyards and sailors from earlier times kept the people of Port Royal economically afloat. In that same year, Port Royal's connection with the mountain regions near Kingston was first severed by an act of the legislature which separated the country from the town. One consequence of the British naval presence in Port Royal was the growth of an influential local coloured community on intimate terms with the higher echelon of the governing classes. Lady Nugent in her diary for March 1805 made an interesting reference to one member of this group who was sufficiently distinguished to be called 'the Duchess of Port Royal'. She refers to her as Martin's daughter. 'It is a sad thing', wrote this governor's American-born wife, 'to see even this good kind woman in other respects so easy on the subject of what a decent kind of woman in England would be ashamed of and shocked at. She told me of all her children by different fathers, with the greatest sang-froid. The mother is quite looked up to at Port

Royal, and yet her life has been most profligate, as we should think, at least in England!' So looked up to was the Duchess in fact that she had no hesitation in calling to see Lady Nugent at King's House in Spanish Town and leaving her presents.

Much of rebuilt Port Royal was destroyed by fire in 1815, but seven years later there were some 120 slave owners and 800 slaves in the town, besides free coloured people and a floating population of persons who were enrolled as soldiers, sailors or dock workers. It was after the fire of 1815 that modern Port Royal's 'Old Naval Hospital' was constructed, and in 1821 the Navy began to train Port Royal coloured boys as dockyard workers. From the curate to the rector and chaplain to the Naval Hospital, Richard Bickell, we learn that in 1825 Port Royal had two or three thousand inhabitants and that St Peter's church could accommodate 500 people and was usually well filled every Sunday morning 'chiefly by free people of colour and free blacks and the soldiers of the garrison'. When the Rev. James Philippo saw the town in 1843 he found it a 'miserable wreck of its former greatness', but it still presented an 'imposing appearance from the sea; groves of coconut trees in stately columns, waving their verdant branches amongst the buildings'. The town was then 'ornamented with several large and beautiful buildings belonging to the naval and military departments, together with some handsome and capacious private houses'. By 1848 conditions must have changed radically if we are to believe Lord Dundoland's estimate. 'Never', he says, 'have I seen a place so disgustingly filthy, or which could give so bad an opinion to foreigners of British colonial administration as the town of Port Royal'. Some of the dirt he noticed may have been due to the establishment of a coaling station which had been put there in an effort to relieve local unemployment, but it is probably true to say that Port Royal, like the rest of Jamaica, reached its lowest level of material prosperity during the two decades which followed the withdrawal of the British navy in 1836. Today, despite the title of 'Buccaneers Banquet' given to Thursday evening feasts at Fort Charles, the most celebrated name in Port Royal is that of Horatio Nelson. His quarters there on the long quarterdeck are being reconstructed, while a memorial tablet on the wall reminds visitors: 'In this place dwelt Horatio Nelson, ye who tread his footprints remember his glory'. On Nelson's quarterdeck I was approached by a coloured lady who introduced herself as 'the number two guide, wife of the number one guide'. She told me nothing new or old about Nelson, but she rattled off the distances in miles which separated Port Royal from the Equator, England, Germany, North America, Australia, New Zealand and other lands. Perhaps if I had waited she might have told me something about the brass watch which was made in 1688 and recovered from the sea in 1959 with its hands pointing to 11.43, the time when in 1692 Port Royal's buildings sank below the waves during an earthquake. Other items recovered by divers in 1959 included an ancient Spanish swivel gun, barrels, spoons, onion-shaped bottles and many relics of a 'boom' town; until that year the drowned city had chiefly been represented in Kingston by a Spanish bell preserved in the Institute building and labelled as possibly the one which Morgan and others used to hear as it chimed out the hours for services in the church of old Port Royal. Encouraged both by the success of the 1959 diving expedition which had been sponsored by the National Geographic Society and the Smithsonian Institution, and by their own subsequent explorations, the government of Jamaica have embarked upon a 20-year redevelopment scheme which is intended to make Port Royal one of the major tourist attractions of the Caribbean. Besides excavations on the site of Port Royal which should be completed before 1980, offices and air-conditioned 'laboratories' for visitors are being equipped in ground-floor rooms of the old naval hospital. By 1974 there were sufficient relics in the form of coins, pewter vessels, pottery, glass and other artifacts to offer a one-hour tour of what will eventually be a Port Royal Museum, complete with three-dimensional exhibition windows of the rise and fall of the 'Wickedest City in Christendom'.

From the National Trust Tower, Kingston is seen spread out on the right and Port Henderson on the left across the waters of the fenced-in (palisadoed) harbour. Behind Port Henderson and Dawkins' Lagoon is Passage Fort, which looks on to the waters of Hunts Bay, where the ships of England's invasion fleet cast their anchors in the year 1655. Passage Fort, six miles from Spanish Town, was the only defensive outpost maintained by the Spaniards of St Iago de la Vega. Its inability to stop the earlier attacks launched by Shirley, Newport and Jackson, ought to have prepared them for the final victorious march of the men commanded by Penn and Venables. Modern Jamaican maps show a point at 716 feet above sea level where Rodney kept a lookout to the rear of Port Henderson; they also show the locations of later forts – Clarence, to guard the approach to Port Royal and Augusta, to protect Hunts Bay. From his lookout Rodney would have often enjoyed a most spectacular panoramic view of Kingston, of delicately pink-tinted Port Royal and of the Blue Mountains illuminated by rays of the setting sun. Similar vistas of great beauty were more easily accessible to guests on the top floors of the Intercontinental Forum Hotel at Port Henderson, which, after little more than a year's trading, closed its doors in early 1975, but which, because of its favoured location and accessible sporting amenities may yet fulfil the hopes of those who hailed it as Kingston's first resort hotel.

The foreshore harbour road, now called Marcus Garvey Drive, runs behind Newport East past the Esso refinery and behind the new harbour of Newport West to rejoin the Spanish Town road on the right and to meet with the new causeway which crosses the entrance to Hunts Bay and continues through to Port Henderson and the Hellshire Hills by Augusta Drive or to Passage Fort and Independence City along Dawkins Drive. The road along Passage Fort Drive leads into Caymanas Boulevard which skirts Caymanas Park, where about 15 horse-race meetings are held each year on public holidays and preceding or succeeding Saturdays, and where polo matches are played.

From the junction of Slipe Road and Old Hope Road the motorist drives in a north-westerly direction along a road called Half Way Tree to a place of that name once recognised as the capital of St Andrew's parish. Tradition has it that Half Way Tree was named for the large cotton tree (ceiba) which dominated the crossroads between the church and the courthouse at the junction of the ways to Spanish Town, St Mary and St George. The recent church which lost its tower in the earthquake of 1907 and was much altered in the latter half of the nineteenth-century dates back to 1700 and its records to 1666.

Not far from Jamaica House, on Montrose Road is one of the island's most historic mansions. It was formerly used by the chief secretary as a residence but was later reconditioned for the Prime Minister's use. Known as Prospect Penn and later as Vale Royal it is supposed to have been constructed in 1694. One of its owners told Lady Nugent, who lived in Jamaica from 1801 to 1805, that his chief ambition was to make his son Simon Taylor, then in Germany, the 'richest commoner in England'.

Among the houses of special interest in the hills which look down upon Kingston from heights of 1,000 feet or more are Bellevue and Mont Salus in the Red Hills. The second of these was used as a rest home by British admirals from Port Royal and may have been the 'Admiral's Mount' to which Nelson was sent to convalesce after being nursed back to health by the freed slave Cuba Cornwallis. Bellevue was selected by a representative of the Georgian Society in 1950 as a fine Jamaican example of Georgian architecture.

Overlooking the Liguanea Plain and Hope Gardens in the region of Jack's Hill, Jamaican hero, George William Gordon, once lived at Cherry Gardens in a house where the historian, James Anthony Froude was later made welcome in 1887. 'No mortal', wrote Froude, 'ever selected a lovelier spot for a residence than did Gordon in choosing Cherry Garden. How often had his round dark eyes wondered over the scenes at which I was gazing, watched the early rays of the sun slanting upwards to the high peaks of the Blue Mountains, or the last as it sank in gold and crimson behind the hills at Mandeville; watched the great steamers entering or leaving Port Royal, and at night the gleam of the lighthouse from among the palm trees on the spit. Poor fellow! one felt very sorry for him, and sorry for Mr Eyre too.'

Beyond Constant Spring Golf Club off Old Stony Hill Road is Casa Monte Hotel, 1,360 feet above sea level. There on Sunday mornings between 9.30 and 11.30 the management put on a brawta (extra special) breakfast, which includes fresh fruit, saltfish and ackee (the national dish), mackerel and green banana, pork, roasted breadfruit, fried dumplings and much more.

Kingston was a prime holiday destination in 1901 when the Constant Spring Hotel stood in splendid isolation in green meadows beneath the o'ershadowing Blue Mountains and when the Myrtle Bank Hotel in Harbour Street was within easy walking distance of a Parade then dominated by Queen Victoria's statue. It was the centre of social life in the capital. That leisurely Kingston of the horse cab, long gowns, tight collars and hats is no more; today's sprawling capital has undergone many changes as the city has spread sideways and upwards into the hills, pushing down, transforming or bypassing old relics of its past, creating new towns and building new residences to attract new generations of men and women anxious to obtain their shares in new wealth which has been more generally distributed than ever before in Kingston's history.

TRAVELLERS' DIGEST

Airlines: Air Jamaica, British Airways, Air Canada, B.W.I.A., Pan American, Lufthansa, Cayman Airways, A.L.M., Delta, Eastern, Mexicana, T.A.C.A.

Airports: Norman Manley International, Palisadoes, about 10 miles from centre.
Tinson Pen, behind Newport West.

Antique Shops: Connoisseur, Mahogany House, Fourposter.

Art Galleries: Institute of Jamaica, Hill Galleries, Jamaica School of Arts, Devon House Museum.

Banks: Bank of Nova Scotia, Barclays, Canadian Imperial Bank of Commerce, Royal Bank of Canada, Bank of Montreal, First National City Bank of New York, First National City Bank of Chicago, Jamaica Citizens Bank.
Open weekdays, 9 a.m. to noon (and 2.30 – 5 p.m. Fridays). Branches in some hotels.

Shipping Services: Alcoa, Saguenay, Elders and Fyffes, West Indies Shipping Service, Spanish Line, Norwegian Caribbean Line.

Shopping Hours: Kingston: 8.30 a.m. to 4 p.m. (Wednesday till noon).
New Kingston: 9 a.m. to 5 p.m. Saturdays 9 a.m. to 5.30 p.m. (Thursday till 1 p.m.)

American Embassy: 43 Duke Street.

U.K. High Commission: 58 Duke Street.

Canadian High Commission: Dominion Life Building, New Kingston.

Chamber of Commerce: 8 East Parade.

Religion: Places of worship maintained by many denominations. Among these are Anglican, Church of God, Congregationalist, Baptist, Society of Friends, Methodist, Presbyterian, Moravian, Roman Catholic, Salvation Army, and Jewish.

Newspapers: The Daily Gleaner, The Jamaica Daily News, The Star (evening).

Radio and TV: Jamaica Broadcasting Corporation, Radio

Jamaica and Rediffusion transmit radio programmes daily. JBC transmits TV programmes in the evening.

Credit Cards: Many hotels accept credit cards.

Tipping: Charges added to hotel bills. For other services between 10 and 15 per cent.

Departure Tax: All visitors must pay departure tax at airport.

Customs: Personal belongings are duty free, as are tobacco ($\frac{1}{2}$ lb: 200 cigarettes: 25 cigars); 1 pint liquor other than rum: 1 quart wine. Other goods subject to duty.

In-Bond Shopping: Shops in hotels and nearby shopping centres sell at duty free prices spirits and liquor, Swiss watches, French perfumes, British woollens and cashmeres, leather goods, silverware, fine china, jewellery, cameras, radios, tape recorders and other items.

Taxis: By arrangement with hotels, or by radio-controlled meter cabs. Check that meter is working. Fares to airport and other popular destinations are displayed at some hotel entrances.

Self-Drive: Cars may be rented from Avis Rent-a-Car or Martins Jamaica. Persons over 17 who hold valid driving licences or international driving permits can drive in Jamaica. Others have to undergo a test and pay the current fee. Petrol stations are open from 7 a.m. till 9 p.m. Monday to Saturday and from 7 a.m. till noon on Sunday. Credit cards not accepted.

Rules of the Road: Drive on the left.
Speed limit for cars in towns and built-up areas 30 m.p.h.; on highways 50 m.p.h.

Trains: The Jamaica Railway Corporation operates diesel services daily between Kingston and Montego Bay and between Kingston and Port Antonio.

Boats: Daily ferry services between Kingston and Port Royal. Boats can be hired at Morgan's Harbour for picnics on Lime

Cay, Rackham Cay or Drunken Man's Cay. Glass-bottomed boats also available for hire.

Currency: Bank notes 50Jc, J$1, J$2, J$5, J$10. Coins 1c, 5c, 10c, 20c, 25c.

Service Clubs: Kingston Jaycees, 10 Altamont Crescent; Rotary Club, 21 Hope Road; Kiwanis, 2 Lady Musgrave Road; Lions, 31 Trafalgar Road.

Public Holidays: January 1, Ash Wednesday, Good Friday, Easter Monday, Labour Day (May 23), Independence Day (August 1st), National Heroes Day (3rd Monday in October), Christmas, Boxing Day.

Laundry: Hotels provide laundry, dry cleaning and pressing services. Clothes line in bathrooms for small items, (do not hang on balconies!).

Hairdressing: Facilities in New Kingston hotels.

Electricity: 220v 50 cycles. Adapters for curlers and dryers obtainable in some hotels, where special outlets with automatic resets (220v or 110v) are provided in bathrooms.

Radio Hams: Headquarters of the Jamaica Amateur Radio Association is at the Red Cross Building, Cross Roads.

Time: Same as Eastern Standard Time or 5 hours behind GMT. Daylight saving was introduced on January 6, 1974.

Vaccinations: None needed to enter Jamaica or to return to U.S.A. or Canada if whole stay has been in Jamaica. UK visitors require vaccination certifiate on return to their country.

Passports: Citizens of UK require passports. American and Canadian citizens require only return air tickets and proof of their citizenship.

Water: All pipe water is chlorinated and filtered and safe to drink. Other water should be treated with caution.

Milk: Pasteurised in hotels.

Clothing: Light summer all year round. At least two swimsuits or trunks and two pairs of shorts should be packed, also cotton shirts. Long-sleeved shirts and slacks recommended as protection against too much sun.
Ladies will want lightweight evening dresses and men cotton or linen jackets. Ties are worn in the evening. Ready-made suits, or slacks made to measure within 24 hours.

Nursemaids: Available through hotels.

Sports
Yachting: Visitors with introductions can become temporary members of the Royal Jamaica Yacht Club (Yachts include 'O' class, Snapper and Cruiser). Morgan's Harbour Beach Club have sailing boats on hire for deep-sea fishing or cruising. Races are held at stated times in Kingston Harbour.

Waterskiing: Morgan's Harbour Beach Club have motor boats for hire. Instructors available.

Tennis: Caribbean championships held once yearly, usually in March. Some hotels have own courts and can arrange temporary membership for visitors at some local clubs.

Swimming: In hotel pools or on beaches (Morgan's Harbour, Lime Cay, other cays).

Spear Fishing and Skin Diving: Facilities provided at Morgan's Harbour Beach Club. Underwater excursions to old Port Royal.

Polo: The All Jamaica Polo Association has three clubs in the capital, The Kingston, The Caymanas and The Garrison. Inter-club matches are played the year round and visitors are made welcome as spectators or players.

Flying: The Jamaica Flying Club at Palisadoes Airport has over 200 members, many with their own planes. Visitors are welcome. Canadian and U.S. licences are valid in Jamaica. Incoming flyers have to go through formalities at Kingston or Montego Bay, but there are over 30 airstrips on the island. Those near Tower Isle, Port Antonio and Silver Sands Beach

Club are 3,000 ft long while two at Mandeville and one at Caymanas are 2,000 ft in length.

Horse Racing: Saturdays, most public holidays and every other Wednesday at the modern Caymanas race track six miles from the city centre.

Riding: Information from Saddle and Polo Club, Up Park Camp or Belcour Riding Lodge, Marylands.

Golf: 18-hole course at Constant Spring and Caymanas, and the 9-hole Liguanea.

Fishing: No licence required. Charter boats and completely equipped cruisers available for hire. Usually sought are blue marlin, sailfish, dolphin, wahoo (kingfish), albacore and barracuda.

Boxing: Usually on Saturday nights at the new National Stadium.

Shooting: Open season for birds is 1 September to 14 October. Wild pigeons and doves.

Eating Out
Duppy Night at Devon House, Monday. Country music during dinner. Folklore show afterwards (Jamaican dishes served at lunch daily).

Buccaneers Banquet at Fort Charles, Port Royal every Thursday evening. Rum punch served on boat across Kingston Harbour. Dinner includes roast suckling pig, curried goat and special Jamaican dishes. Steelband for jump-up dancing and floor show.

One thousand feet above Kingston on the banks of the Mammee River, dine (jacket and tie for men, wrap for ladies) at the exclusive Blue Mountain Inn.

Self-service buffet in Skyline Pub.

The House of Chen, New Kingston.

Golden Dragon, Mona Plaza.

Talk of the Town, Jamaican Pegasus, New Kingston.

Panoramic Views: Gaslite Roof, Sheraton, Kingston; Casa Monte Gardens, Strawberry Hill on Road to Newcastle, Hardwar Gap (4,380 feet).

Places to Visit: Devon House (and African Museum at back), Port Royal, Hope Gardens, Castleton Gardens, Lime Cay, University of West Indies on Mona Heights (note chapel reconstructed from Gale's sugar works, and aqueduct), Institute of Jamaica, Arawak Indian Museum, White Marl (between Kingston and Spanish Town), Spanish Town Georgian Buildings (see Rodney's monument and Folk Museum), The Mill, Manor Park Plaza (modern Jamaican Georgian with acqueduct and water wheel).

Jamaica Souvenirs: Straw goods, tortoiseshell, shellwork, woodwork, Blue Mountain Gems, Pickapeppa sauce, cigars, rum and other articles.

Sightseeing Tours from New Kingston: Martins offer $3\frac{1}{2}$-hour tour through residential areas to Spanish Town, a 7-hour tour through the 'best' of Kingston, a 3-hour tour of Devon House, Hope Gardens, through the U.W.I. campus to the National Stadium.
A 3-hour tour of the Blue Mountains makes stops at Hope Gardens and Newcastle.

Famous Places within 25 miles of Kingston city: Constant Spring (6 miles), Hope Gardens (6 miles) Mona (6 miles), Stony Hill (9 miles), Spanish Town (13 miles), Newcastle (19 miles), Castleton Gardens (19 miles), Hardwar Gap (22 miles), Bog Walk (23 miles).

The County of Middlesex

Middlesex, the largest of Jamaica's three counties, extends over 2,026 square miles of land from north to south, and includes the five parishes of St Catherine, St Mary, Clarendon, St Ann, and Manchester. Within its boundaries are found Jamaica's third largest city, Spanish Town, as well as important towns like May Pen and Mandeville, and holiday centres like Ocho Rios and St Ann's Bay. When the handbook of the Institute of Jamaica was published in 1896 every parish of Middlesex was supplied with hotels or lodging houses and several with livery stables. Regular tourist establishments were then operating at Castleton Gardens, Annotto Bay, and Port Maria in St Mary's parish; at St Ann's Bay, Moneague, Ocho Rios and Brown's Town in St Ann's; at Spanish Town, Linstead, Bog Walk, Ewarton, Old Harbour and Old Harbour Bay in St Catherine; at Chapelton in Clarendon, and at Mandeville and Porus in Manchester. Tourists moved around Jamaica by horse and buggy and hotels were needed at places along the routes they followed. By 1901 tourism had developed sufficiently for another hotel, the Rio Cobre, to claim to offer 'a good table and fairly good rooms' in the neighbourhood of Spanish Town. Visitors were frankly told, however, that neglect was the main feature of the former capital especially with regard to the former governor's residence, King's House, and the old House of Assembly. By 1901, too, it was possible to take a train from Spanish Town to Ewarton, where a carriage (ordered in advance by telegraph) was available for the scenic crossing of Mount Diablo to the comfortable

Moneague Hotel, run then and for many years afterwards 'so as to give satisfaction'. An early start might be made the following morning for Fern Gulley and St Ann's Bay. On the way the traveller would see the Roaring River Falls which 'had a beauty all their own, quite as well worth seeing as Niagara'. Stops were also made at the village of Ocho Rios, the town of St Ann's Bay and Claremont.

Travellers to Jamaica at the beginning of this century were also urged to visit the hill resort of Mandeville, where the air was 'restorative and curative'. The place to stay then was Brook's Hotel, where everyone was 'satisfied with the excellent table and general looking after the comfort of the guest'. Jamaica was not then an island for fun seekers. It was promoted as 'God's hospital for a sick man or woman who comes from the harsher air and the thick of the fight of life's battle'. No one had yet heard of the 'rat race', but Americans arriving on ships (the only way of coming) were told to 'bring warm clothes for the voyage' (since it was winter), and warned not to go in for 'late suppers with friends who want to say farewell'. Too much drink, according to the writer in the handbook was bad in the tropics, 'the less alcohol the better'. Clothes recommended for ladies were 'white dresses, with a dark suit, shirt waists, a dinner gown and an evening dress'. Also required was thin underclothing and 'a sailor hat!' Finally a warning was given to travellers who expected to find in Jamaica what they had left at home. It was summed up in an envoi which said:

> 'To Jamaica God has given
> Just a little touch of Heaven,
> To the earth and sea and sky
> So just pack up and travel
> Now, do not stop to cavil
> But see a little Heaven ere you die.'

The advice today would be heartily applauded by many who find in Jamaica as much of heaven as they expect ever to find on earth.

Twenty years later another edition of the handbook was

promoting Jamaica more professionally. 'There are several ways', the visitor was told, 'of seeing Jamaica. The most comfortable is to reside for some time in some centre, view its beauties, and then pass on to fresh woods and pastures new. The most convenient centres are Kingston for the town and plain of Liguanea, with trips to Castleton and the Blue Mountains; Port Antonio for the east end of the island; Moneague for St Ann; Mandeville for the centre of the island; and Montego Bay for the west end'. The emphasis was still heavy on Jamaica's scenic beauty. So, for example, the traveller is told: 'From Annotto Bay the coast road passes through most beautiful scenery some way inland through banana land to Port Maria, the centre of the north-side banana trade; then by Oracabessa and Rio Novo (where D'Oyley defeated the Spanish in 1659) past White River which divides St Mary from St Ann, to Ocho Rios. Here a branch of the great road from Spanish Town, through Linstead and Moneague to St Ann's Bay, comes from Moneague and connects the north and south sides of the island.... From Moneague the great interior road passes through Claremont and Brown's Town.' A halt is recommended at the Dry Harbour Caves, the interior of which, according to the writer, resembles 'now the Roman catacombs, now a Gothic crypt' and possessed a 'piano' formed from stalactites, which, when struck, gave out notes like those of 'tubular bells'. On the way to the southern shores of Jamaica the visitor could drive by motor through Brown's Town and Cave Valley and arrive underneath the Bull Head Mountain peak (2,782 feet) in the very centre of the island. From there the road led past Chapelton to May Pen which was no more than ten miles distant from the old Port Esquivel. Near there Columbus had a conversation with an Arawak Indian who wanted to go with him to Spain.

The roads of Jamaica have been greatly improved and new highways constructed since 1928, but the advice recommended then still holds good for the traveller who wants to get the feel of Jamaica's largest and earliest developed county.

In the neighbourhood of Old Harbour Bay, which has a race course, are the ruins of Colbeck Castle. It was constructed before the end of the seventeenth century and was surrounded by a moat. It was a fortified castle consisting of four square three-storey turreted structures joined together by a series of arcades. The building occupied an area 114 feet long and 90 feet wide. In each corner there were lookouts and underneath were dungeons. There were probably several of these large castle homes in areas likely to be attacked by Spaniards, maroons or sea rovers during the decades which followed British occupation. Colbeck Castle is not far from Monymusk, second largest of Jamaican sugar estates. Further south at Alley near Carlisle Bay is an English-style church whose rector in the years 1770-72 was also a physician and writer. John Wolcot, a Devon man by birth, had studied medicine in Cornwall. He was ordained in 1769, two years after obtaining a licence to practise medicine in Aberdeen. He accompanied Sir William Trelawney as personal physician when Sir William went out to Jamaica as governor, and was promoted to the office of physician general in 1770. He seems to have become active in the Church in order to have time for his writings, for his *Persian Love Elegies* appeared in 1773 while he was still resident on the island. On his return to England soon afterwards, he practised medicine for a time in Truro. He moved to London in 1781. There he wrote satires which established his reputation as a man of letters. Among the best known are *Mr Whitbread's Brewhouse* (1787), and *Bozzy and Piozzi, or the British Biographers* (1786).

In Carlisle Bay there is a fort and breastwork which remind today's traveller of the time when Jamaica was invaded by French forces under du Casse, in 1694. Five miles west of Alley is the Milk River Spa, which is described on a modern Esso map as the world's 'most radio active mineral bath, 54 times more so than the waters of Baden Baden'.

May Pen is the capital of Clarendon parish. Over 30,000 persons live in the town, which has a mayor. Situated on the banks of the Rio Minho about 35 miles west of Kingston,

19. Christmas street band passing the Rodney Memorial, Spanish Town.

May Pen is a packaging centre for citrus fruit is close to Denbigh, where Jamaica's agricultural and industrial exhibition is held annually in August. Frankfield, a banana town, lies to the north-west in the vicinity of the Bull Head Mountains and is a terminus for the 24-mile railway branch line that runs from May Pen. Spaldings, further west, is popular with Jamaicans as a health resort in the mountains. The road from Spaldings through Frankfield to Chapelton is full of panoramic views of the Bull Head Mountains. Tobacco plants grow well in Clarendon, which also produces sisal that is processed in a factory at the Cross near May Pen.

Middlesex, which from earliest Spanish times has been a great agricultural county, is now the heartland of bauxite and alumina. Before bauxite mining was started in Jamaica in 1952 the export of sugar and bananas chiefly contributed to the island's economic growth. By mid-1973 Jamaica's economy had been revolutionised radically and it was not only exporting about 7 million tons of bauxite that year, but had also established an oil refinery, cement and steel plants and a complex of 1,500 factories which produced processed foods, chemicals, plastics, furniture, electronic equipment and many other previously imported goods. At the same time a powerful thrust had been given to the growth of an agricultural industry through the establishment of an 'Operation Grow' programme which was intended to have brought an additional 20,000 acres into production before the end of 1975.

As far back as 1869 the first geological survey of Jamaica had reported that 'its red ferruginous earth' was principally a mixture of iron and alumina. But when closer attention was given to Jamaica's red earth in 1938, it was only the agricultural chemistry division of the department of agriculture trying to discover how to make soils produce more food. It was not until four years later, in 1942, that Sir Alfred D'Costa, owner of large cattle ranches in St Ann's parish, decided to ask the department of agriculture to analyse his soil, with a view to increasing its agricultural productivity. The chemistry division carried out studies on

20. King Street, Kingston, with the Blue Mountains in the background.

his Lydford properties and reported that they contained between 45 and 50 per cent alumina. Impressed by the information Sir Alfred and the Department took steps to discover how the lands might be best exploited. It took a decade and an expenditure of one million dollars by Reynolds Metals Company of the United States before Jamaica began shipping bauxite to the United States at a time of increased demand during the Korean War. By that time a mining and drying area had been established at Belmont and a six-mile overhead cable tramway constructed to carry bauxite to storage sites close to a new deep-water pier which was built at the western end of Ocho Rios Bay. Before operations began, it had been suggested by a Reynolds official that bauxite 'could turn out to be a first-class attractions to tourists who wanted to see how bauxite was mined'. No doubt increasing numbers of tourists to Jamaica are continually being impressed by the inescapable evidence of bauxite activities in the Ocho Rios area, but a much more important asset to Jamaica's tourist growth has been Reynolds' contribution to agricultural development. As early as 1951 the Jamaican division of the company had announced in a report to the government that 'it would put more back into the land than is withdrawn from it'. The fact that in 20 years beef production rose from under 100,000 pounds to nearly 2½ million shows how beneficial was the company's decision to improve cattle breeding on those cattle lands which they had been compelled to acquire in their efforts to get access to bauxite. Besides cattle raising, Reynolds' Lydford Enterprises also engaged in commercial poultry production, hog and sheep farming, the cultivation of orchards including avocados and coffee plants, and in afforestation. By 1970, out of 600 acres of mined bauxite land, 500 had been restored.

The production of bauxite and alumina was being conducted in 1974 by six companies, whose operations were in the Ocho Rios and Belmont area, near Ewarton, and an area north and south of May Pen and around Mandeville. By that time the Jamaican government had imposed a levy which was expected to produce $200 million by March 1975 and had also made arrangements with the governments of Trinidad and Guyana for aluminium to be smelted in each of those territories. Later, agreement was reached with Mexico and Venezuela for the production of alumina in Jamaica.

Manchester parish, the homeland of Jamaican national hero Norman Washington Manley, was created during the regime of William, 5th duke of Manchester, who governed Jamaica between 1808 and 1827. The duke has been described by a successor in office of this century as a 'begetter of numerous brown skinned illegitimate progeny' as well as being a 'reckless gambler, a hard drinker and a hard rider'. The parish which commemorates his name was best known for its capital, Mandeville, a place long regarded as a health resort because of its situation more than 2,000 feet above sea level. It is still described as a 'quiet cool mountain resort, popular for golf, strolling and horse back riding', but the proximity of bauxite operations has transformed it from a sleepy English-style country village with a green and courthouse into a bustling garden suburb. Christiana, higher up at 3,000 feet, is now more eagerly sought by Jamaican residents in search of a mountain retreat far removed from the summer heat of the plains.

The countryside between Christiana and Old Harbour recalls several old Jamaican families who had achieved fame and fortune by the late seventeenth or eighteenth centuries. Some of these family names are still remembered in Colbeck: Morant, Collier, Long, Sutton, Dawkins, Beckford, Bright, Pennant, Gale, Sinclair and Morgan. The parish of Clarendon was named for the great English statesman who controlled England's policy in the years immediately following the Restoration. It appealed particularly to Englishmen because of its fine climate. The Spaniards instead had concentrated upon St Catherine parish as it was the land most easy of access when the decision was taken early in the sixteenth century to forsake their settlements on the north coast. Around Linstead, a busy little market town which is celebrated in song, four rivers retain their Spanish names of Cobre (copper), Pedro (Peter), Doro (golden) and Magno (great). Near Bog Walk on the way south to Spanish Town water and trees combine to provide a scenic view which has often drawn appreciation from the brushes of painters and the pens of writers. For most of the year the gorge between Bog Walk and Flat Bridge carries a placid stream, but there are moments when the water churns across Flat Bridge in torrents foaming with spray. In February 1802 Lady Nugent and her retinue went by way of Bog Walk in 'curricles, gigs or kittereens'. She described it as the 'most romantic, beautiful and picturesque road' she ever saw. There was then 'a precipice on one side and the rocky mountain hanging overhead'. At the bottom was a clear, beautiful and rapid river.

Spanish Town was undoubtedly selected by the Spaniards because of its proximity to the waters of the Rio Cobre. The water from this river is today directed through the Dam and Irrigation Works, two miles from Flat Bridge, into the fields of St Catherine, which produce a great variety of Jamaican produce. Spanish Town has changed greatly since Trollope's visit in the mid-nineteenth century. He described it then as a city of the dead, where nothing entered but 'sunbeams – and such sunbeams! The glare from these walls seems to forbid that men and women shall come there.' Worse, Trollope found in Spanish Town the most frightfully hideous race of pigs: 'the very ghosts of swine, consisting entirely of bones and bristles. Their backs are long, their ribs are long, their legs are long, but above all their heads and noses are long.... These brutes prowl about in the sun, and glare at the unfrequent strangers with their starved eyes.' As for the square around which stood the Governor's House, House of Assembly, Council House and public buildings, Trollope judged it might have some pretension 'did it not seem to be stricken with eternal death... there are no sounds; men and women never frequent it'. With two hours to kill he spent the time 'without a book' miserably in the Wellington tavern, hoping that when he next visited Jamaica the seat of government might be moved to Kingston. Before the century ended Kingston had indeed become the capital city and from that city today tours are available to the most ancient surviving city of Jamaica, where the Georgian architecture around its square is now much admired. The cathedral which was altered several times during the nineteenth century was built in 1714 and was first dedicated to St Catherine. Inside are some monuments by Bacon and other British sculptors. Today's pilgrim may like, as he admires the 'graceful aspect' and 'beautiful east window' of the cathedral to imagine the sight which Lady Nugent recorded in 1802. In mid-May, during extreme heat, there was an immense congregation of soldiers dressed all in scarlet for the ten o'clock service. 'The poor Jews, she noted wryly, looked very uncomfortable . . . but they would have lost their pay of five shillings a day if they had not attended.'

King's House, which Trollope visited and in which Lady Nugent received all the ladies and the principal officers of the navy and the army, councillors and assemblymen, had been built in 1762; before its destruction by fire in 1926 it was generally considered to be one of the most splendid of British colonial buildings. Only the façade of King's House remains today on the west of King's Square, not far from the red-brick cathedral which replaced the church that had been destroyed in 1712. The Jamaica Folk Museum, which is open on Wednesdays from ten till five, occupies the former stables of King's House. Bacon's marble statue of Rodney is on the north side. The cupola, which encloses it, was designed locally and added later, as was the block of office buildings. The reconditioned House of Assembly building is on the east side of the square and the old Court House on the south. Trollope would have enjoyed today's garden in the centre, which is known as the Park. The archives of Jamaica are housed in buildings alongside the Rodney memorial. An old Arawak village between Spanish Town and the Ferry is the site of the White Marl Arawak Indian Museum which is open on weekdays from ten till five. It is approached by an ancient path across the sugar and banana lands of Caymanas

Estates. Tom Cringle's cotton tree, which is called after the hero of Michael Scott's novel, is one of the very large silk cotton trees which are abundant throughout the island, and which have long life spans. The Ferry Inn nearby got its name from the ferry service across the Fresh River which, according to tradition, was started by William Parker in 1677. In the pastures around the inn are some of Jamaica's large shade trees called guangos. These trees are also found in Trinidad and other islands of the South Caribbean where they are known as samans. When James Stark wrote his guide in 1898, the Rio Cobre Hotel in the vicinity of Spanish Town had established a reputation for Jamaica salmon (calipever) which with 'Salt Pond Mutton' were then great delicacies of the great salt pond. The hotel was equally renowned for serving ginger, pineapples, oranges, limes, guavas, cashews, mangoes and tropical preserves. The Ferry Inn today also enjoys an excellent reputation for food, and is strategically situated for a rafting trip on the river.

The northern parish of St Ann's was early and still is distinguished by the pleasing title of Jamaica's garden parish. For many decades Jamaica's best hotel was in the mountains at Moneague, 17 miles south-east of St Ann's Bay. Today it is used as a training college for primary school teachers. Built in the last decade of the nineteenth century, Moneague Hotel was a spacious building with wide balconies from which thick vines fell in clusters to a verandah below. From Moneague scenic drives were made in horse-drawn buggies to Fern Gully, Roaring River Falls, and 'Cherreras' (as Ocho Rios was called). Today St Ann's seashore has replaced the mountains as the favourite choice of holiday makers, and from many attractive air-conditioned modern hotels by the sea delightful excursions are made instead by car or bus into the mountains behind. One of the most rewarding of such excursions is the Plantation Tour at Brimmer Hall which lies above Bailey's Vale in the hills above Port Maria. This tour passes by groves of coconut trees, bordered by gay flowering bougainvillea, hibiscus, and crotons, and meanders along fields which are sometimes planted with pineapples, cocoa trees, bananas and ackees. The journey is made in an open trailer drawn by a slow-moving diesel-powered tractor. It was enlivened for me by the friendly instructions given by the Rev. Jones, a pastor of the Church of God. Each time he stopped he gave us a well rehearsed potted version of the plants we were seeing and always ended his speech with a promise to take us on to 'further places'. Particularly interesting was his dissection of the various layers of banana tree; when he reached the fibrous material that resembles cotton thread he laughed and told us that it wouldn't be long before women in our party would be 'wearing bananas'. His interest in fibres was again in evidence when he disembowelled a cocoa pod which he had picked from the 'chocolate tree'; he showed us its purple spots set against a white fluffy cotton wool substance surrounding the seeds. The highlight of the tour, however, was a sequence of picking and drinking water coconuts. The skill of the man who shinned up the tree, pressing with circling arms and pushing with feet fastened together by a cotton rag, was rivalled only by the dexterity with which Pastor Jones slashed off the tops of dozens of green shells in turn, inserted a manufactured straw and poured in liberal quantities of rum. As he handed me one such refreshing beverage – like nectar on a hot Saturday afternoon – he told me with a conspiratorial chuckle 'I don't give this to my congregation!' The plantation tour at Brimmer Hall was started by Major Vaughan who had modernised an old Jamaican great house, furnished it in good taste and begun a collection of maps and books (including the Letters of Cardinal Vaughan!).

The countryside of St Ann's has a great appeal for settlers from the United Kingdom. Not far from Port Maria, Noel Coward once owned two houses (one at sea level and one in the mountains!). Ian Fleming was married at Port Maria in 1952 and lived for many years near Oracabessa at Golden Eye, where many famous men and women have stayed. Another meeting place of famous people is Prospect, the estate of the former British M.P., Sir Harold Mitchell. In

1953 Sir Winston Churchill was his guest. Today any visitor to Jamaica can go over the estate on a plantation tour first organised in 1975. Besides offering insights into the cultivation of sugar cane, bananas, citrus, coconuts, and pimento (spice), the tour includes an inspection of Red Poll cattle and the operation of a beef-feed lot. Prospect extends over 1,200 acres and provides views of the White River gorge and the seashores of St Ann's. A training centre for young Jamaicans is located on the property and visitors who go on the tour are shown the chapel which is used by Jamaican cadets.

The Kaiser Bauxite Company have constructed Port Rhoades at Puerto Seco on the far side of Discovery Bay for the shipment of bauxite. They have also created a small park (named for Columbus) on the other side of the bay and equipped it with cannon, and replicas of utensils and machines used by Jamaicans through the centuries. Less than three miles from the park is the Kaiser Mystery House which stands beside a 48-acre lagoon that is supplied by fresh water springs and reaches the sea through underground caves.

Between Discovery Bay, where Columbus is believed to have landed in 1494, and Runaway Bay, from which the last Spanish guerillas are said to have escaped to Cuba in 1660, are the Green Grotto limestone caves. For the visitor with time to spare, the caves, which are four miles west of Runaway Bay, are very well worth visiting. Some rock formations inside are recognisable as an eagle, a man's face and a Madonna and Child. One of them, known as Big Ben, chimes the time in calypso rhythm when struck by the guide, while the Indian Fire Dance instrument gives out a whole series of tuneful musical notes when tapped. Legend has grown around a 'limbo hollow rock' and you are shown the passage through which the last Spanish governor went on his way way to the sea and Cuba. The people at the caves are very welcoming and the tour begins with the offer of a limeade or punch. Wise visitors are those who choose the limade, for the journey to the Green Grotto is partly through a forest path that is humid and hot for most of the day. At the bottom of the grotto a small pool of cold fresh water may be explored in a flat bottomed boat. It is a very modest pool when compared to the grotto near Amalfi or to the Blue Grotto at Capri, but it should not be missed by anyone who explores the caves. I was impressed by the number of small trees growing inside the caves, from seeds dropped by bats. You must not fear attacks from the bats because, as the guide will tell you if you ask, 'the rat bats are more afraid of you than you afraid of the rat bats'. In any case the bats are proclaimed as friendly by the proprietor of the caves whose card contains the prayer 'May a golden rat bat kiss you and all your dreams come true'. The caves are open from 9 a.m. till 6 p.m.

In the hills overlooking Discovery Bay and Runaway Bay another Jamaican 'bangerang' trip may be made in a tractor-drawn open vehicle through orchards of mangoes, sappodilla, soursop, naseberry, star apple and other Jamaican trees. As you pass through the Avenue of History you are reminded of men who preceeded you, Columbus, Bligh, Morgan and others. Topside, as the Jamaicans say, you will find a great house landscaped amongst colourful flowers. And if you keep a sharp lookout you should see quick darting humming birds as they fly from tropical flower to tropical flower.

Near Runaway Bay Hotel is Cardiff Hall great house, long owned by the Blagrove family and for a time by the duke of Newcastle, who modernised it. An 18-hole golf course is part of the Cardiff Hall development. A little beyond the Runaway Bay Hotel is the Club Caribbean, an informal collection of beach kraals or circular houses landscaped among fruit and flowering trees. The sea off the brown sandy beach is particularly invigorating and reminded me of the coast of Bathsheba in Barbados. A bronze figure of Columbus, cast in Genoa, commemorates the old Spanish town of New Seville. It is on the right of the highway leading to St Ann's Bay and was erected in 1957, through the efforts of a Jesuit priest Neil Donahue. Further along a driveway, a shrine built by another Jesuit, Ray Sullivan, contains stones taken from Peter Martyr's unfinished church. On the way to

Dunn's River Falls the road from the Club Caribbean goes through sugar lands, and skirts pimento orchards and pastures where cattle graze. On the high lands above, beautiful modern houses are landscaped among the trees. On St Ann's polo ground polo is played on Saturday afternoon throughout the year. Visitors from north coast hotels are welcome to watch the games. My friendly taxi driver, whose analysis of Jamaica's problems was simple ('a too rich top crust unwilling to share with bottom, who have a hard time') stopped his magnificent limousine on the way back from the Dunn's River Feast, picked out a black crab with his light, switched off the engine and proceeded to show me how to catch it. I watched his hands skilfully avoid the crab's backbiting claws and thanked him for the display. He was grateful and threw the crab back over the road where it was less likely to be crushed by a passing vehicle. St Ann's Bay town is the capital of the parish and birthplace of a Jamaican national hero, Marcus Garvey. Between St Ann's Bay and Dunn's River Falls the villas of Mammee Bay offer a way of life far removed from that of the neighbouring Hilton hotel or the high-storey hotels of Ocho Rios.

The Dunn's River Feast is an occasion especially organised for tourists by the friendly North Coast Tourist Board. A beach barbecue, rum punches, floodlit falls and the lapping of waves on soft sands prepare even the most sophisticated traveller for a barefoot romp to the captivating drumbeats of a Jamaican calypso band. The atmosphere unfortunately proved too seductive for a teenage English girl the evening I was there. She picked herself a handsome young Jamaican beau and literally offered herself in an impromptu series of unmistakeable sexual advances which the prudent young Jamaican was too well behaved to accept. Later in the evening her ardour may have been cooled in the refreshing waters of the falls, where bathers are expertly conducted by guides. The spectacular Roaring River Falls are now used to supply water and electricity. In 1898, when Stark wrote his guide to Jamaica, the Roaring River, which could be heard a long way off, was described as 'one of the loveliest objects in a land of beautiful things'. The falls were 175 feet in breadth and discharged 'a myriad of small cascades, feathery and brilliant, massed together, clustered, glancing at a hundred different angles, breaking into a thousand foam jets'. Waterfalls are understandably a feature of a district named after eight rivers, and the sight of water tumbling into the sea or rushing over an inland precipice will be a bonus for anyone who explores the neighbourhood. A restaurant at the Ruin, below the gardens of Mantalent Inn, is situated beneath the Eden Falls. One of the greatest losses of the Ocho Rios district has been the destruction of the old great house of Shaw Park on the hill overlooking the town. There T. S. Eliot and many other famous men and women once found temporary retreat from the pressures of modern living. But the modern taste for establishments on the seashore has today transformed the old Shaw Park site into a garden stop where fashion shows, afternoon tea and the music of a Zouave-uniformed Jamaican military band are dished up to tourists who want to imagine what they hope might be memories of a Jamaica that has vanished into history.

Hotels, villas and inns are found at intervals along the shoreline stretching from Ocho Rios to Oracabessa. There is to be found the Gold Coast of Jamaica's resort life and there is a great variety of places where you may stay. My own choice for a long time will be the Jamaica Inn, a place shaped by nature and landscaped by man for the delectation of those who want to live simply and elegantly at the same time. Nowhere have I found in the Caribbean a beach so perfectly formed and so naturally protected at both sides. It is a crescent-shaped cove with a sandy beach and low coral cliffs made colourful by flowers of frangipani and bougainvillea. Blue-green mountains tower in the far west and deep blue sea faces north. The rest is a harmony of trees, shrubs, and buildings arranged for the comfort and pleasure of guests who enjoy indoor-outdoor living. Plantation Inn and Sans Souci also cater for selective holiday makers who appreciate elegance, décor and personal service in settings of tropical beauty. For others there are the large American-styled hotels at Ocho Rios and St Ann's Bay, while beyond the White River, Shaw Park Beach Club, Tower Isle, the Playboy Club and others appeal more directly to those who want 'fun-in-the-sun'. As one brochure puts it: 'There is so much to do at Tower Isle! Skindive and explore the coral reef ... water ski ... climb a mountain. Better still climb a waterfall ... enjoy ... sailing, archery, tennis, shuffleboard, cycling, movies.' There is something for everybody on the popular north coast between St Ann's Bay and Oracabessa. Even a Scandinavian establishment for those who seek natural holidays in the buff!

Because the hotels and inns around Ocho Rios developed as scattered oases, pedestrians have to share the narrow roads with motor cars that take corners sharply. It is only in the modern villages which are springing up in the hotel districts that pedestrians are encouraged to saunter along sidewalks which connect small shops, banks and travel offices. There progress may be held up for a while by the importunities of those who sell bead necklaces and other souvenirs from street stalls.

On the north coast I took counsel of a North American lady who had adopted the island and was the mother of Jamaican children. What advice had she to give the visitor? They should behave as they would at home, she replied. Jamaicans could easily recognise innocents abroad, and if strangers behaved without reserve they were likely to be taken at face value. Girls who accepted offers to drive to lonely beaches were inviting the consequences which would surely happen. My companion through Fern Gully, a tree-shaded avenue about three miles long, was a young lady from Grenada. From her I learnt that Jamaicans in the countryside are always willing to help visitors, but that young and old men alike prefer to be addressed as 'Sir'. She used this address when we stopped in the hills near Lydford to ask directions from a venerable peasant seated on an ass. We got a civil reply, but I never had any problem with Jamaicans other than a complete inability to understand their usual speech. I asked another friend exactly what

Jamaican dialect was. His reply 'mispronounced English' amused me but didn't teach me how to communicate. Fortunately for the ordinary visitor everyone directly engaged in the tourist industry speaks two tongues, one recognisable English, the other unrecognisable Jamaican Creole.

Besides the English tea in the old Shaw Park and the feast and swim on Dunn's River beach, holiday makers on the popular north coast are also entertained on Sunday with a Jamaican night on the White River. A floor show and a boat ride by torchlight are the highlights of this pleasant sponsored entertainment.

Sixteen miles south of St Ann's Bay in the Pedro hills there is a ruin known as Edinburgh Castle. For about a decade in the late eighteenth century the castle was the residence of a Scot, Lewis Hutchinson, who was eventually hanged in Spanish Town for a series of murders committed upon lonely travellers whose bodies according to legend, were thrown in a 'sink hole' of his estate!

Between the White River and Port Maria the northern Gold Coast runs into St Mary's parish, which claims the Tower Isle, the Playboy Club and the Golden Head hotels. More than 100,000 people live in St Mary's parish, which has an area of 254 square miles and is planted with bananas, sugar, citrus, pimento, cocoa, coconuts and coffee. Castleton Botanic Gardens are near the southern boundary along the banks of the Wag Water River. The capital of St Mary's, Port Maria, has a good harbour that is protected by Cabaritta Isle which stands squat and square to the north. Oracabessa on the western side of the promontory also has a sheltered harbour that was once used for the shipment of bananas. The coastline between Oracabessa and Port Maria is rugged and picturesque and for these reasons appealed to creative writers like Coward and Fleming. Cabaritta Isle is part of Llanrumney Estate, a property which once belonged to Henry Morgan. Annotto Bay was named after an orange dye (usually spelt annatto) and was once a busy port used by dozens of estates within the parish. One of the great houses on a neighbouring estate, Agualta Vale was built as recently as 1907. In the eighteenth century the property belonged to Thomas Hibbert, who went to Jamaica from Manchester and prospered greatly. Windsor Castle, which has a small factory for processing pimento, is the boundary between St Mary's and Portland parishes along the shore. The name recalls the strong English impact of a parish which also glories in names like Whitehall, Hampstead, Highgate, Islington, Epsom and Richmond.

TRAVELLERS' DIGEST

MANCHESTER PARISH.

Area: 339 square miles.

Population: Over 123,000.

Chief Town: Mandeville (2,061 feet above sea level).

Second Town: Christiana, 14 miles north of Mandeville, centre for ginger, bananas, Irish potatoes.

Mountains: Don Figuerero, May Day and Carpenter.

Main Crops: Bananas, coffee, pimento.

Major Industry: Bauxite mining.

Airports or Airstrips: Marlborough, Cedar Grove, Kendal, Dump.

Hotels: Mandeville, Belair (has swimming pool, shops and pub).

Golf: Mandeville Country Club.

Entertainment: Friday night dance and feast at Astra's Revival Room.

Special Interest: Spur Tree Ridge, Christiana, Alcan's Kirkvine Alumina Plant, Mandeville, Monticello (birds, animals, orchids), Abbey Caves.

CLARENDON PARISH.

Area: 467 square miles.

Population: Over 177,000.

Chief Town: May Pen, 35 miles from Kingston.

Other Towns: Frankfield, Chapelton, Spaldings.

Mountains: Bull Head, Mocho, May Day.

Main Crops: Sugar cane, bananas, citrus, tobacco.

Major Industry: Bauxite mining.

Special Interest: Monymusk Sugar Refinery, Alley Church, Milk River Bath, Bull Head Mountain (centre of island), Denbigh Agricultural Show Grounds.

Airstrips: Sandy Gully, Hayes, Birds Hill.

Rivers: Rio Minho, Thomas, Milk, Baldwins, Hilliards, Rock, Pindars.

ST CATHERINE PARISH.

Area: 483 square miles.

Population: Over 186,000.

Chief Town: Spanish Town. Capital of Jamaica till 1872; population over 41,000; seat of mayor; archives.

Other Towns: Linstead, Ewarton.

Villages: Lluidas Vale, Troja, Glengoffe, Port Henderson, Passage Fort, Old Harbour Bay.

Main Crops: Sugar cane, coffee, bananas, rice, citrus, tobacco, cocoa.

Industries: Sugar, rum, alumina, citrus processing, condensery, pineapple cannery, textile mill, bagasse plant, steel mill.

Special Interest: Twickenham Park School of Agriculture; Bodles Agricultural Station;
In Spanish Town: Rodney memorial, old government buildings, old House of Assembly, courthouse, cathedral, Jamaica Folk Museum, Baptist church; Colbeck Castle; White Marl Arawak Museum; Ferry Inn, Tom Cringle's Cotton Tree; old Jewish cemetery, Hunt's Bay; Waterfront, Port Henderson; Rodney's Lookout; Caymanas Park Race Course; Bog Walk; Devil's Race Course.

Airstrips: Old Harbour, Spring Village, Salt Island Creek, Innswood, Windsor Park, Tulloch, Worthy Park, Ewarton, Caymanas Estate.

Rivers: Rio Magno, Rio Cobre, Rio d'Oro, Rio Pedro.

Mountains: Juan de Bolas, Guy's Hill, St John, St Dorothy, Hollymount.

ST ANN, THE GARDEN PARISH.

Area: 482 square miles.

Population: Over 121,000.

Chief Town: St Ann's Bay (seat of mayor).

Other Towns: Brown's Town, Claremont, Moneague, Discovery Bay, Ocho Rios, Llandovery.

Rivers: Roaring River, Llandovery, Rio Bueno, Cave.

Mountains: Pedro and Dry Harbour (Albion 2759).

Airstrip: Moneague.

Ports: Ocho Rios, Port Rhoades.

Industries: Bauxite, tourism, cattle raising.

Agriculture: Bananas, pimento, sugar cane, coconuts, coffee, citrus, sisal.

Special Interest: Columbus Park, Discovery Bay; Runaway

21. (*above*) A view in the Blue Mountains.
22. (*below*) The Jamaica Hope Herd of cattle.

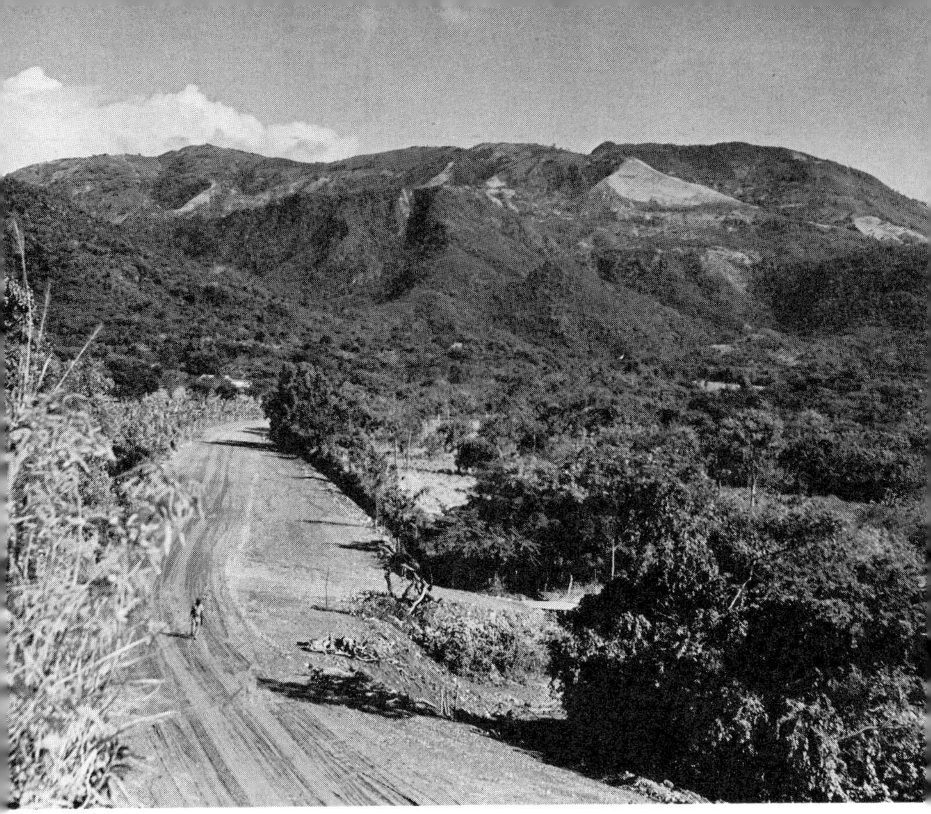

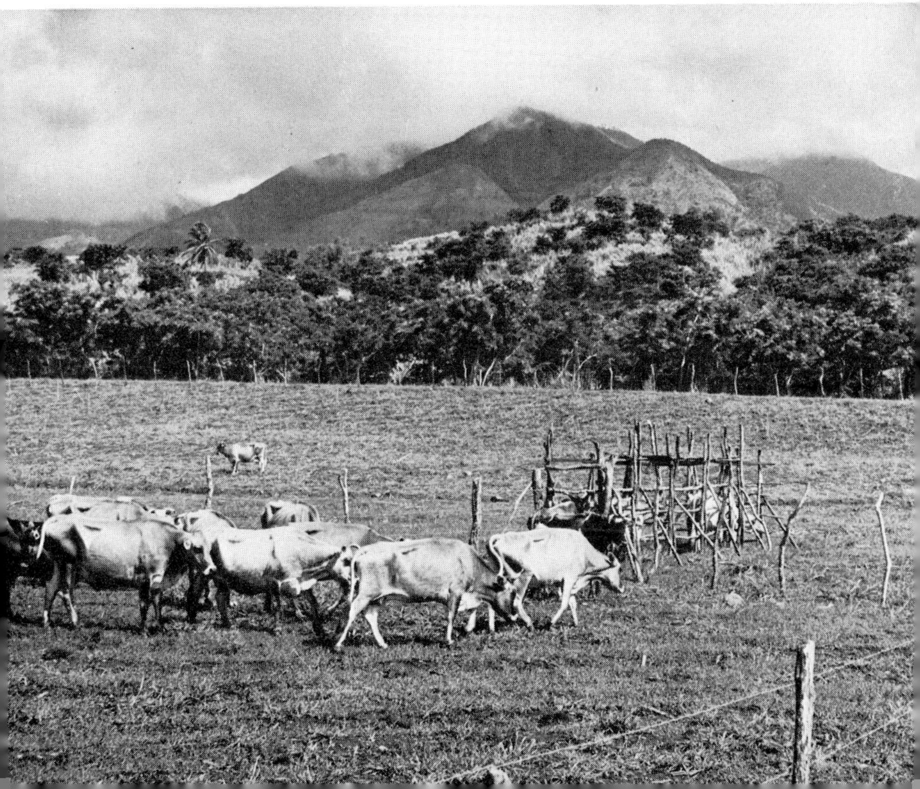

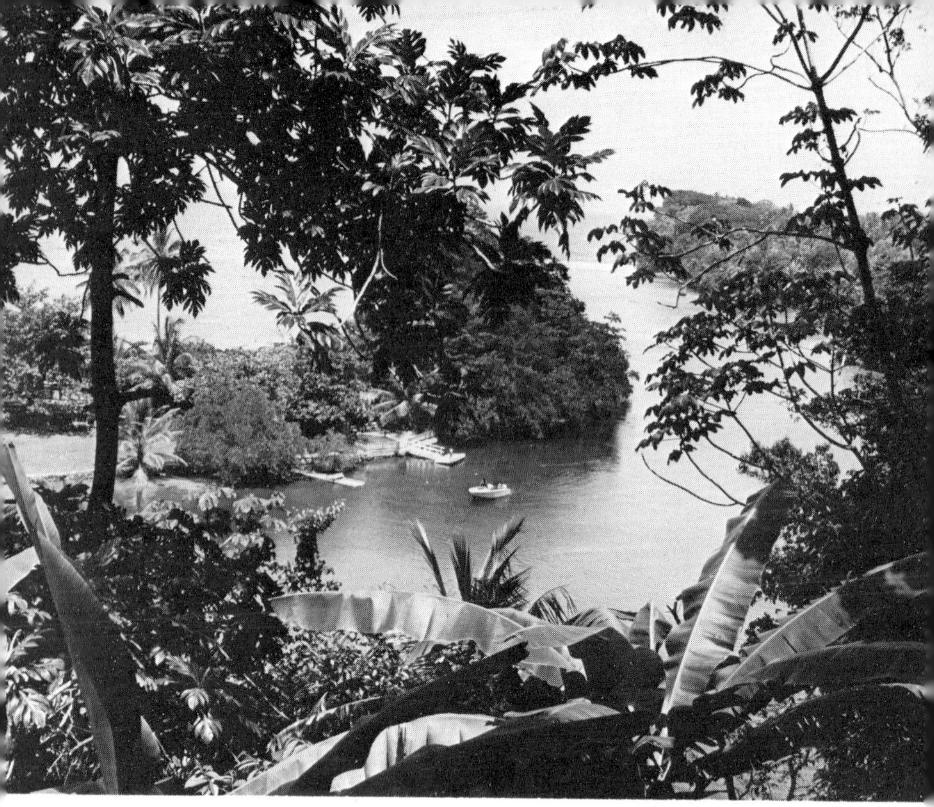

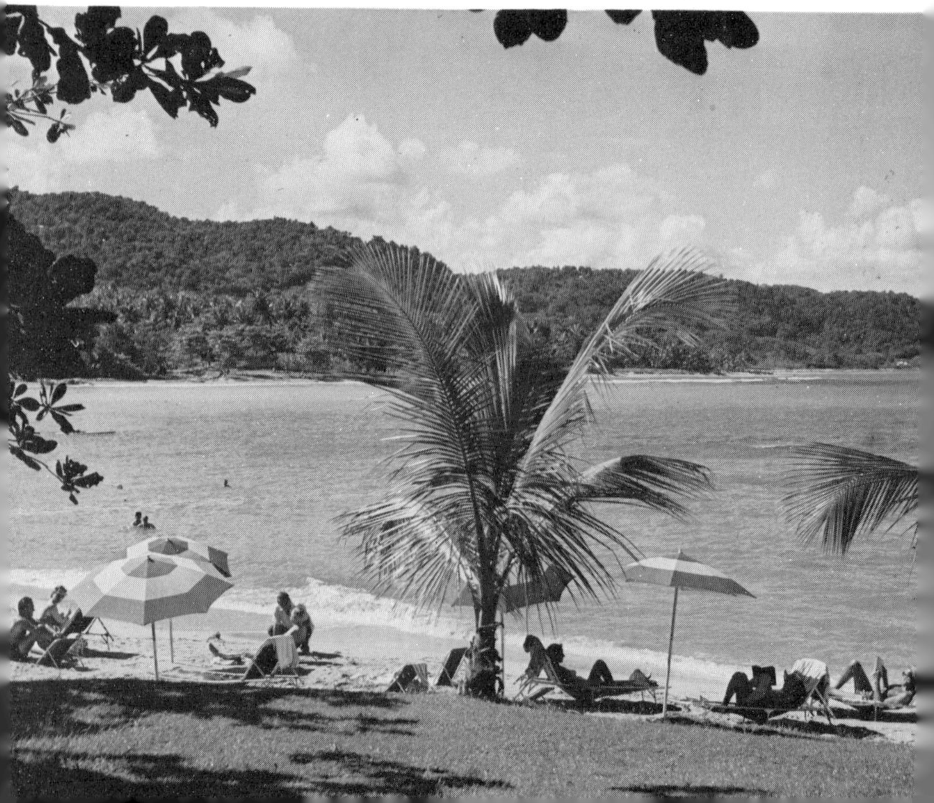

East Jamaica

Jamaica's smallest county, Surrey, is the most densely populated of the three. Its 820 square miles contain the four parishes of Kingston (including Port Royal), St Andrew, St Thomas and Portland. The two most easterly of these parishes, Portland and St Thomas, occupy 628 square miles and their combined population exceeds 140,000. The Grand Ridge of the Blue Mountains divides Portland from St Thomas on its southern boundaries. From Dover Point on the northern shores, the sea coast follows through a series of indented bays gently southwards as far as North East Point. The land then begins to fall sharply in a southerly direction. Hectors River marks the boundary between Portland and St Thomas and the John Crow Mountains divide the coastal plains from the interior valley of the Rio Grande.

Portland was named for the Duke who was governing Jamaica in 1723 when the parish was formed. The Duke was responsible for the capital town being called Titchfield after a town in Hampshire which was then in use as a small seaport. Titchfield has survived in Port Antonio as the name of a residential area, Upper Titchfield, and in the administrative and commercial centre, Lower Titchfield. But Port Antonio has for long been the description of the town, which is recognised as the cradle of the banana and tourist industries. Stark, writing in 1898, found Port Antonio a bustling banana town, provided with Jamaica's only modern luxury hotel, the Titchfield, where guests were served 'northern products' and were waited upon by New England waitresses who served 'daintily'. The Americans arrived by sea in vessels

Caves and Grotto; Cardiff Hall; Columbus Monument and Catholic Shrine, Seville Estate; Seville great house; Dunn's River Falls; Pineapple Place Shopping Village near Ocho Rios; Shaw Park Gardens; Fern Gully; Pine Forests; Mount Diablo; Friends Craft Centre, Highgate.

Golf: Upton Country Club and Golf Course Runaway Club.

St Mary Parish.

Area: 254 square miles.

Population: Over 100,000.

Capital: Port Maria.

Other Towns: Highgate, Richmond, Oracabessa, Annotto Bay.

Administration: Mayor and council.

Agriculture: Bananas, sugar cane, citrus, pimento, cocoa, coconuts, coffee.

Industries: Copra, tourism.

Mountains: Blue Mountain Ridge (Mount Telegraph 4183).

Rivers: White River, Rio Nuevo, Rio Sambre, Wag Water, Flint Water, Dry River.

Special Interest: Prospect Estate; The Botanical Drive; Rio Nuevo Bay; Oracabessa, Port Maria, Brimmer Hall plantation, Highgate, Clermont, Don Christopher's Point, Agualta Vale, Castleton Botanic Gardens, Annotto Bay, Windsor Castle.

Airstrips: Boscobel, Highgate.

23. *(above)* Blue Lagoon, near Port Antonio.
24. *(below)* North Shore Beach with almond tree and coconuts.

which Stark said came 'bounding in on the swell; rushing apparently to certain destruction, when suddenly swinging under the lee of the island that guards the mouth of the west harbour, she glides along past the hotel on an even keel over the unruffled surface of the harbour, till she anchors along-side one of the wharves'. Such a description today might in part be applied to some stages of the eight-mile rafting trip from Berrydale in the hills behind Port Antonio to St Margaret's Bay where cruise passengers arrive in sleek modern motor vessels. Stark himself had reached Port Antonio by rail from Bog Walk. He had followed the coast eastwards from Annotto Bay and was duly impressed during his journey by inland views of cloud-tipped mountains and lofty trees covered with creepers. At Buff Bay he had noticed 'coral pavements' in its translucent waters. It took him four hours to travel 46 miles on the new branch line.

My journey to Port Antonio's airport took only 15 minutes of flying time. I had been picked up at Boscobel airport near Oracabessa by a Cessna of the Jamaican Air Taxi Service which had come in especially from Montego Bay. The 22-year-old Jamaican pilot kept well out to sea at a height of 2,500 feet so that when I looked inland I could distinguish only a back-drop of tree-clad mountains, white twisting roads, railway tracks, fields of sugar cane, banana and coconut groves and clusters of buildings and houses in isolated coves. Just before landing near St Margaret's Bay I saw patterns of flat coral which might possibly have been mistaken for 'undersea pavements' by anyone unfamiliar with Caribbean waters. The plane was much too far from land for me to get a glimpse of the beautiful scenic road which winds its way over the watershed at Hardwar Gap up to the heights of Greenwich and Newcastle overlooking Kingston. There's nothing like a plane journey to dramatise the change between one place and another. In that short trip by Cessna, while the pilot talked through his radio to his headquarters, I began to feel the pulse of a new Jamaica where people wanted to move around in a hurry. The holiday feeling which had been uppermost during my stay at the Jamaica Inn fell away and I was ready to explore a region which everyone in Montego Bay and the Ocho Rios neighbourhood had told me was the wettest place in Jamaica. I landed in brilliant sunshine and the Cessna was back in the air before I could say 'Ken Jones', the name of the airport. There was no one there to meet me so I had time to savour the peaceful quiet of the place. I might have been on a remote island of the Bahamas. There were two people on duty in the little hut which served for a terminal building and they greeted me with a friendliness which is always found in places where there is time to stand and stare. One of the things that I stared at for some minutes was a weighing machine, which had Spanish markings on its dial. A minute later I was surprised to read the word 'caballeros' on the door of the men's loo. Spain, it seems, lingers on at Port Antonio, at least in Spanish words. I never got to the bottom of the mystery, if mystery it was, but perhaps there was no more significance there than in the survival of so many Spanish names elsewhere in Jamaica. Yet why has Titchfield given way to Port Antonio? While I pondered about this a large station wagon pulled up and I was officially welcomed by Mr Bramhall, one of nature's gentlemen, who had forsaken his office on one of his busiest cruise-ship days to show me a hospitality which came as much from the heart as from the job. I was to meet several others like him during my stay in Jamaica, not a few in the Port Antonio area.

Mr Bramhall supplied me with a rafting ticket and within minutes I was bowling along the road in a Volkswagen mini-bus which passed through bustling streets in the centre of Port Antonio before climbing upwards into fertile planted hills with twisting roads that led to the tree-shaded rafting station at Berrydale. There as many as one hundred rafts are assembled at certain times of the year to take ticket holders on an eight-mile river journey which has moments of excitement for everyone and offers a unique experience to lovers of natural beauty. A cruise passenger who had made the journey on the same day as myself summed up his experience by saying 'It's what I expected from Jamaica'. I understood exactly what he meant, and would go further and say 'It was more than I expected, for it is worth going to Jamaica just to go rafting on the Rio Grande.' The bamboo rafts in which voyages are made from Berrydale to the sea are each 30 feet in length. They are made from bamboo poles which are securely fastened together, but which are kept individually mobile in the front so as to pass smoothly over rounded stones in rapids without obstruction. The skill with which a raft captain treads barefoot over the rounded poles as he hops from one side to another of the narrow (less than four feet) flat 'prow' is an art passed down from father to sons through generations of river folk. For hundreds of years the produce of the steep Portland hills has been carried down by river to the coast, but only in relatively modern times did it occur to anyone that the rafting skills thus learnt might be used for entertainment as well as business. According to local tradition pleasure rafting derived from the happy decision of one banana grower to let two of his guests accompany a load of bananas which he was sending down river to St Margaret's Bay. The joy they expressed on their return has made rafting popular ever since. Errol Flynn, the film star, added another dimension to pleasure rafting by organising an annual rafting regatta on the Rio Grande. Competition encouraged the rafting 'gondoliers' to new efforts and the most famous of all, 'Red' Grant was acknowledged by his fellows as King of the River. Among those whom he piloted safely along rills, rapids and bends was Sir Winston Churchill.

My gondolier wore a cocked hat shaped like an admiral's; he was barefoot, having stowed his shoes under the box where I sat. His bicycle was lashed securely behind the raised platform. He used two bamboo poles to propel his raft, one about four feet shorter than the other, which was between 15 and 20 feet in length. The short pole was used when the water was fairly shallow and the long pole in deep pools and at sharp bends. Both were used sometimes almost like rudders to steer the raft in the right direction. As a young man I had watched the seemingly effortless way in which a Venetian gondolier had propelled me along the Grand Canal pullulating with 'duks' and sleek motor launches before swinging his strange bark into the quiet back waters of the town. On the Rio Grande I was somewhat in the position of a surf rider who has surrendered his board to a man who understands every secret of the river and who approaches what seemed to me like certain hazards with the skill of one who knew just when and where the wave would curl as it swept relentlessly towards the shore. I believe his name was King. He was certainly a sovereign of his art and no Venetian gondolier could have spun his craft around in more than 60 degree bends with such unerring accuracy. Seldom have I seen a man put so much effort into any task. I was only sorry that he had to make a sunbaked journey all the way back to Berrydale by bicycle and that he could earn no more fees until his raft was brought back up river to him by a boy who had to be paid one third of the cost of a ticket. Throughout the 8-mile journey, scenery and activities change as in slow moving pictures. We passed women unashamedly dressing after a swim, we passed workers building walls against river floods; we saw bushes being cleared on the slopes and heard the loud pops of bamboo joints as they exploded in flames; we met other rafts carrying ice-cold beer and soft drinks; we were pursued for a while by naked boys who invited us to throw a 'co-in'. Overhead flew herons, black and white; the pale green fronds of bamboos whispered in the breeze, bright immortelles and other flowers illumined the tops of flowering trees, many of which trailed long tendrils through their branches; at water level we passed beside wild canes in a row and clusters of gay yellow balisiers. In one deep pool a boy was fishing for mullet which streaked past us in shoals through crystal clear ponds. In the early afternoon the sun's rays penetrated the tissues of my exposed skin and it was a pleasant relief to pause for ten minutes on a shaded strand of the river where another guide had stopped before us and baked a piece of breadfruit which his riders were eating with relish, washing it down with ice-cold beer. Little boys near us were turning over rocks in their search for janggas, tiny river shrimps. As the river draws near to the sea it widens and spits of land appear. On these islands I saw dozens of John Crows, the large birds which seem part turkeys, part vultures. They are best seen hovering above the tree tops for on the ground they resemble surly undertakers splashed with red. They look more menacing than they really are for they are often attacked by the much smaller migrant petchary which spends part of each year in Jamaica. The Jamaican proverb 'John Crow say him a dandy man but him only have so-so feather' aptly expresses my own feeling for a bird who may be useful as a scavenger but who has no obvious social graces.

The earl of Mansfield was responsible for the development of Rafter's Rest at Burlington where the river meets the sea. Showers, dressing rooms, swimming pool, bar, restaurant and souvenir shop are available for rafters, cruise passengers, or sightseers by bus or car. In the open-to-air restaurant cooled by breezes I lingered over cold Red Stripe beer and hamburgers with as much enjoyment as though I were dining at Jamaica Inn, Sans Souci, Goblin Hill or Half Moon where Jamaican cuisine is at its best. The Jamaican Tourist Board supervises rafting from Rafter's Rest and the Berrydale Starting Point is controlled by friendly, uniformed Jamaican policemen. At Berrydale, if you are lucky, you may be offered a small bamboo model of a raft, accurate in every detail. Cameras in cases slung around the neck are recommended for those who want to make a record of their memorable journey. Water from a dripping pole or spray from splashes caused by diving boys, or rainfall can penetrate exposed cameras and there is always a possibility, if not a likelihood, of unexpected contact with water. The river pilots protest that there is no risk of water getting into your camera, but my own experience on a sunny calm June day is that you have to be careful all the way if you carry an expensive camera. Lenses should certainly be cleaned at the end of the journey, which takes two and a half hours. The town of Port Antonio has interesting architectural styles.

Most conspicuous is that of the square brick courthouse, ornamented with iron verandah rails and a cupola. It is the dominant building in the centre of the town. At the eastern end of Harbour Street, on a raised ground, Christ Church recalls the aims of the Anglican religion in the early years which followed the abolition of slavery. It was designed by Annesley Voysey and built in 1840. Olivier Park at the far eastern end of Port Antonio commemorates the Fabian socialist Lord Olivier, who was governor in the years 1907-13 and dedicated his term of office to the advancement of the peasant growers of the 'blessed isle'.

Because of its twin harbour, separated by an island, Port Antonio was early established as a defensive stronghold. A fort was built and the extremity of the peninsula and the island which was used as a naval station became known as Navy Island. The defences of Port Antonio were also beneficial for planters who were periodically attacked by maroons. From their base at Nanny Town in the mountains they terrorised the inhabitants of Port Antonio in the early years of the eighteenth century. Not until 1739 was peace made and only after big guns had been dragged up the mountains and fired against Nanny Town.

The natural beauty of Port Antonio attracted the attention of Lady Brassey who called there in the yacht *Sunbeam* with her husband during a world cruise in 1883. 'We entered', she wrote, 'one of the prettiest small harbours in the world.' From the decks she saw low hills covered with vegetation, with little houses dotted about their slopes, while in the background rose tier upon tier of the 'evergreen ranges of the lovely Blue Mountains high in the air'. The fruit trade had just started with America and people ashore were hopeful that Port Antonio might become the future port of Jamaica. The cultivation of bananas for export in Port Antonio had been started in 1867 by Captain Baker of Boston. It developed steadily and Baker with friends and associates formed the Boston Fruit Company which acquired or rented abandoned sugar estates between the banks of the Rio Grande and the foothills of the Blue Mountains for planting with banana suckers. In 1899 the United Fruit Company of New Jersey was formed to exploit the boom in bananas which had replaced sugar as the chief export. Other American competing companies had been formed and in 1901 Sir Alfred Jones formed an English company and a shipping line, Elders and Fyffes, to obtain a share of the profits for English investors. The United Fruit Company was too powerful, however, and obtained control of Elders and Fyffes. In 1903 a hurricane laid waste the banana plantations. In 1929 the Jamaica Producers' Association was formed to exploit the banana trade for the benefit of Jamaican growers, but their efforts were handicapped by an outbreak of Panama disease in the 'forties. Exports fell from 23 million stems in 1938 to six and a half million in 1949. Baker's vision more than one hundred years ago was fully justified, however, and bananas are still profitably grown in the neighbourhood of Port Antonio and other parts of Jamaica. The Titchfield Hotel which his Boston Fruit Company constructed as a group of cottages on top of a hill, with separate amenities elsewhere, also happily set a pattern for the modern resort complexes which contribute to the special charm of Port Antonio's holiday district. For this reason Jamaicans leave Kingston and go to Goblin Hill at San San in search of the real Jamaica. Goblin Hill reminded me of a Caribbean I had glimpsed on holiday in the mid-forties on St Kitts, Montserrat, Antigua and Dominica before the Cuban revolution had caused a tidal wave of American style 'tourism' to undiscovered paradises. The magnificent spacious accommodations are American enough in their luxury bathrooms, giant refrigerators and air-conditioned bedrooms and living rooms but their sun balconies open on to a Jamaica of songbirds, handsome shade and flowering trees, dark blue seas, and hillside villas designed by architects who have learnt how to blend elegance with rustic simplicity. The sea at San San is not in truth as appealing as the sea on the golden, central northern shores, but it is a great deal cleaner than and as invigorating as many of the famous seaside resorts of Southern Europe. Walking from Goblin

Hill to San San beach through a landscaped forest garden is good for health and much more relaxing than lying on beach chairs surrounded by hordes of sun-soakers. If you keep to the main road, instead of nipping through a hole in the hedge, and walk for a few hundred yards towards the main beach gate at San San you will be rewarded by greetings from friendly Jamaicans as they move at slow speeds on bicycles or in motor vehicles which have no reason to hurry. There is no rat race at Goblin Hill, only blessed tranquillity, excellent food, simple entertainment and (while I was there) unending tennis. Even when the rain came rushing through the tropical undergrowth in swathes of hissing sound I relaxed still more and enjoyed the cool breeze from the gardens, conscious that I was protected by large canvas awnings from getting wet. Rain should never be feared in the Caribbean, it is always cool and only occasionally and in certain months of the year does it outstay its welcome. For it stops often as suddenly as it starts, leaving the land sweet smelling and clean, and the sea as rounded and smooth as a velvet cushion. Jamaica's mocking bird sings so sweetly at Goblin Hill and elsewhere that the islanders call it *their* nightingale. Not so the untidy grackle aptly described as kling-kling; the sound of these words nearly describes the harsh clang of their unending chatter. Their presence at Goblin Hill seems to be due to some heavenly supervisor who is suspicious of earthly paradises.

Although Goblin Hill is truly an escapist's paradise for people of all ages it is also an ideal centre for young people who go down to the sea in snorkel gear, or want to row boats or sail in them. San San Bay, at the foot of the hill, is conveniently equipped with a princess island, a reef and a picturesque headland. Not far away is Boston Beach and the Blue Lagoon, with calm dark blue surface perfect for water skiing. It is over 200 feet deep. Close by a white sandy beach there is a restaurant. The approach to this haven of peace is lined on the seaside by a collection of modern villas, equipped with private landing stages. On the road above there is a small layby where photographers can capture the contrasts between the deep 'blue hole' water and a variety of greens in the surrounding foliage. Photographing beautiful scenery can be practised within the grounds of Goblin Hill or at many points within a radius of two miles.

Lovers of horses can combine their enjoyment of riding with a photographic tour on horseback into the Blue Mountains. Called Camera Safari the tour lasts for two and a half hours. It passes through groves of coconuts and bananas and includes lunch at the Rafter's Rest. Only one mile from Turtle Crawle Harbour, which lies between Folly Point and Burnetts Point I saw humming birds darting between the bougainvillea and oleander flowers of Athenry, a modern plantation house 700 feet above sea level with an uninterrupted view of Navy Island. Athenry is a 185-acre plantation largely given over to coconuts. It was bought by an American who saw it advertised in the *Wall Street Journal.* The plantation might have continued as a typical Jamaican estate in the hills but for the accidental discovery of a cave. According to my guide (who had learnt his piece by heart and said it slowly) the cave was discoverd by someone who was looking for a goat that had been lost. He heard it bleating behind a thick vine and entered an opening which is now the main entrance of Nonsuch Cave. Compared to the large caves near Runaway Bay the cave at Nonsuch is very modest, but the interior is spotlessly clean, lit by electricity, adequately provided with concrete walks and has stairways in places where stooping or bending would otherwise have been necessary. As you walk in one side and come out at the other the guide tells the tale of the discovering goat, and how the entrance and exit were dug by hand. He also points out sediments and fossils which were formed when the cave was under the sea. Signs of volcanic activity are visible in the rock structure and there are curiously shaped stalagmites and stalactites. One group of these dripstone formations has been aptly likened to a frozen waterfall. The gardens of Athenry are small but plants and trees are labelled. At the far end of the garden a pavilion gives an unimpeded view of Navy Island and Port Antonio's harbour. It is a good place to sit and sip some ice-cold drink, surrounded by seven hills on the slopes of which grow limes, papayas, mangoes, bananas, coconuts and avocado pears and pineapples. In the warm scented air you even grow drowsy and wonder whether Nonsuch is not really part of a dream induced by the fact that you did go there by way of Fairy Hill, Sherwood Forest and Cambridge?

The Jamaican Tourist Board's promotional literature refers to Port Antonio as the island's smallest resort, and this explains its charm. People in Kingston visit the resorts near Port Antonio as they go into the Blue Mountains to re-discover the old Jamaica of their own or their parents' youth. Tourists who go there may be organised but they are never 'packaged'. There is always time wherever you are to relax. No one hurries near Port Antonio. In a resort like Frenchman's Cove the Jamaican stone houses where you find every comfort are so far from the main road that you are given a golf cart and map on arrival. You need it because the property extends over 40 acres. The wall of an old sugar mill, an empty syrup tayche, cannon on the cliff create an old-world atmosphere that blends with cultivated gardens and is yet compatible with a coconut-fringed sandy beach as remote from other worlds as that on which Crusoe first discovered the footprints of Friday.

Between Frenchman's Cove and Boston Bay on another 40-acre estate 32 houses form a village near a beach only seven miles from Port Antonio. The resort is named after Dragon Bay. On the slope above its beach the great house of an early nineteenth-century Jamaica planter, William Betts, once stood. However grand it may have been before its collapse it could never have been more impressive than today's main shingle-roofed building through which guests enter an elaborate 'village square' that is surrounded with arcades and arches. All around this square the houses offer a variety of architectural features which include French jalousies, enclosed verandahs, open roof balconies, stone stairs, and panelled sash glass windows. But for its modernity it might have been designed as a stage setting for *Figaro*. The name Dragon Bay supposedly derives from the frothing, hissing waves which in full tide come bounding through an opening in the reef. During my visit the dragon was fast asleep and only a quiet lap of water advanced and receded on a sandy beach which lay below well tended lawns, shaded by tall almond and seagrape trees. It was a tranquil setting suited to a landscape painter and indeed a lady from South Carolina was hard at work on the grass, sketching outlines of gnarled seagrape branches, placid blue sea water and a tree-flanked promontory on which stands the winter restaurant. A landscape artist, Leo Sullivan, is the man responsible for the park-like look of the grounds at Dragon Bay. There among other trees you will see traveller's palm, night blooming cereus, lime, mango, pimento, coffee, ackee, breadfruit, and bamboo, while splashes of colour are provided by flower-bearing hibiscus, jasmine, anthuriums, cassias and leaf-tinted crotons. In an aviary near the beach some exotic birds have been collected, among them crested cranes, cockatoos, lories, macaws, mynahs, parrots and toucans. They are decorative but in some ways unnecessary, for the free Jamaican birds fly swiftly about singing sweetly between the branches of the trees when they are not queuing up and chirping for breakfast or lunch scraps from the tables of friendly visitors. Dragon Bay has its own small marina. At Dragon Cove there is a boat landing where water taxis call to pick up passengers on their way to the Blue Lagoon; there arrangements for many kinds of watersports can be made. Residents at Dragon Bay are given membership facilities at the San San Golf Club which is only three miles away.

An old sugar plantation, Spring Garden Estate, between Buff Bay and Orange Bay was once owned by Quintin Hogg, founder of the London Polytechnic and partner of the sugar trading firm of Hogg, Curtis and Campbell. A road from Spring Garden provides a 13-mile detour through the Spanish and Swift river valleys by way of Skibo, Chepstow and Ythanstide. It offers splendid views of towering Blue Mountain heights before rejoining the main road at Hope Bay. The condition of the road should however be checked, as it is quite steep and rough in places. Somerset Falls, nine miles west of Port Antonio, are located just half a mile to the east of Hope Bay. The falls are cascades of water which drop several hundred feet down through a deep forested gorge of natural rock in the Daniels River. Platforms have been erected for about 200 yards overlooking a spot where the waters plunge 280 feet before forming green pools in the river below.

Some of the names of places in Portland parish have undergone strange changes. The district now known as Shotover (at about 1,000 feet, in the hills overlooking Port Antonio) derived its name from the original French title of Château Vert, a property owned by a Frenchman who escaped to Jamaica during the Jacobin persecution on other Caribbean islands. Cornwall Barracks, deep in the interior of the valley of the Rio Grande recalls an army outpost during the maroon wars, while Cuffie Head, in the hill district of Mount Pleasant overlooking St Margaret's Bay is named after the maroon leader who was beheaded there. Another maroon leader, Quao, who used to control the mountainous country around Moore Town (which lies in the interior between Seamans Valley and Cornwall Barracks) is remembered by Quaw Hill which overlooks Holland Bay. Names like Millbank, Windsor, Norwich Halt, Burlington, Shrewsbury, Maidstone, Durham and Chelsea evoke memories of the years when the English in Jamaica considered themselves as only temporary exiles from the familiar places they or their fore-fathers regarded as their real homes. These names have long outlived the reasons for their being used. Others, like Nanny Town near St Ann's Bay, have survived as historical sites. The isolation of Jamaican maroons is officially ended but memories, like ghosts, linger on and in the parish of Portland the nature of the land tends to perpetuate those states of mind which were first responsible for names like Two Claw Peak, Pumpkin Hill, Corn Husk River, Hog Meat Bottom, Hard Dog Bump, Snake River and Alligator Church.

The Eastern Jamaican Anglers Association has a club

house on the waterfront overlooking Boundbrook wharf. Each year two deep-sea fishing tournaments are organised there. The International Fishing Tournament is usually held in October and is followed by a Blue Marlin team tournament. Marlins usually weigh between 400 and 200 pounds, but the record catch is over 600 pounds. Although fishing is an all-year-round activity, the most favoured months around Port Antonio are September and October.

On leaving Port Antonio I took the coastal road which follows the seashore as far south as Hectors River and then goes by way of Quaw Hill to the banana port of Bowden. About five miles beyond Boston Bay there is a sudden spectacular view of Long Bay, a wild windswept coastline of outstanding beauty where white spumed waves dash on to sands made picturesque by tall coconut palms. The eye follows a sequence of sea sand and vegetation as far as Sail Rock in the spray-lined distance. The beauty of Long Bay is similar to that of the beauty of Barbados' eastern shores near Bathsheba, but it is much more rugged. Manchioneal near Sharpnose Point has a small stone church. My chauffeur guide found rooms there at eight dollars for the night and three for breakfast. A few miles along the coastal road good views of the seashore may be seen from Belle Castle. When seas are high, incoming breakers dash against the crags and push white spray upwards in columns of 100 feet. As I followed the coast in its semi-circular path to Kingston I became aware of towering headless trunks of coconut trees. At first I thought they had lost their heads in some tropical storm or hurricane, but I soon learnt that they were victims of a dreaded yellow lethal disease which had played havoc with coconut groves in eastern Jamaica. They are being replaced by shorter, hardier Malayan varieties but for years perhaps visitors may see acres of headless lofty poles standing sentinels against the Jamaican skyline as if in mourning for their once gay, waving, green-golden, plumed branches that murmured and whispered in the trade winds. I have other memories like snapshots, of picturesque coves, fine houses, a modern farm, the Quaker school at Happy Grove, modern churches, sugar cane fields, banana groves and woodlands. In St Thomas' parish the density of traffic increased and as the road widened lorries packed high with bottles went roaring by, their tyres shrieking under pressure at sharp bends. At one major junction I was not at all surprised to read on a notice prominently displayed where to obtain ready made coffins. I could understand that it might have been intended as a bona fide service to those who had failed to keep death off the road, but it was probably no more than a happy coincidence. For any driver who saw it was likely to slow down, at least, for the next corner. Jamaican frenzy on the road seemed to contrast strangely with another characteristic I noted, the ability of the ordinary Jamaican to curl up and rest, perchance to sleep, almost anywhere. I saw some apparently asleep on oil drums and one upon a motor car bonnet!

Lady Nugent, who spent four years in Jamaica (1801-5), had found the negro houses she saw in St Thomas extremely pretty, especially along the Plantain River. As I passed by, I was reminded of the long barrack-like buildings I had seen sugar workers use near Georgetown in Guyana. Lady Nugent left a record of her visit to Golden Grove, Simon Taylor's sugar plantation near Holland Bay in east Jamaica. 'I believe he takes me for a boy', she wrote, 'as I constantly wear a habit, and have a short cropped head.' It was very hot at Golden Grove, so Lady Nugent put on a dressing gown and attempted to rest but was 'every instant interrupted by mulatto ladies', whom she found very tiresome, 'constantly liable to miscarry and subject to a thousand little complaints'. Dinner at Golden Grove was served at 5 p.m. It was substantial: a great variety of fish, barbecued hog, fried conch, black crab and pepper pot. 'Very good indeed,' Lady Nugent wrote in her diary. At Rocky Point, where there was a good harbour, she dined the following day at 6 p.m. In the centre of the table there was 'jerked hog (pork prepared in the manner of the Quichua Indians)'. The first course was black crab pepper pot; this was 'capon stewed down, large pieces of beef, another of ham also stewed to a jelly, six dozen land crabs picked fine with their eggs and fat, onions, peppers, ochras, sweetbreads and other vegetables cut small, *all well stewed.'* The second course consisted of turtle, mutton, beef, turkey, goose, ducks, chicken, capons, ham, tongue crab patties, etc. The third was sweets and fruits. After facing this gargantuan meal it is a relief to read that Lady Nugent the next day had a fine view of the sea and Manchioneal Harbour. Five days later she was off visiting a maroon settlement at Charlestown. 'The women danced', she wrote in her diary, 'and the men went through their war exercises'. The 'band was composed of all sorts of rude instruments'; one of these was a 'Coromantee flute', a long black reed played with the nose. In the midst of the mountains Lady Nugent spent a night in a house which was new and neat and 'perfectly in the Creole style'. Only there were 'a number of negros, men women and children running about in all parts of it. Never did I smell so many'. Later she wrote, 'the negros in the Creole houses sleep always on the floors, in the passages and galleries'. Throughout her stay in Jamaica Lady Nugent found more to praise in the scenery than in the people, whom she found 'uncongenial to us'. To reach Bath she had taken a most beautiful and romantic drive over the mountains. She had gone there to drink the waters and found it a lovely village at the foot of an immense mountain. To get to the bathing house, where each of four rooms had a marble bath, she rode off on horseback wearing 'her night cap, dressing gown and pokey bonnet'. The botanic garden at Bath which Lady Nugent saw was the first established in Jamaica in 1779. Among the trees she saw was the Otaheite apple, star apple, breadfruit, jackfruit, cinnamon, and cabbage and sago palms. The water, which is today piped into the baths, derives from a mineral spring and is radioactive and recommended for treatment of rheumatic patients. It is possible to ride through the Cuna Cuna Pass or Corn Puss Gap which separate the Blue and John Crow Mountains and descend to the valley of the Rio Grande.

The ruin of Stokes Hall on the road between Golden Grove and Pleasant Hill is the only reminder of the fortress house – with four solid stone towers – built by descendants of Luke Stokes, the governor of Nevis who brought 1,600 people from Nevis in 1656 to settle near Port Morant. At Morant Bay the eye can sweep along the banks of the Negro River and upwards through the Blue Mountain valley in a northwesterly direction to seek out the highest peak of the mountains near Portland Gap. Morant Bay is the capital town and shipping port of the parish of St Thomas. In front of the courthouse is Edna Manley's statue of Paul Bogle, one of Jamaica's five national war heroes.

After the hurricane of 1951 the Yallahs Land Authority was formed to curb soil erosion and develop farming over 70 square miles extending from Silver Hill Gap near Newcastle down to the shorelines of St Thomas where the Yallahs reaches the sea. Yallahs is thought to be a corruption of a Spanish name for a proprietor or his estate. When I saw the Yallahs where it enters the sea it was brown coloured and flecked with spume as it churned its waters along. At other times its channel is nearly dry. This sometimes quiet, sometimes turbulent river epitomises a parish which has witnessed periods of tranquillity and times of violence by nature and by men. For St Thomas has been struck several times by hurricanes that swept inland from the south-eastern Caribbean Sea, and it has seen periods of high productivity of sugar, when Belvedere, and Albion, Lyssons and Hordley and Golden Grove were synonyms for wealth. It has also witnessed one of the worst explosions of racial conflict in the island when desperate men took the law into their own hands and triggered off repressive measures which led to the Governor's recall to England, to years of legal controversy about his action, and to the surrender of powers by the island's House of Assembly.

TRAVELLER'S DIGEST

St Thomas Parish.

Area: 300 square miles.

Population: Over 71,000.

Capital: Morant Bay.

Main Crops: Sugar cane, bananas, coffee, nutmeg.

Mountains: Blue Mountains (Mossman's Peak over 6700, Blue Mountain Peak over 7402).

Rivers: Plantain Garden, Yallahs, Morant, Negro, Green, Morgans, West Arm, White.

Airstrips: Dalvey.

Special Interest: Bath Mineral Spring and Botanic Garden; Port Morant, Edna Manley's statue of Paul Bogle; Albion, where Albion sugar was made; Rozelle waterfall; Quaw Hill; Morant Cays, four islets about 33 miles southeast of Morant Point.

PORTLAND PARISH.

Area: 328 square miles.

Population: Over 68,000.

Capital: Port Antonio.

Other Towns: St Margaret's Bay; Buff Bay, Manchioneal.

Main Crops: Bananas and coconuts.

Mountains: Blue Mountains, John Crow, Sugar Loaf Peak (in Blue Mountains over 7000 feet).

Rivers: White, Buff Bay, Spanish, Swift, Back Rio Grande, Stony, Guava, Rio Grande, Priestmans, Drivers, Hectors.

Airstrips: Buff Bay, Ken Jones Airport, Boston Bay, Manchioneal.

Special Interest: Somerset Falls, Rafter's Rest, Bonnie View Hotel, San San Golf Club, Frenchman's Cove, Trident Villas, Dragon Bay, Blue Lagoon, Boston Beach, Long Bay, Nonsuch Caves, Moore Town.

Things to do: Horse Riding, Walking, Fishing, Golf, Rafting on Rio Grande, Yachting, Water Skiing, Swimming, Tennis.

The County of Cornwall

If Surrey may be likened to the tail and Middlesex the hind flippers and carapace of turtle-shaped Jamaica, Cornwall can be described as its head and front flippers. Second largest of Jamaica's three counties, Cornwall (1,565 square miles) comprises the five parishes of St Elizabeth, Westmoreland, Hanover, St James and Trelawny. The largest parish, St Elizabeth (474 square miles), has a population in excess of 127,000 persons. Industrialisation is marked by the alumina plant at Nain. It was constructed by Alumina Partners of Jamaica (ALPART) at a cost of $124 million. Its products are exported from the deep-water pier which the consortium of companies constructed at Port Kaiser, near Alligator Pond Bay. The excellent climate of the Santa Cruz mountains has often been praised, but never more highly than by Dr Charles Reinhardt, who said 'there is no other such place that I have ever heard of where there is so exceedingly equable and so pleasant a climate'. From Lacovia in the Black River Valley the Santa Cruz mountains run down towards the south eastern coast where they suddenly terminate at a place called Lovers' Leap, 1,660 feet above the sea. Malvern, 2,400 feet above sea level, was once a favourite hill station for Jamaicans. The drive up to Malvern from Black River Town offers splendid panoramic views of the coastline. Fifty acres of early Jamaican forest on Stanmore estate near Malvern have been recommended by the National Trust of Jamaica for preservation. Several educational institutions are located around Malvern. They include St Elizabeth's Technical High School, the Moravian Bethlehem

Training College for Women, Munro College and Hampton School. A road from Wilton crosses the Horse Savanna and runs in a circular direction around the banks of the Black River. From logwood trees in this region, dye was formerly extracted in factories at Lacovia and Elim. Several estates, of which Bogue is one, were the first in Jamaica to receive Moravian missionaries in 1754. Horse Savanna to the north and Bull Savanna in the south were named after the horses and cattle reared on their grasslands. Dairying is encouraged by the government at a training centre in Goshen and at Pepper a large dairy herd is maintained by the Kaiser Bauxite Company.

At the turn of the nineteenth century the town of Black River was important as the centre of a booming dye export trade which continued until the late 'thirties. It is reported to have been the first of Jamaican towns to be lit by electricity. Today it is a part of that 'undeveloped Jamaica' which increasingly finds favour with all Jamaicans who do not want to see their entire island transformed into a playground for tourists. The river which gave the town its name has its source in the mountains of southern Trelawny, flows underground until it emerges near Balaclava and then winds its way for over 40 miles to the sea. In earlier times small boats used its waters to travel as far as 25 miles into the interior. Crocodiles (commonly called alligators in Jamaica) used to frequent the river, but their numbers have been reduced considerably. The Great Morass east of Black River Town is a fresh-water swamp dotted with islands covered intermittently with reeds, rushes and trees. It is a popular base for sportsmen who shoot marsh birds or fish in the sea or river. Between the town and Pedro Cays to the south deep-sea fishing is generally rewarding. Some hotel and cottage accommodations are available at Treasure Beach. Middle Quarters, north of Black River is known as the shrimp capital of Jamaica. There live many families of fishermen who fish for mullet and fresh-water shrimps in the waters of the Y.S. (originally Wyess) and Middle Quarters rivers. The Holland sugar estate nearby was once owned by the father of

William Gladstone, the Liberal statesman. The two-mile avenue which leads to Lacovia is shaded by graceful overhanging canopies of bamboos, descendants of the oriental plants which were introduced into Jamaica by way of Haiti at the beginning of the eighteenth century. For some 50 years of that century Lacovia disputed with Black River Town for primacy as the most important town in St Elizabeth's parish. Some Jewish tombstones seem to corroborate Long's claim that it was once 'mostly inhabited by Jews'. One of two tombstones at the junction road leading to Maggotty (once famous for its falls) records the death of a young man who has been claimed as a member of the Spencer family which was connected by marriage to that of the Churchills.

The Nassau Valley in the north east of St Elizabeth is famous for the sugar canes which extend for miles in a mountain-ringed bowl of land. The distillery at Appleton, which may be visited by governor's coach along the railway track from Montego Bay, makes several of Jamaica's finest rums and liqueurs, as well as vodka and gin. Accompong, some miles to the north-west of Appleton, and close to the boundaries of Trelawny parish, was named after a maroon chief. It is approached by a narrow steep road which has sudden sharp turnings and skirts precipices. Physical isolation from the plains below symbolises the spiritual isolation of its people who have been described as the most African of all Jamaicans. The town's history goes back to the treaty of 1739, which is still celebrated every year with feasting and dancing on 6 January.

Near Appleton the governor's coach in which I travelled pulled in beside a shed alongside the Black River, not far from the bauxite plant at Revere. Before entering the shed and sitting on benches lunch boxes and a coke were distributed to each passenger. Rum punches, limeade and cold beer had been made available earlier after the stop at Ipswich Caves where I saw swallows flying outside and had to run the gauntlet of many wood carvers, anxious to sell their birds, plaques, trees, and other objects at a dollar apiece

Three entertainers played and sang for us at lunch, like
minstrels of old, while we ate our hardboiled eggs, sand-
wiches, a piece of corn bread and a banana: simple fare
indeed, but particularly suited to the relaxed atmosphere of
persons taking a holiday.

Westmoreland, the most westerly of all Jamaica's parishes,
was until modern times predominantly a parish of large
cattle and sugar estates. Trollope in 1859 referred to its
'lovely park-like landscapes'. On the Great River Valley lay
the rich estates that were raided in the great slave rebellion
of 1831. Between the banks of the Great River and
Savanna-la-Mar were the plantations of Beckfords, Lewis,
Vassalls, Ricketts and others whose wealth brought fame and
fortune in England. Among them were Lady Holland, the
great Whig hostess who inherited Friendship Estate, Vis-
count St Vincent, a grandson of George Ricketts, William
Beckford, twice Lord Mayor of London and Matthew Lewis,
owner of Cornwall Estate. The democratic open way of life
on these plantations in the early nineteenth century con-
trasted strongly with that of the elegant upper classes in
Regency England. Matthew Lewis, of whom Lord Byron
wrote affectionately:

> *I would give many a sugar cane*
> *Mat Lewis were alive again,'*

has left us in his *Journal of a West Indian Proprietor* (1834) a
vivid description of a great house:

> The houses are absolutely transparent; the walls are
> nothing but windows – and all the doors stand open. No
> servants are in waiting to announce arrivals: visitors,
> negroes, dogs, cats, poultry, all walk in and out, and up
> and down your livingrooms, without the slightest
> ceremony.... Many a time has my delicacy been put to
> the blush by the ill-timed civility of some old woman or
> other, who wandering that way... has stopped her course
> to curtsy very gravely and pay me the passing compliment
> of 'Ah, massa! Bless you, massa! How day?'

In 1909 a large factory was erected at Frome to grind canes grown on Belle Isle, Fontabelle and Frome plantations. From this factory has developed the large central factory which was established by a subsidiary of Tate & Lyle of London, in the late thirties of this century to accommodate the greatly expanded growth of canes in Westmoreland and neighbouring Hanover.

Banister Bay between Bluefields and Scott's Cove recalls the landing of sugar planters who came from Surinam with Banister, after the British government gave Lord Willoughby's Guianese plantation to the Dutch by the Treaty of Breda (which brought New Amsterdam, later New York under the English flag). The coastal area between Bluefields and Whitehouse is still called Surinam Quarters. Bluefields which is generally believed to have been built on the site of an early Spanish settlement, Oristan, marks the end of an Old Spanish road which ran from the mouth of the Martha Brae, where Falmouth was built. For eighteen months the great house at Bluefields was the residence of Philip Henry Gosse, author of the colourful *Birds of Jamaica* (1847) and *A Naturalist's Sojourn in Jamaica* (1851). The mountain scenery and the wooded hills above Bluefields Bay which delighted the zoologist from Worcester still fascinate lovers of natural beauty. A magnificent view of the sugar plains of Westmoreland and the western shores of Jamaica may be had by anyone prepared to drive up the twisting road which leads from Whithorn Village to the tobacco-growing district near Darliston.

Savanna-La-Mar, with a population of approximately 12,000, is the port used by the West India Sugar Company's factory at Frome. There is a constant movement of trucks near the pier during the first six months of the year. A modern power generating station and telecommunications have prepared the way for the gradual growth of Savanna-La-Mar as an important industrial centre in south-western Jamaica. Cattle raising, sugar cane culture and fishing have been the traditional occupations of a town which has suffered extensively and often from hurricanes. Admiral

Knowles, who inspected the port in 1755, judged it to be the worst in the island and was contemptuous of an unfinished fort, a third of which had fallen under the sea. Among places of special interest are 22 Beckford Street, where some old Jewish tombstones record earlier times; 54 Beckford Street, headquarters of the Hope Lodge 2813 of the English Craft Masons; and Manning's School, which was first endowed by a Westmoreland slave owner in 1710.

There is a golf course at Ferris, five miles east of Savanna-La-Mar where the Paradise Club offers a plantation tour, horseback riding and a visit to Palm Jungle Gardens.

The strangely named Little London, about six miles north-west of Savanna-La-Mar, is populated largely by East Indians who are descended from immigrants who came to Jamaica in the nineteenth century. German immigrants who were introduced by the absentee proprietor, Baron Seaford, were settled in eastern Westmoreland at the town which still bears his name. The oriental stone gateways at New Hope Estate have been attributed to a mason from Barbados and were erected soon after the end of the First World War. Not far from New Hope is the Anglican church of St Paul's, which is surrounded by fields of sugar cane.

South Negril Point is the most westerly point in Jamaica and lies between the lighthouse and Negril village, which is famous as the port from which West Indian regiments sailed against New Orleans in 1814. The boundaries of Westmoreland and Hanover (the northern half of the turtle's head) meet halfway along the five-mile-long white sandy beach fringed with palms. For most of Jamaica's history this beach was neglected by residents because the Great Morass behind it bred mosquitoes and resisted the advance of modern communications and general amenities. In modern times the government set up a Negril Land Authority which prepared the way for development by draining the Morass and building roads. Today the scenic road from Montego Bay brings Negril beach within one and a quarter hour's driving distance from that town. One tour operator offers a seven-hour circle tour, with a three-hour stop at Negril for swimming and lunch, and a return trip through Savanna-La-Mar and into the interior by way of Whithorn, Knockalva and the cattle ranches of Shettlewood and Montpelier.

Jamaicans want to keep Negril as a holiday resort where visitors from overseas do not take precedence over Jamaican workers, and their families. The government selected Negril and Hellshire (near Port Henderson) as sites for a two million pound beach cottage development within the reach of Jamaican workers and their families, and at the same time available for rental to visitors from abroad. Special emphasis has been laid on appeals to trade union members and their families from overseas to take holidays near these beaches.

Long Bay separates Negril village in Westmoreland from Negril Harbour in Hanover. On the hill overlooking Negril village is Whitehall great house with rooms to let. Between Whitehall and the modern Sundowner Hotel in the centre of the bay are many thatched-roof huts for rental. Other places which welcome visitors are the Negril Yacht Club and the Negril Sands Club. Horses for riding are available from Whitehall.

The determination that the west coasts of Jamaica will not become like Montego Bay was given official voice early in 1975 when the Jamaican minister whose portfolio includes tourism, said that the original plans for a 450-room hotel at Rutland Point near the 600-yard Negril airstrip 'would have been a disaster'. Instead, he said, the new 250-room hotel which would be operated by Issa Hotels was designed to attract young active visitors in search of informality, water and land sports at rates within the reach of 'modest budgets'.

Except for Kingston, Hanover (177 square miles) is the smallest parish in Jamaica. It is well watered and there are hills rising to 1,809 feet at Birchs Hill and 1789 at Dolphin Head. At Round Hill, just across the Great River that divides Hanover from St James, one of the early modern cottage-type hotel colonies was established in the early 'fifties of this century. Before the 'fifties were out, another winter colony had followed at the neighbouring Tryall Estate where a 19-hole championship golf course was also laid out. An old mill wheel turned by water brought by aqueducts and gutters from the Flint River was restored at the same time. In the nineteenth century it had been used to produce power for the sugar factory at Tryall. Parts of an old estate house were utilised in the hotel complex.

Hanover Polo Club field at Blue Hole, a little over a mile from Sandy Bay is often used during the winter months, especially on Thursdays. There are old sugar works on Kenilworth Estate, previously owned by the Blagrove family who also owned Cardiff Hall in St Ann's.

Lucea, the chief town, is picturesquely set on the western side of an almost landlocked harbour. It is famous for its yams. Fort Charlotte is well maintained and has two cannons made during the reign of George III. The monument to Sir Simon Clarke in the church was sculpted by John Flaxman, who also sculpted the memorial to his wife Lady Clarke in Tewkesbury Abbey. Haughton Court estate, which is just outside Lucea, recalls one of the earliest settlers from Barbados. Blenheim, not far from Davis Cove, is the birthplace of national hero and first Prime Minister of Jamaica, Sir Alexander Bustamante. His father was an overseer on Blenheim Estate. The village of Dias, about two miles farther, commemorates an eighteenth-century Jewish landowning family.

Bloody Bay, or Negril Harbour, probably got its name from the blood of whales killed in the harbour area. It is an extension of Long Bay, which is associated in Jamaican history with several adventurous exploits and particularly with the arrests of the pirate Rackham, his mistress Ann Bonney and her female companion Mary Read.

Booby Bay, or Gibraltar, at the northern end of Long Bay, was used by the Walt Disney team which made the film *Twenty Thousand Leagues Under the Sea*. Around the eastern boundaries of Hanover near the Great River are famous grazing lands like Shettlewood and Haughton Grove. The Indian cattle of Shettlewood were one of the breeds preferred by planters because of their strength and immunity to ticks.

Shettlewood and Montpelier on the other side of the river were stocked by the Hon. Evelyn Ellis in the last decade of the nineteenth century with imported Zebu and Mysore cattle. Mr Ellis also built an elaborate hotel at Montpelier which Stark described in 1898 as the 'most richly furnished' in Jamaica. The 200-acre estate at Knockalva is today used as a practical agricultural training centre. Good views of the cattle-grazing country on both sides of the Great River are obtained from the governor's coach, which runs three times weekly between Montego Bay and Appleton especially for visitors. The station from which the coach starts is genuine old Jamaica, built in quarters which were typical of pre-war West Indian towns throughout the Caribbean. The coach when I travelled was grey-green. Inside the car the mood was friendly but the seats were hard. A large poster greeted us with an invitation to make love without becoming a family man. Our guide welcomed us with a loud hailer through which he spoke continuously, retailing anecdotes and information. He only took a rest near the Anglican church at Catadupa on the outskirts of the Cockpit country. There the local clergyman and his wife encouraged us to join in singing and playing the organ, a useful preliminary to the collection which was taken outside. Our first stop had been at Anchovy, where the Bogue islands are visible in green-grey water, and behind them, the high-rise Heritage Beach condominiums and ships at Montego Freeport. At Anchovy Miss Lisa Salmon's bird sanctuary should be visited at feed time (4 p.m.). Between Anchovy and Montpelier the countryside is fairly tidy and in places enclosed. Bamboos are plentiful and on many trees clusters of wild orchids are visible from the coach. I could also recognise mangos, golden apples, citrus trees and coconuts. Only once did I see men on horses rounding up cattle. As we approached Cambridge the forest became dense and only an occasional bunch of mauve flowers on a tall palm tree or white frangipani flowers relieved the perpetual green vegetation which stretched unbroken eastwards to the Cockpit country. Catadupa, where coffee beans are washed and pulped between September and February, was expecting us. There village women had hung out gay printed dresses, shirts and lengths of cloth. On both sides of the street wood carvings, straw baskets, necklaces and other souvenirs were also laid out for inspection.

Outside the area of active selling, beside a stone on which I read the inscription 'Psalms 109' and the word 'SNOBS' in capital letters, I spoke with a few young men. When I asked them what life in Catadupa was like, one replied, the church people get everything and we are squeezed out. After a pause for shopping the guide took us to a small planted area where he briefly told us about the plants we saw. He then warned us never to eat ackee fruit from a tree because it is deadly poisonous. Catadupa is as near as most visitors to Jamaica will ever get to the Cockpit country where places with names like the District of Look Behind, Quick Step, Me No Sen You No Come, Rest and Be Thankful indicate a quality of life far removed from that of Jamaica's No. 1 tourist resort which sprawls above, around, through and outwards from the islands' second largest town at Montego Bay in the parish of St James.

The fame of Montego Bay as a holiday resort originated with a cave that had a sandy floor beneath. This cave was responsible for the name of the popular Doctor's Cave Bathing Beach, where the water is very salt and buoyant and which has been recommended to sufferers from rheumatic complaints. Before the Second World War a number of good small hotels had begun to attract visitors in increasing numbers each year and in 1949 I was able to fly there directly from Nassau in a small plane which took a long time to get across Cuba. Twenty five years later in a sleek Air Jamaica plane I landed at an airport which had acquired an imposing runway, but with terminal buildings and general amenities that seemed to me far behind those of other famous airports in the Caribbean. Not surprisingly the Jamaican government announced soon after plans for major improvements at the Montego Bay and Kingston airports. These improvements should go a long way to complement the remarkable efforts that Air Jamaica and the Jamaica Tourist Board have both made to promote the island's attractions as an all-year-round holiday resort.

The pace of hotel building in Montego Bay was so rapid in the 'sixties that the beautiful Doctor's Cave Beach and the buildings around it and the magnificent bay now look like survivals of a past age. One reason for the extension of the hotel district eastwards has been the pursuit of beaches. In the 'fifties Crescent Beach was acquired by a group of shareholders brought together by a Jamaican, Harold de Lisser. Today this beach is incorporated into Half Moon Hotel, which is a beautiful landscaped, tree-shaded cottage-type resort standing on fields once used for growing sugar cane. The excellence of Half Moon is perhaps best realised by the 30 per cent of its winter visitors who are happy to return each year. There is a golf course across the road, laid out by Robert Trent Jones; the club house is built near to a disused water-wheel. The golf course is a part of the 6,000-acre Rose Hall property owned by Mr John Rollins of Wilmington, Delaware. Mr Rollins also rebuilt Rose Hall great house, which was famous in Jamaican legend for the so-called 'white witch', who died by strangling in 1827 during an insurrection of her slaves. Beautiful but cruel sums her up. Rose Hall, which was built in the mid-eighteenth century, had become a ruin before the end of the nineteenth century. A description in the Journal of the Institute of Jamaica, quoted by Stark in his *Jamaica Guide* of 1898, still holds good for the imposing flight of stone steps which leads to the main entrance of the mansion. Through massive folding doors of solid mahogany four inches thick, access was given to a hall 40 feet long, 30 feet wide and 18 feet high. There was a magnificent staircase, highly polished, with rails, balustrades and mouldings carved out of sandalwood.

Anne Palmer was the white witch of Rose Hall, but an earlier Mrs Rose Palmer was the first mistress of Rose Hall mansion. Rose was greatly beloved by her husband John, who, on her death, commissioned the famous English sculptor John Bacon to carve her profile on a medallion which still hangs in the parish church of Montego Bay. Unlike the notorious Anne, who later married a grand-nephew of John Palmer, Rose was 'open, cheerful and agreeable'. Anne by contrast was cruel and self indulgent.

Like the Greeks, who gave pleasant names to places in hopes of propitiating local spirits, Jamaican planters chose friendly names for their estates. Encircling Montego Bay are plantations with ingratiating titles like Golden Grove, Friendship, Canaan, Paradise, Amity, Hope, Loveliest and Sweet Water. I expected to find roses at Rose Hall and was very disappointed to discover that the weeds had run wild in the garden near the artificial lake. The welcoming stone steps leading up to the entrance were magnificent, but inside Rose Hall had become a museum piece, a place reconstructed for visitors, who were also invited to buy a large colourfully illustrated souvenir volume of the mansion. The old Rose Hall legend has now been transformed into a novelty for visitors to the hotel and other developments that have sprung up around Rose Hall, but something has been lost in the process. At Sam Lord's Castle in Barbados, old mirrors, original ceilings and fine specimens of Regency furniture give the impression of a Georgian mansion where gracious living is still possible. At Rose Hall enormous sums of money have been spent to create a style of old West Indian living which seems at great variance with the contemporary records of observers like Lady Nugent and Matt Lewis. Four-poster beds, imitation Chippendale chairs, elaborate wallpapers, and fine stairways give impressions of opulence, but of late nineteenth century *nouveau-riche* opulence rather than of the age of elegance. And because it is a show place the quiet dignity of the mansion is irretrievably lost.

Up a winding country road five miles from Montego Bay another more successful attempt has been made to give visitors the sensation of living in a gracious Jamaican past. There, over 60 acres of an old plantation of pimento trees, an Englishman, Jack Gold and his American-born wife Annette have made Sign great house a place of spacious relaxation for those who enjoy natural surroundings tamed by man.

Modern accommodations equipped with four-poster beds and furnished in Jamaican style ensure comfortable backgrounds for activities which include horseback riding and fishing or boating on a lake fed by mountain water. The taming of the acres on Sign Plantation may have encouraged the Tourist Board to create another beautiful park downhill at Irwin. There Dr Jack Regan has created much beauty at the splendid Tropic Gardens, which are approached from Montego Bay by way of a bamboo canopied road. Towering bamboo trees provide refreshing shade at the back of the gardens where an artificial waterfall is pumped up from the river below. Songbirds and gay flowering plants are attractions of a park which is equipped with refreshment bars and souvenir shops.

Ten miles west of Montego Bay the Great River, which divides Hanover from St James' parish flows into the Caribbean sea. On this river, when the weather is suitable, the Jamaican Tourist Board organises evenings of entertainment, which include torchlit boat journeys, Jamaican style dinner, floorshow, music for dancing, and shopping for nutmegs, brown sugar and other Jamaican specialities at a country store. East of Montego Bay in the area of the Rose Hall Intercontinental Hotel, tuition in riding and excursions over selected trails is available at the Spot Valley Equestrian Centre, where show-jumping and gymkhana events are put on during special seasons of the year. Riding is also arranged for guests of the Fairfield Hotel and Country Club which is inland from Montego Bay on the west of the Montego River. Guests at Fairfield are also entitled to use the hotel's 9-hole golf course and the facilities of the Montego Bay Racquet Club, where tennis can be played at night on seven teleflex courts. Montego Bay is a centre for sea sports. Up to 50 people at a time can go cruising through the Bogue islands to Montego Freeport or can take advantage of other facilities for sailing, fishing or scuba diving. There is a marina east of the town near the highway junction. The Montego Bay Yacht Club organises an annual Easter regatta and every second year the Pineapple Trophy is awarded to the winner of the Miami-Montego Bay Race. The club also arranges an annual marlin-fishing tournament every September.

Two companies operate private flying services from Montego Bay's airport. Jamaica Air Service has daily flights to Ocho Rios, Port Antonio and Kingston, while Jamaica Air Taxi Service is ready at any reasonable time to fly visitors to a choice of more than 40 destinations where landings are possible on Jamaica.

St James' tourist strips run roughly from the western to the eastern boundaries at the northern end of the parish. There is, however, a choice of rides or drives into the interior either along the railway route taken by the governor's coach or by car, bus or taxi. St James was the parish of famous Jamaican families like the Barretts, Scarletts, Moultons and Lawrences. One member of these related families, Sarah Goodin Moulton, has been made immortal in the painting, 'Pinkie', which Sir Thomas Lawrence exhibited at the Royal Academy in 1797. Sarah was the sister of Edward Moulton who took the name of Barrett when he inherited Jamaican estates, and was the father of the poet Elizabeth who married another poet Robert Browning. A cemetery on Cinnamon Hall Estate above Rose Hall is still used by members of the Barrett family. The Queen of Spain's Valley runs from the eastern parts of St James across the boundary into Trelawny parish. Hampden Estate was once a large sugar plantation on which the Gale's Valley sugar factory stood for years like a Roman ruin until it was removed to Mona, stone by stone to be erected as a special chapel donated to the first chancellor of the University of the West Indies, Princess Alice, Countess of Athlone.

The Martha Brae, Jamaica's third largest river, rises in the Cockpit country which forms a great portion of southern Trelawny. Windsor Castle, on the borders of the Cockpits, once was famous for its well-furnished great house. The caves at Windsor are large and open to the public. There is a ten-mile bush trail leading from Windsor to Troy in the parish of Manchester. Only the adventurous should consider taking it. Arawak rock carvings have been found at caves in

Pontrepant some miles further west. The house at Good Hope, five miles inland from Falmouth, is well preserved and is opened as a hotel during the winter months. Guided tours are offered during the summer and private motorists starting from Falmouth may include Hampden, Wakefield, Bunkers Hill and Adelphi on their return to Montego Bay.

Good Hope has earned the name of a dude ranch because 200 miles of marked trails radiate from the plantation's centre. In 1974 there were 70 horses available for riding.

One of Cornwall's most exciting places to visit is the crocodile farm near Salt Marsh Bay on the outskirts of Falmouth town. Crocodiles were unknown on the north coast of Jamaica until the arrival some years ago of Ross Kananga, who claims descent from Seminole Indians on the mainland of America. Today's tourist brochures claim that up to 1,000 crocodiles and nine alligators roam Kananga's ranch. I did not attempt to count them, but as I crossed a small roadway that could also be used by crocodiles on either side of a small forest I appreciated the point of Ross's printed warning: 'Trespassers will be eaten'. The teeth of the saurians I saw (it matters not whether crocodile or alligator) were made more frightening because Ross told me he had received no less than 92 stitches after contact with one of them. Nothing went wrong on the morning of my visit, however, and I was free to admire (at a safe distance) Ross's feeding of a jumping saurian, his pier for motor boat trips through the swamps, his thatched hut with relics, his act with a Jamaican snake, and his lion and black panther (in cages). Kananga's ranch is a great antidote for any holiday maker who finds Jamaica too relaxing a place, but no place for children. The place to leave them is in the play area of Rafter's Village. From there bamboo rafts may be taken for two miles down the Martha Brae river to Rock on the coast. Rafters are met at Rock and taken back to Rafter's Village where rafting certificates are issued as souvenirs. Restaurant shops and a swimming pool are some of the amenities provided at the village. Rock has water which gives off a luminous glow when struck; trips over its lagoon are sometimes made after dark from the Fisherman's Inn restaurant. Visitors are also invited to see the processing of cloth at the Caribatik factory in Rock. Falmouth, the capital of Trelawny parish, was an important sugar port in 1837 when Trelawny still contained 76 sugar estates, two coffee plantations and several livestock farms, or pens. Falmouth in England had been the birthplace of William Trelawny, the governor of Jamaica after whom the parish was named. The court house, built in 1815 and restored in 1926 after a fire, is evidence of the importance of a town which has other fine surviving buildings.

The imposing parish church in Duke Street was begun in 1796 and extended in 1842. The Baptist church was completed in 1948 as a memorial to William Knibb, the son of a Kettering tailor, who toured the British Isles in support of the abolition of slavery, and who died in a village near Falmouth named Kettering after his birthplace. The Catholic church of St Joseph in Rodney Street was consecrated in 1966. Some upper balconied houses have survived on Market Street and there are some old warehouses rooted in past history.

The development at New Falmouth of the high-rise 350-room Trelawny Beach Hotel, with its new 18-hole golf course has completed a progress of tourism on the north coast of Jamaica which has been advancing steadily for 20 years. It was very new and lacking in shade trees when I saw it and I was most surprised to find that the price of a beer (not particularly cold) was 15 cents higher than in the best hotels of Montego Bay. But all hotels go through a teething stage and Trelawny as a parish should benefit greatly from the establishment of a hotel along one of Jamaica's best sandy beaches.

TRAVELLERS' DIGEST

St Elizabeth Parish

Area: 474 square miles

Population: Over 126,600

Capital: Black River

Other Towns: Lacovia, Santa Cruz, Newmarket, Siloah, Malvern, Maggotty

Maroon Settlement: Accompong

Mountains: Lacovia, Nassau, Santa Cruz

Rivers: Black, Broad, YS, Smith

Agriculture: Sugar cane, rice

Industries: Bauxite, sugar, liquors, tomato canning

Other Activities: Horse and mule breeding, fishing

Special interest: Lovers' Leap, Treasure Beach Hotel, Black River, Bamboo Avenue, Appleton, Port Kaiser, Malvern.

Airstrips: Nain, Lovely Point, Union, Appleton, New Holland

Heights: Malvern (2,378 feet); Blackwood Hill (2,292 feet)

WESTMORELAND PARISH

Area: 320 square miles

Population: Over 113,000

Capital: Savanna-La-Mar

Other Towns: Little London, Petersfield, Bethel, Williamsfield, Darliston

Fishing Ports: Bluefields, Little Bay, Negril, Cave, Whitehouse

Rivers: Negril, New Savanna, Morgans, Thicket, Cabarita, Roaring, Robins

Heights: Pinnock Wood (2,533 feet); Orange Hill (2,104 feet); Burnt Savanna (500 feet).

Agriculture: Sugar cane, rice, bananas, ginger, pimentos, logwood, bee-keeping.

Industry: Sugar and rum factory at Frome

Airstrips: Banister Bay, Crab Pond Bay, Savanna-La-Mar, Frome, Alma, Grange Hill

Special Interest: Negril Beach, Frome Central Factory, Paradise Park and Club, Savanna-La-Mar, Bluefields, Roaring River Source, Seaford Town (settled by German immigrants).

HANOVER PARISH

Area: 177 square miles

Population: Approximately 60,000

Capital: Lucea

Rivers: Orange, Grand Island, Davis Cove, Lucea East, Lucea West, Flint, Great

Heights: Birchs Hill (1,809 feet); Dolphin Head (1,789 feet); Old Pen (1,569 feet).

Airstrips: Long Bay, Sandy Bay

Main Crops: Bananas, ginger, sugar cane, pimento, yams, arrowroot

Other Economic Activities: Rum, cattle breeding, tourism.

Special Interest: Blenheim (birthplace of Sir William Bustamante), Green Island, Hopewell (tourist resort), Bloody Bay, Long Bay, Lucea, Grazing pens at Shettlewood and Houghton Grove, Old Waterwheel at Tryall; 18-hole golf course at Tryall; evening on the Great River.

ST JAMES' PARISH

Area: 240 square miles

Population: Approximately 105,000

Capital: Montego Bay

Other Towns: Cambridge, Ducketts, Seven Rivers, Chesterfield, Adelphi, Montpelier, Catadupa

Airport: Sangster International

Freeport: around Bogue Islands

Main Crops: Sugar cane, bananas, coffee

Industry: Tourism, light industries (at Ironshore and Bogue Industrial Estate, Freeport).

Railway: through St James, St Elizabeth, Manchester, Clarendon and St Catherine to Kingston.

Rivers: Great, Montego

Heights: Kempshot Hill (1,850 feet); Palmyra (1,366 feet); Spot Valley (1,103 feet).

Special Interest: Rocklands Bird Sanctuary at Anchovy, Rose Hall Great House, Sign Great House, Tropic Gardens, Governors Coach trip to Appleton, Montego Freeport, Parish Church, County of Cornwall Hospital, Richmond Hill, Half Moon Club House, Calymento Botanical Gardens, Meet the People Programme—Mrs Lawrence, telephone 952-4425

Sailing: Montego Bay Yacht Club, Annual Easter Regatta, Miami-Montego Bay Race, Monta Ray Cruises from Casa Blanca pier, D. Jolly Dolphin Cruises

Fishing: Marlin tournament in September

Scuba Diving: Instructions for beginners. Pond House Reef, Point Reef, Unity Hall Reef.

Golf: Half Moon/Rose Hall 18-hole course: Ironshore 18-hole course; Fairfield Golf and Tennis Club 9-hole course

Tennis: Montego Bay Racquet Club, Fairfield Golf and Tennis Club.

Riding: Fairfield Golf and Tennis Club, Sign Great House, Spot Valley.

Eating Places: Half Moon Club House Grill, Admiral's Inn, Town House, Rose Hall Great House, Ramparts Inn, Buddles, Villa's Rum Barrel, Richmond Hill.

TRELAWNY PARISH

Area: 352 square miles

Population: Approximately 63,000

Capital: Falmouth

Other Towns: Clark's Town, Stewart Town, Rio Bueno, Duncans, Albert Town, Ulster Spring

Cockpit Villages: Troy, Wait-a-Bit, Warsop

Rivers: Martha Brae, Hectors

Airstrips: Hampden, Braco

Main Crops: Sugar cane, pimento, ginger, bananas.

Industries: Tourism, sugar, rum

Special Interest: Cockpit county, Rafting and Fishing on Martha Brae, Falmouth Town, Florida Bathing Beach, Derby Beach, Windsor Caves, Good Hope Plantation, Jamaica Safari Crocodile Farm, Shell craft centre, Hampden Sugar Estate, Caribatik factory and Luminous Lagoon at Rock.

Golf: Trelawny Beach 18-hole course.

CHRONOLOGY

4 May	1494	Columbus landed at Dry Harbour
	1510	Sevilla Nueva founded
	1517	Negroes first imported from Africa
	1523	Diego Columbus suppressed Indian revolt
	1534	Villa de la Vega founded
	1597	Sir Anthony Shirley marched on Villa de la Vega
	1600	Newport attacked Villa de la Vega
	1624	Bishopric of Jamaica annexed to archbishopric of San Domingo
	1626	Attempted invasion by Dutch off Negril Point
	1643	Jackson attacked Villa de la Vega
	1655	Venables' army landed at Passage Fort. March on Villa de la Vega
11 May	1655	Spaniards surrender to Penn and Venables. Jamaica 'became a ship anchored in the middle of the Caribbean sea, pointed at the Spanish Empire'.
	1656	Settlement of Nevis planters near Port Morant
	1661	D'Oyley appointed first governor
	1664	First meeting of general assembly Governor Modyford brought 1,000 settlers from Barbados.
	1665	First factor of Royal African Company arrived in Jamaica
	1670	Spain recognises English right to Jamaica
	1675	1,200 settlers from Surinam land at Surinam Quarters in the then parish of St Elizabeth (now Westmoreland)
	1678	Assembly resist constitutional changes put forward by the earl of Carlisle

	1681	Sir Henry Morgan puts down pirates in Cow Bay
	1685	Negro revolt
	1687	Sir Hans Sloane arrives with 2nd duke of Albemarle
		First Postmaster appointed
	1692	Port Royal destroyed by earthquake
	1693	Foundation of Kingston
	1694	Du Casse landed at Cow Bay and sacked neighbourhood
	1699	Refugees from Scotch colony of Darien settle in the then St Elizabeth parish
	1703	Formation of parish of Westmoreland
	1710	Thomas Manning bequeathed estate for foundation of parish school
	1711	Western Jamaica struck by hurricane. Losses of £700,000 in parish of Westmoreland
	1713	England obtains contract to supply Spanish colonies with slaves
	1715	Fire causes destruction of Port Royal
28 August	1722	Hurricane severely damaged Kingston and new Port Royal
	1723	Formation of parish of Portland
	1726	Over 4,000 seamen die of sickness off Port Royal
	1730 ⎫ 1732 ⎬ 1734 ⎭	Skirmishes with maroons
	1736	Wolmer School founded, Kingston
	1738	Maroons granted 2,500 acres of land
	1740	Charitable school founded in Vere
20 October	1744	Storm and earthquake. Savanna-La-Mar wrecked. Severe damage done to Port Royal, Kingston, Old Harbour and Passage Fort
	1744	Peter Beckford school founded, Spanish Town

1750	British replaced by Spanish contractors as suppliers of slaves to Spanish American colonies. Expansion of Cuban sugar industry which rose from 50,000 quintals in 1750 to 650,000 in 1800
1753	Moravian missionaries given 1,000 acres in St Elizabeth
1756	School founded at Old Woman's Savannah, Clarendon
1758	Formation of counties of Cornwall, Middlesex and Surrey
1760	Slave rebellion in parish of St Mary. 600 Africans transported to Bay of Honduras
1762	Havana fell to the English
1768	Jamaica has 651 sugar estates
1770	Martin Rusea school founded, Hanover
1774	Jamaican assembly asked English government to stop importation of slaves into Jamaica
1776–83	England at war with thirteen American colonies
1778	Nelson took part in unsuccessful expedition from Jamaica against San Juan de Nicaragua
	Spain grants freedom of trade with American colonies to all Spanish towns
1779–83	Spain at war with England
1780	Jamaica has 150 coffee plantations
1782	Rodney wins sea battle of des Saintes, and saves Jamaica
1783	Loyalist families leave America for Jamaica
1784–86	Severe storms. Many negroes died of famine
1786	Jamaica has 1,061 sugar estates
1789	Spaniards decreed freedom of trade in negroes

Revolution in Hispaniola and France

Arrival of first Wesleyan missionary

1793   Bligh introduced fruit trees and new sugar cane varieties from South Seas

1795–96   Maroon rebellion. Five hundred maroons shipped to Nova Scotia (later transferred to Sierra Leone)

1796–1802   Spain at war with England

1796   Jamaica has 769 sugar plantations (mostly in hands of attorneys)

1797   Spain allows Spanish colonies to trade with neutrals

1799   Jamaica has 686 coffee plantations

1800   Scottish Missionary Society established

1807   Slave trade abolished by Parliament of United Kingdom

1814   English Baptist missionaries arrive

1824   Dr Lipscomb becomes first bishop of Jamaica

1831   Negro uprising in Cornwall

1833   Parliament granted Jamaican slave-holders £5,853,975 as compensation for freeing 300,000 slaves

1 August   1834   Abolition of slavery. Introduction of apprenticeship system

1837   Jamaica has 670 sugar factories

1838   Total abolition of slavery

1842   Indian and German immigrants established on plantations

Royal Mail Steam Packet Company established

1845   Opening of Jamaican Railway

1846   Withdrawal of British tariff protection of sugar

1850   Death of 32,000 persons in cholera epidemic

1853   Formation of Royal Agricultural Society

	1854	Formation of Royal Society of Arts
	1855	Formation of Jamaica Militia
	1856	Jamaica relinquishes responsibility for Mosquito Shore protectorate
	1861	Religious revival. Price rises caused by American Civil War
		Moravian Training College for Women Teachers opened
	1863	Floods, followed by drought
11 October	1865	Outbreak at Morant Bay. Martial law declared
		Jamaica becomes a Crown Colony
	1866	Jamaica given new constitution
		Parishes reduced to 14. Organisation of semi-military police, medical services and department of public works
	1868	Fruit trade established between Port Antonio and the United States
	1869	Telegraphic communications opened to Europe via Havana
	1870	Disestablishment of Anglican Church
		Kingston chosen as seat of government
	1872	Mongoose introduced
		Beginning of West Indian Reference Library
	1874	Turks and Caicos islands annexed to Jamaica
		Formation of Institute of Jamaica
	1881	Bridging of rivers along north coast of Portland
11 December	1882	Great fire in Kingston
	1881–1921	Years of migration to United States and Panama
	1883	Increase in number of elected members of legislative council
		Crossman Commission to investigate finance

	1889	Jamaican Railway sold to American syndicate
27 January	1891	Prince George of Wales opened Jamaican International Exhibition Opening of first Teachers' Institute
	1892	Free elementary education introduced
	1894	Jamaican Railway extended to Montego Bay
	1896	Widening of franchise for fourteen members elected to legislative council
	1897	Jamaica and other sugar-producing islands in the West Indies visited by Royal Commission
	1898	Direct telegraphic communications established with England
	1900	Government re-acquired control of Jamaica Railway
	1901	Agricultural and commercial depression. £20,000 spent on tourist promotion. Direct steamship service established between Jamaica and England
	1903	Hurricane destroys banana fields
	1906	Jamaica Militia disbanded
	1907	Earthquake kills 800 and causes over £2 million loss of property in Kingston
	1907–13	Rebuilding of Kingston
	1910	Visit of Canadian mission
	1911	Formation of Boy Scouts Establishment of central governing body for secondary schools
	1912	Hurricane Formation of Agricultural Loan Bank
	1914–18	Ten thousand Jamaicans served overseas in World War One
	1914	Garvey founded United Negro Improvement Association
	1922	YWCA formed

	Tourist Trade Development Board formed
1924	YMCA formed
1929	Jamaica Banana Producers Association formed
1934–38	Economic depression. Emigration outlets to Panama and Cuba closed
1938	Riots
1939–46	Jamaicans served overseas in World War Two
1942	Public Health training centre established
1944	Representative government established under adult suffrage
	Hotel Aids Law
1947	Textile Industry Encouragement Act
1948	Cement Industry Law
1949	Pioneer Industries Encouragement Law
1950	Jamaica has 24 sugar factories
	Bauxite and Alumina Industries Encouragement Law
1950–68	Emigration (mostly to U.K.) accounts for over 30 per cent of natural growth of population
1952	Industrial Development Corporation
1955	Reconstitution of Tourist Board
1956	Industrial Incentives Law – outright tax holidays
	Export Industries Encouragement Law
	Small Business Loans Board
1958–62	Jamaica a member of West Indies Federation
1959	Development Finance Corporation
1961	Central Bank established
August 1962	Jamaica becomes independent monarchy within the Commonwealth
1963-64	Esso petroleum refinery built

1969 Air Jamaica inaugurates service to United States
1972 Election of PNP Government
1974 Air Jamaica inaugurates service to United Kingdom
1975 Air Jamaica inaugurates service to West Germany

BIBLIOGRAPHY

When Jamaica was chosen in the 'forties of this century to be the site of the University of the West Indies it was partly in recognition of Jamaica's importance as a pacesetter of West Indian culture. Early writers like H. G. de Lisser and Claude McKay were forerunners of a stream of creative painters, dancers, poets and novelists. Some modern writers like Andrew Salky, Orlando Patterson, John Hearne, Rex Nettleford and Evan Jones have established themselves in the front rank of modern English writers, while others like Louise Bennet and Vic Reid have turned towards the enrichment of Jamaican dialect and folk customs which have been influenced by African culture.

Other Jamaicans have written books about the history, sociology and economy of their island and have also contributed articles to journals, magazines and newspapers which chronicle the island's past and present progress and sometimes suggest patterns for the future development. Among recent books I find especially stimulating *The Politics of Change: A Jamaican Testimony,* by Michael Manley, who became Prime Minister in February 1972. His political testament, published in 1974, may be described as an act of faith in the creation of a classless Jamaican society. It ought to be read in conjunction with Owen Jefferson's *The Post-War Economic Development of Jamaica* (1974). A companion book to these two modern assessments of the Jamaican social, political and economic condition might be *Jamaica The Old and New* (1963), by Mary Manning Carley.

For those who are content to savour something of the Jamaican background without deep probing there can hardly be a better guide than the slim booklet, *Jamaica Way* written by Philip Sherlock, a former principal of the University of the West Indies.

One volume of outstanding beauty contains 120 colour plates of the birds of Jamaica which were designed to accompany Philip Gosse's *The Birds of Jamaica* (1849). Gosse, who was later pitilessly portrayed by his son Edmund in the book *Father and Son* (1907), also wrote *A Naturalist's Sojourn in Jamaica* (1851) in which he praised the 'lovely Eden-like scenes' he saw in Jamaica, especially in the Bluefields region. Earlier during the years 1820 and 1821 James Hakewill (author of *The Picturesque Tour of Italy*) had visited Jamaica. As a consequence there appeared in 1825 *A Picturesque Tour of the island of Jamaica from drawings made in the years 1820 and 1821,* dedicated to the noblemen and gentlemen proprietors of estates in the West Indies, to the Resident Gentlemen, and to the merchants of the United Kingdom. This volume and that of the Birds of Jamaica may be seen in excellent condition at the Royal Commonwealth Library in London. Edward Long's *History of Jamaica* (1774) has fortunately been reprinted by Frank Cass in three volumes. It is indispensable reading for anyone who wants to obtain a comprehensive understanding of the first century of Jamaica after the displacement of the Spaniards. An intriguing but less accessible volume is an account published in 1707 of Hans Sloane's *Voyage to the islands of Madera, Barbados, Nevis, St Christopher and Jamaica with the Natural History of the Herbs and Trees, Four Footed Beasts, Fishes, Birds, Insects, Reptiles, etc. of Jamaica.*

A Spanish appreciation of Jamaica from the time of Columbus to the British Conquest was published in Seville in 1952. It is written in Spanish by Morales Padron and entitled *Jamaica Española*. Relevant chapters of *An Economic History of Spain* by Vicens Vives helps towards the understanding of Spanish-English relations before and after the conquest.

A. P. Thornton, who lectured for a time at the University of the West Indies, sheds light upon a critical period of Jamaican history in *West Indian Policy under the Restoration.*

An optimistic late nineteenth-century study is *A History of Jamaica from its Discovery to 1872,* by W. J. Gardner. This history emphasises the extent of social and educational progress which had followed the civilising mission of religious leaders. *The Governor Eyre Controversy* by Bernard Semnell (1962) is an account of an event in Jamaican history which in the opinion of most Jamaicans today signalled the end of imperial domination and gave Jamaicans two of their honoured national heroes.

In 1936 an account of *Jamaica: The Blessed Isles* by Lord Olivier, a former governor and eminent Fabian socialist, focussed attention on the potential of Jamaica as a country of peasant farmers. Like so many writers about the island Lord Olivier was captivated by its magnificent scenery and charmed by the Jamaican way of living.

Twentieth Century Jamaica by H. G. de Lisser represents the viewpoints of an illustrious Jamaican journalist and author who recognised the need for changes but who was proud that Jamaica 'with its independent land owning peasants, its freedom from race hatred, its respect for the law and love of order, its diminishing superstition and developing intelligence, has more than once been held up as a pattern to the United States'.

Jamaica, Land of Wood and Waters, by Fernando Henriques is of especial interest today because it was written on the eve of the Federation of the West Indies and reflected the enthusiasm and hopes of educated Jamaicans for a wider West Indian future.

The Arts of an Island (1970) by Ivy Baxter is a fascinating account of African influences on a culture which for centuries has been predominantly oriented towards Europe.

Fascinating accounts of Jamaica in the heyday of British overlordship in the early years of the nineteenth century are Matthew Lewis' *Journal of a West Indian Proprietor* (1834) and Lady Nugent's *Journal of her residence in Jamaica from 1801-1803* (revised in 1966). Eyewitness descriptions of Jamaica in the first quarter of the century are also frequent in *Tom Cringle's Log* (1836), written by Michael Scott who once lived and worked in Jamaica. Smollett, who married Nancy Lascelles, daughter of a Jamaican planter, has also left picturesque glimpses of the island in *Roderick Random,* which was first published in 1748. Trollope's observations on Jamaica and Jamaicans in *The West Indies and the Spanish Main* (1859) have literary and historic value, while Froude in 1887 had much to say about Jamaica and the empire in *The English in the West Indies.*

How Jamaica looked to the tourist travelling by yacht in 1885 is preserved in many interesting pages of Lady Brassey's *In the Tropics and the Roaring Forties.*

There is no end to a list of books about Jamaica and selection in reading will depend upon individual tastes.

In my reading I found those mentioned above especially helpful in guiding me through the mosaic of Jamaican progress to modern times. I would like to close this list with *The Gleaner Geography and History of Jamaica* (1973). With this slim volume and copies of the Esso and Texaco maps of Jamaica in your possession, Jamaica becomes far more than a geographical expression. It is a land awaiting exploration.

Index